COGNITIVE
DIMENSIONS OF
SOCIAL SCIENCE

COGNITIVE DIMENSIONS OF SOCIAL SCIENCE

MARK TURNER

OXFORD
UNIVERSITY PRESS
2001

OXFORD

UNIVERSITY PRESS

Oxford   New York
Athens   Auckland   Bangkok   Bogotá   Buenos Aires   Cape Town
Chennai   Dar es Salaam   Delhi   Florence   Hong Kong   Istanbul   Karachi
Kolkata   Kuala Lumpur   Madrid   Melbourne   Mexico City   Mumbai
Nairobi   Paris   São Paulo   Shanghai   Singapore   Taipei   Tokyo   Toronto   Warsaw

and associated companies in
Berlin   Ibadan

Published by Oxford University Press, Inc.,
198 Madison Avenue, New York, New York 10016

Oxford is a registered trademark of Oxford University Press

Library of Congress Cataloging-in-Publication Data
Turner, Mark, 1954–
Cognitive dimensions of social science / Mark Turner.
p. cm.
Includes bibliographical references and index.
ISBN 0-19-513904-6
1. Social Sciences.   2. Cognition.   I. Title.
H61 .T97 2001
300—dc21   00-048366

9 8 7 6 5 4 3 2 1

Printed in the United States of America
on acid-free paper

✍ ACKNOWLEDGMENTS ✎

I AM GRATEFUL to the faculty, members, and visitors of the School of Social Science at the Institute for Advanced Study during 1996–1997, where this book was conceived and formed. I thank Agnes Gund, Trustee of the Institute for Advanced Study and President of the Museum of Modern Art, for her financial support, and the University of Maryland, for assigning me to research leave.

This book is based on theories that are the result of my collaboration with Gilles Fauconnier, who deserves an exceptionally public acknowledgment of his influence.

Of the many scholars who have responded to drafts of parts of this book or who have provided me with superior opportunities to present this work publicly, I especially thank Aaron Belkin, Henry Brady, Per Aage Brandt, Bruce Bueno de Mesquita, David Collier, Finn Collin, Seana Coulson, Gary Cox, Gerald Edelman, James Fearon, Monika Fludernik, Dedre Gentner, Samuel Glucksberg, Joseph Goguen, Adele Goldberg, Joseph Grady, Richard Grush, Paul Hernadi, Douglas Hofstadter, Daniel Kahneman, Kristian Ditlev Jensen, Mark Johnson, George Lakoff, Arthur Lupia, Mat McCubbins, Nili Mandelblit, Harold Morowitz, Chrystopher Nehaniv, Todd Oakley, Andrew Ortony, Sam Popkin, Alan Richardson, Tim Rohrer, John Robert Ross, Ellen Spolsky, Francis Steen, Eve Sweetser, Sarah Taub, Philip E. Tetlock, Francis-Noël Thomas, and Lisa Zunshine.

Parts of this book draw on earlier talks and articles. Chapter two draws on a talk at the MacArthur conference on counterfactual thought experiments in political science in 1995, on an article in Philip E. Tetlock and Aaron Belkin, editors, *Counterfactual Thought Experiments in World Politics* (Princeton University Press, 1996), and on parts of an article by Turner and Fauconnier in John-Pierre Koenig, editor, *Conceptual Structure, Discourse, and Language II* (Stanford: Center for the Study of Language and Information, 1998). Chapter three draws on a talk at the Colloquium on Political Reasoning at the University of California, San

Diego in 1996 and a talk at the annual meeting of the American Political Science Association in 1997. Chapters two and three draw on an article in Arthur Lupia, Mathew D. McCubbins, and Samuel Popkin, editors, *Elements of Reason: Cognition, Choice, and the Bounds of Rationality* (Cambridge University Press, 2000). Chapter four draws on talks I gave at the Institute for Advanced Study in 1996, at the National Election Survey Conference on Cognition, Emotions, and Communication at the University of California, San Diego in 1997, at the annual meeting of the American Political Science Association in 1997, and at the Conference on Computation of Metaphor, Analogy, and Agents at the University of Aizu in Japan in 1998. Chapter five draws on a seminar paper presented at the School of Social Science at the Institute for Advanced Study in 1997, parts of which were published in Mark Turner and Gilles Fauconnier, "A Mechanism of Creativity," *Poetics Today* 20: 3 (1999), pages 397–418, and also on a talk at a symposium on Body, Mind, and Brain at the University of Oregon Institute for Cognitive and Decision Sciences in 1997.

Excerpts from Clifford Geertz, *After the Fact: Two Countries, Four Decades, One Anthropologist* (Cambridge: Harvard University Press) are copyright © 1995 by the President and Fellows of Harvard College and are reprinted by permission of the publishers.

Excerpts from Clifford Geertz, "Deep Play: Notes on the Balinese Cockfight" are reprinted by permission of *Dædalus*, Journal of the American Academy of Arts and Sciences, from the issue entitled, "Myth, Symbol, and Culture," Winter 1972, volume 101, number 1.

CONTENTS

COGNITIVE DIMENSIONS OF SOCIAL SCIENCE

ᗒ 1 ᗕ

DEEP PLAY

THE INSTITUTE

E ARLY in April of 1996, my wife and I arrived, curious and invisible, at a research institute we intended, as prospective residents, to study. A small place,
about two hundred people, and relatively remote, it was its own world. We were
intruders, professional ones, uninvited and unannounced, but also practically un-
noticed, since the Institute for Advanced Study's annual purge of most of its
population and replenishment with fresh recruits makes it a gathering of inter-
changeable anonymities. Their status, the only one necessary, is that they are "at
the Institute." To all appearances, we were at the Institute, too, where outsiders,
to a comfortable degree, become insiders exactly by being there.

Uninvited visitors have no place in this world, so there are few signs to direct
them, but the pattern of the Institute buildings is conventional, and the recep-
tionist, conditioned to look right through anything resembling an absent-minded
professor, dealt with us as though we were not there. Nobody greeted us, but
nobody scowled or said anything unpleasant to us either, and that was fine.

We located immediately the common room, with its wooden racks of newspapers and periodicals, which in other circumstances would have distracted us
for hours; the mathematics library, with its high windows, spiritual and restful,
where, it turned out, I would pass week after week reading by the natural light;
the glass-and-concrete dining hall, where a bust of Einstein impassively oversaw
the discreet promotional sale of sweatshirts and T-shirts, each carrying an image
of a full-frontal naked Truth heraldically matched by a diaphanously veiled but
no less anatomically emphatic full-frontal Beauty; the sloping lawns; the serene,
kidney-shaped pond; and the five-hundred-acre wood through which our own

two Christopher Robins would later pursue the mallard ducks, the Canada geese, the herd of deer, the legend of the baby black bear, and—the chief attraction, aside from the bow hunters who thinned the herd—the April eruption of frogs, toads, and salamanders.

We found our goal, the Institute preschool, and handed over a check to enroll our three-year-old son in the next term's morning program. My first duty on arriving in September would be to hire someone—she turned out to be a young woman fresh from St. Petersburg, Russia—to come to our residence in the mornings to care for our one-year-old son while my wife, a writer of fiction for young adults, plied her careful art, but my tasks for the day were completed. We drove past the playground, between Einstein Drive on one side and von Neumann Drive on the other, and I nearly ran the car into the curb as we gaped at the apartments. The elegance of the Institute buildings, the pleasure of the woods, and the perfection of the grounds had left us aesthetically unprepared for their full-frontal presentation of ugly. (Actually, I would later come to view them as the appropriate neutral and functional background for work at the Institute, and regret to hear that they were to be gutted.) Before we left that afternoon, it had begun to snow—on us, on the Institute, and on the amphibians.

The School of Social Science in the Institute for Advanced Study had announced its intentions for 1996–1997 in a call for applications:

> In 1996–1997 the School will be celebrating its twenty-fifth year. Over these years the School has been associated with the development of "interpretive social science" (the attempt to supplement models of natural science with explanations for social change drawn from humanities disciplines such as history, literature, and philosophy). In an effort both to review our past and anticipate our future, we will be looking for projects that exemplify the best of existing interpretive approaches to the social sciences, or that point the way to new kinds of social scientific interpretation, or that assess the strengths and weaknesses of "interpretive social science." Our interest is in the application of interpretive approaches to substantive issues and examples (with an awareness, of course, of the methods being employed), not in the elaboration of abstract theoretical proposals. We will also welcome proposals that critically examine the history of the social sciences during the past twenty-five years.

My own work consists of trying to make sense of acts of meaning and, especially, of trying to explain the mental abilities possessed by cognitively modern human beings that make those acts of meaning possible. "Modern" in this context means roughly the last fifty thousand years. My method consists of deploying any research instrument that seems promising. My hobby-horse preoccupation is Erving Goffman's "What is going on here?" So I guessed that I was a logical candidate for the School, and it turned out that I was right.

Around me that year were other squirrels working on other nuts: civil society in Argentina, Mexico, Peru, and Cuba from 1780 to 1880; the social dimension of laboratory design; boredom in Germany in the nineteenth century; the writing of ethnography on Central America; reform in Morocco; the history of the history of science in the United States; whistleblowing in organizations; Mayan public intellectuals; theocratic thought in China from 1885 to 1924; the social earmarking of money; a biography of the tobacco mosaic virus; segregation in Yonkers; how immigrants in the *banlieue* of Paris justify their racism; aesthetic constraints on the development of physics; morality internal to capitalism; and one last project whose bogey was the representation of AIDS but whose principled ambition was to escape being labeled or understood.

A conference on "25 Years of Social Science," to be sponsored by the School and held in the Institute's absolutely gorgeous Wolfensohn Hall, was scheduled for May 1997. The announcement of the conference offered, as its grand finale, a breathtaking swash of impossibly broad questions about the future of social science, questions which the conference participants—no wonder—found difficult to address, much less to answer.

I have written this book in an attempt to answer those questions: where is social science? where should it go? how should it get there? My answer, in a nutshell, is that social science is headed for an alliance with cognitive science. In the chapters of this book I investigate what "cognitive social science" might look like. Here, in this chapter, I take up questions of interpretive social science. In subsequent chapters, I take up central themes of qualitative social science. Each chapter offers pictures of the kind of research we might expect to see if we supplemented the kind of research done by social scientists with the kind of research done by their cousins in the cognitive sciences. I conclude the book with a look at some prospects for cognitive social science.

My story begins with the Institute for Advanced Study's announcement of its conference on "25 Years of Social Science":

> Our invited speakers are men and women who have sustained an interest in the larger society while working successfully in their own disciplines. As former members, they know the School of Social Science well (though at different stages of its history). We have asked them to reflect on their own work—its material conditions, disciplinary approach, intellectual goals—in this doubled context, social and academic. How has their research, their discipline, their world changed

in the last 25 years—and what do they see as the critical tasks of the next 25?

The conference should open into a collective intellectual stock-taking, so that we come out of it with a better sense of what the School should be doing right now and in the foreseeable future. Where exactly do we stand, and where do we go from here? What kind of work do we want to sponsor? What kinds of problems should we be addressing, with what kinds of approaches and arguments?

For anyone familiar even in passing with the fabulous, tumultuous history of the School, or developments in contemporary anthropology, or the influence of the "interpretive turn" in the social sciences, or even the Sunday *New York Times Magazine*, this depopulated prose had to be interpreted as pointing off-stage to an overtowering main actor, Clifford Geertz. The Institute for Advanced Study, unlike the Center for Advanced Study in the Behavioral Sciences, which is modeled on the Institute, and unlike the National Humanities Center, which is modeled on both of them, has a permanent faculty. In this way, it resembles the Collège de France, on which it is in fact modeled. Carl Kaysen, director of the Institute, recruited Geertz to its faculty in 1970, with the purpose of moving toward the creation of a new branch of the Institute, a School of Social Science. After an attempt to secure a second appointment died in Dantesque darkling flames, Geertz threatened to resign. The Board of Trustees of the Institute convened to create the School of Social Science, with Geertz as its lone faculty member.

A quarter of a century later, a few days before the members of the class of 1996–1997 occupied their offices, Clifford Geertz attained the canonical age of three score years and ten. By temperament unlikely to march at all, much less under any banner, Geertz had nonetheless in his solitary eminence cut, sewn, and hoisted an intellectual flag—*Interpretatio*—found at the front of several academic forces, some of whom were passionately hacking one another to bits.

One might have thought that the 1996–1997 year and its conference would focus, at least implicitly, on Geertz. To be sure, Albert O. Hirschman, Joan Scott, and Michael Walzer would be equally present as faculty members, equally engaged in interpretive social science. Scott, energetic and solicitous, frank and responsive, would serve as presiding officer and run the May conference; Walzer, polished and thoughtful, would conduct both the large, public, Thursday luncheon seminar and the small biweekly seminar reserved for participants in the School; the astonishingly resilient Hirschman would extend the saga of his prodigious "retirement," and all three would publish constantly. But Geertz was the one who had been with the School throughout its history, the one who had brought the others there and bound them together. For most outsiders, Geertz and the School were synonymous.

Consumers of academic rumor knew how, some years back, the Institute's scientists had scuttled the School's unanimous effort to secure an appointment for Bruno Latour, to assume a professorship in science studies funded in part by the Luce Foundation. Because a school in the Institute with fewer than three active faculty members loses much of its authority over appointments, Geertz could not leave until another appointment was made. After Latour, a second candidate for the professorship in science studies had declined. Throughout my year, external gossip would pass along the hot news of yet a third recommendation, to which the members of the faculty themselves never alluded. Social science was taking stock and so was the School. Geertz, himself relaxed, was at center stage, curtain down, in a tense institutional drama. Readers of Geertz's most recent book, *After the Fact*, knew that he had a refined edge to his views of both social science and the Institute.

But it was anthropologically impossible, given Geertz and the character of the School he launched, that the School would acknowledge overtly a special role for him, even a temporary one. He was present nearly every day, easily approached, prepared to engage without strain in any intellectual discussion or, if that is how it went, equally without strain in *badinage*. He was jolly, at times, which amazed me since I have never otherwise known a jolly academic. He scrutinized paper after paper prepared by the members and visitors. He was robust, tireless, sensitive, but the least directorial or presidory of personalities. He never imposed in any way on anyone. During the year, Hirschman, Scott, and Walzer all gave public presentations of their work, but not Geertz.

During the year, the only near-breach in the strong surface fiction that our gathering had nothing special to do with Geertz occurred at the end of April, during my installment of the biweekly small seminar, whose year-long theme was "The Past and Future of Social Science." In advance of the seminar, as was our custom, I distributed some notes I had put together. They were on the subject of evolutionary theory of meaning, and I paired them with some work by Geertz— his 1962 article, "The Growth of Culture and the Evolution of Mind," a review he had written for the current *New York Review of Books* of a book by Jerome Bruner, and various passages from *The Interpretation of Cultures*, *Local Knowledge*, and *After the Fact*. The theme of my seminar, which preceded by a few days our milestone May conference, was the relation of mind, brain, and meaning in social science, the endurance of that theme over several decades, its association with Geertz, and its importance for the future of social science.

I brought to the seminar, as disciplinary exhibits, *Coevolution: Genes, Culture, and Human Diversity*, by William H. Durham, professor of anthropology and evolutionary biology at Stanford, and *The Adapted Mind: Evolutionary Psychology and the Generation of Culture*, edited by two anthropologists, Jerome Barkow and John Tooby, and a psychologist, Leda Cosmides. Durham cites and quotes Geertz approvingly as having provided, in *The Interpretation of Cultures*, insights that would guide us in combining evolutionary biology with the study of the descent of cultures. But Cosmides and Tooby, in the first chapter of *The Adapted Mind*, give a fiercely opposed portrayal of Geertz as the "literary" wizard who ruined social science by conjuring up the lethal and false "Standard Social Science Model," or "SSSM" for short. Looking for Geertz in these texts was like looking in a fun-house mirror: Tooby and Cosmides endorse Durham as a rare counter-example to the "SSSM," but Durham says he is following Geertz.

At that two-hour Wednesday seminar, no one aside from me so much as referred in as little as a pronoun to either Geertz or the large packet of his work before us on the table. (For the sake of ethnographic completeness, I should record that Michael Walzer, as moderator, did once say "Cliff" to acknowledge Geertz's turn to ask a question, and that the faculty of the School was distracted: the following day, the director of the Institute, by declining to carry an ad-hoc committee's positive but troubled recommendation to the Board, would put a stop to the year-long campaign to make the rumored new appointment in science studies. Upon this third failure, the money offered by the Luce Foundation would go somewhere else. The rejected candidate was a Princeton historian of physics, opposed by the representatives of the Institute's Schools of Historical Studies and Natural Sciences. In an unprecedented tactic, the united faculty of the School of Social Science would explain all this and publicly air its collective grievance in the following week's *Chronicle of Higher Education*.) At my seminar, Geertz also ignored Geertz, but that was expected.

Here was Clifford Geertz, for thirty-five years at the middle of what was now an increasingly pressing debate in social science on the relation of mind, brain, meaning, and culture, an issue which, I argued, should be the focus of the "intellectual stock-taking" to which we were called at the big May conference.

During that seminar, it occurred to me that some of the answers to the questions posed for the conference might be found in what cognitive science and social science might have to say to each other, and that some of what they might have to say to each other might be found in what I have to say to Clifford Geertz, or anyway, in what I have to say about the most famous essay in interpretive social science, "Deep Play," whose author is Clifford Geertz.

OF MEANING AND SOCIAL SCIENCE

In "Deep Play," Clifford Geertz offered a sustained interpretation of a specific sociological entity—the Balinese cockfight. Much more influentially, he laid out—systematically if implicitly—the principles of interpretive social science that have served followers for over twenty-five years.

These principles are now widely institutionalized, and social science as a whole is even more widely institutionalized, not least in having its own school in the Institute for Advanced Study. Social science occupies entire divisions of major universities, a branch of the National Science Foundation, office after office in state and national governments, and what looks like a thousand miles of shelf space in the periodicals section of the library. By contrast, cognitive science is fresh on the scene—the term did not exist until I was a graduate student. Yet mature social science and young cognitive science have begun to flirt, and their intellectual friction is already leading to some fundamental reconsideration of the principles that guide social scientific research. The crux of this reconsideration is "the problem of meaning."

The "problem of meaning" is the riddle of how meaning can come into existence, develop, and descend. What are the basic cognitive operations that human beings use to create new meanings—that is, meanings that do not already exist—and how do those basic cognitive operations work, specifically? Somehow, meanings arise. Somehow, meanings develop. Just as sexual organisms in an environment interact to produce descendents, so meanings in an environment interact to produce new descendent meanings. And somehow, the interplay between existing meanings in contexts creates new, descendent meanings, which may in turn interact with other meanings to create descendents of their own. Meaning descends, and somehow, new meanings are among the descendents.

In conception and nearly in practice, until just lately, biology has chosen to pass over the problem of meaning. Biology's historical achievements are not associated with the problem of meaning—the discovery of the basic neurocognitive mechanisms that human beings use to create new meanings, the specific principles that govern those mechanisms, and how those mechanisms might have evolved during the phylogenetic descent that produced cognitively modern human beings. Biology textbooks do not have chapters with titles like, "How Two Meanings Interact to Create New, Descendent Meaning." Biologists have historically set aside inquiries into the problem of meaning as belonging to an unnamed future branch of research. We do not need answers to the problem of meaning in order to do biology, and biology has plenty of targets at which to aim—viruses, cancer, birth defects, ecology, immune systems—without taking aim at meaning.

Yet meaning is fully biological. It is made by brains, often groups of brains, always in bodies, always in environments. Recently—this is a reversal—neuroscience has begun to take up the study of meaning, and, to an extent, the problem of meaning. During my undergraduate years at Berkeley, it seemed to me that all but a few neurobiologists considered questions of meaning to be in scientific bad taste, premature, given the poverty of our scientific knowledge about the brain. Perhaps they were, and perhaps they still are, but they are becoming professionally acceptable. In the last decade, several adventuresome neurobiologists have begun to work directly on meaning and the brain.

Social science, on the other hand, looks at meaning all the time, but not at the problem of meaning. It offers analyses of meaning as created discursively, or arising between people, or precipitated by interaction between people, or induced according to different "perspectives"—religious, aesthetic, scientific, historical, commonsensical, philosophical, artistic—or negotiated from self-interest. We have learned from social science how certain meanings are transmitted by culture, or selected for their regency by an upper class that sees them as weapons of class struggle, or constituted at the aggregate level by invisible market summations over individual choices made in that market, or modified by generations caught between norms of their parents and their own insufferable conditions. We might want to praise or disparage any of this work on its own terms, but there is no general principle according to which any of it should be devalued or displaced by cognitive science.

Yet all these social scientific approaches have, until recently, assumed, taken for granted, left unexplored the neurocognitive level of operation without which these other social operations would be impossible. Social scientists study meanings and their conditions, but with few exceptions not the basic neurocognitive operations that make those meanings possible. Naturally, there have been social scientists, many more of them now than even a few years ago, who have faced the problem of meaning, and we will encounter some of their refreshing work as we go along. For example, the data and phenomena studied since the late 1950s in what has come to be called cognitive anthropology, surveyed in D'Andrade (1995), have led to the emergence of a vital few anthropologists, like Hutchins (1994), who work simultaneously as social scientists and cognitive scientists. But such cognitive social scientists remain a miniscule minority among those who practice political science, economics, sociology, and anthropology.

Just lately, however, both social science and cognitive neuroscience have started to take a new turn: both have rapidly begun to take note of the problem of meaning. In this respect, they are converging and are accordingly fated to combine. That prediction, in a nutshell, is the view of this book and the motivation for each of its chapters: cognitive science and social science are merging, and the future of social science lies in this blend.

Social science for the most part is built on a tradition that takes meanings as achievements to be interpreted rather than as dynamic results of neurocognitive operations that it is our job to explain. Quite rightly, social scientists usually take it as obvious that people construct meaning—they assign utilities, arrive at conceptions of self, model the behavior of others, categorize and classify, form organizations, set prices, pass laws, create representations, develop rituals, prefer one candidate to another, develop attachments. Also quite rightly, social scientists typically take it as obvious that human beings use mental capacities to do all of this—human beings recognize, see, classify, express, represent, and deploy every other mental capacity conventionally associated with human life. The moment at which social science characteristically unleashes its power comes when there is already some meaning that needs to be interpreted. Social science does not characteristically aspire to explain the neurocognitive mechanisms through which meaning comes to exist.

In this way, the social scientist resembles the textual scholar who takes it as given that a particular text is meaningful and that human capacities were involved in creating its meaning, and who regards it as his task to interpret the text for us. The nature of human neurocognitive capacities, what exactly they are, how their mechanisms work, how it is possible in the first place for meaning to arise and descend—these are not the questions that interpretation addresses. Interpreting a specific meaning—wrestling with it, trying to penetrate and to translate it, looking over the shoulders of those to whom it properly belongs and trying to make sense of it for foreigners—does not require discovering the neurocognitive processes that deliver that specific meaning.

In this respect, social science as a whole is in a position something like biology before the theory of evolution. Biologists, or rather botanists and zoologists, studied flora and fauna in exhaustive detail, in niches, *in situ*, penetrating the mysteries of their local habitations, measuring them, counting them, tracking cycles, writing all this down in the equivalent of field guides, and developing the ability to predict many natural phenomena, including phenomena of change: if frost falls, the bud is harmed; if the soil is enriched, growth improves, and so on. The world of life forms was a text whose meaning the biologist interpreted. But these interpretations did not explain and were not meant to explain the biological processes according to which these species could exist in the first place, or descend, or develop, or differ. To explain these more basic issues required the theory of evolution, which, once it was available, became an indispensable instrument in the professional study of local, narrowly coordinated, *in situ* life forms and the niches they inhabit.

Taking human meaning as given and interpreting it, according to one or another social scientific practice, without referring to the neurocognitive level at which these meanings emerge, is like taking the existence of life forms as given and interpreting them without referring to the theory of evolution. Social science does nothing wrong here, since cognitive science has no theory of emergence and descent of meaning that can begin to compare with the theory of evolution of species. We really are in the position of botanists and zoologists before the theory of evolution, and it is indeed something like the theory of evolution that cognitive science is trying, by gists and piths, with setbacks, to discover.

What cognitive science offers social science, at this moment, is an expectation that interpretation of meanings will eventually go hand-in-hand with explanation of neurocognitive processes of meaning—processes that underlie the objects and the acts of interpretation. Cognitive science offers a few initial, provisional proposals for joining with social science, but it is still in its infancy, and if the theory of evolution is our standard for comparison, cognitive science has very far to go.

Once developed, a cognitive theory of meaning will not displace or dismiss social science, any more than the theory of evolution supplanted the local study of zoological phenomena in their full particularity. I announce as a fact that a child can arrive at an astonishingly detailed, organized, exact, and useful understanding of frogs, toads, and salamanders, and of their differences and relationships, without having recourse to the theory of evolution, and it goes without saying that the theory of evolution alone brings essentially none of this understanding with it. The theory of evolution by itself tells us little in detail about its specific products. In each specific case, we must investigate the contingent details of how evolution played out, and those contingent details are complicated. Still, an understanding of amphibians becomes much fuller once the theory of evolution becomes available.

Just so, an explanation of neurocognitive processes of meaning will tell us little by itself about how those processes play out in any actual complicated case of human culture, because actual cases have intricate and unpredictable boundary conditions. It is clear, from the world's cultures and peoples, that there is a great diversity in human acts of meaning, and that, if we want to analyze all this variety in actual performance, we will need at least all of social science.

Basic human mental operations operate over cultural and personal assemblies of knowledge. Some of these assemblies will be widely shared in a culture, and expressions in the culture's language will evoke them. In our culture, for example, such cultural assemblies of knowledge include *buying and selling, stopping at a red light, moving into a residence, going to the movies.* Cognitive scientists call such assemblies of knowledge "frames." Frames are conventional packets of knowledge that usually include roles (such as *buyer, seller, price, location, time,* and so on) and various interactions between elements. Frames can be quite abstract (*the stronger versus the weaker*) or very specific (*a team climb of Mt. Everest, a pilgrimage to the Vatican, trying to find a parking place in Manhattan, getting through customs at John F. Kennedy International Airport*).

Since basic mental operations operate over cultural frames of knowledge, and those frames can vary dramatically from culture to culture, and purposes and conditions can also vary dramatically, different cultures can and do look strikingly different. *Products* of cognition vary across cultures even though their members share basic cognitive operations. We need every bit of social science to interpret these quite various products, but we need neuroscience and cognitive science to explain the basic mental operations that produce them, and the interpretations offered by social science should become fuller once neurocognitive theory of meaning is brought in. The rest of this chapter and the rest of this book are my attempt to give snapshots of how social science might look if we tried to do that.

BACKSTAGE COGNITION
AND THE BALINESE COCKFIGHT

"Deep Play: Notes on the Balinese Cockfight," by Clifford Geertz, has become by an infinite distance the most famous and successful attempt by a modern anthropologist, perhaps by any social scientist, to explicate a sociological entity. Geertz's beautifully written and finely detailed analysis has become the canonical ideograph for the kind of social science whose purpose is "the analysis of the significance of social actions for those who carry them out and of the beliefs and institutions that lend to those actions that significance" (Geertz 1995, p. 127). This semiotic and hermeneutic approach sees human behavior, or at least the interesting part of human behavior, as symbolic action. It asks what the import of that action is, what it is that is getting said. "The whole point of a semiotic approach to culture is . . . to aid us in gaining access to the conceptual world in which our subjects live so that we can, in some extended sense of the term, converse with them" (Geertz, 1973a, p. 24). This sort of analysis, Geertz explains, is "not an experimental science in search of law but an interpretive one in search of meaning. It is explication I am after, construing social expressions on their surface enigmatical" (p. 5).

This hermeneutical, interpretive impulse results in two features that give interpretive social science its characteristic feel. These features are shared, not surprisingly, with the best historical criticism of texts. The first is *particularity*—a sustained sensitivity to fine nuance and to local elements that are indispensable to the full meaning of the individual, narrowly situated, contingent sociological entity *in situ*. In the manner of Erwin Panofsky on Early Netherlandish painting or C. H. Dodd on the Fourth Gospel, Geertz works through every nuance of the cockfight. No detail that is significant for the actors can be insignificant for the social scientist.

The second feature is *historical retrospection*. This is the feature Geertz emphasizes in calling his book *After the Fact* (1995), and it is the feature with which he begins that book:

> What we can construct, if we keep notes and survive, are hindsight accounts of the connectedness of things that seem to have happened: pieced-together patternings, after the fact. (p. 2)

It is also the feature with which Geertz ends that book:

> A sage is squatted before a real elephant that is standing right in front of him. The sage is saying, "This is *not* an elephant." Only later, as the elephant turns and begins to lumber away, does a doubt begin to arise in the sage's mind about whether there might not be an elephant around after all. Finally, when the elephant has altogether disappeared from view, the sage looks down at the footprints the beast has left behind and declares with certainty, "An elephant *was* here."
>
> For me at least (and that is the "we" we are talking about here), anthropology, ethnographical anthropology, is like that: trying to reconstruct elusive, rather ethereal, and by now wholly departed elephants from the footprints they have left on my mind. "After the fact," is a double pun, two tropological turns on a literal meaning. On the literal level, it means looking for facts, which I have, of course, "in fact" been doing. On the first turning, it means ex-post interpretation, the main way (perhaps the only way) one can come to terms with the sorts of lived-forward, understood-backward phenomena anthropologists are condemned to deal with. On the second (and even more problematical) turning, it means the post-positivist critique of empirical realism, the move away from simple correspondence theories of truth and knowledge which makes of the very term "fact" a delicate matter. There is not much assurance or sense of closure, not even much of a sense of knowing what it is one precisely *is* after, in so indefinite a quest, amid such various people, over such a diversity of times. But it is an excellent way, interesting, dismaying, useful, and amusing, to expend a life. (p. 168)

As far as they go, particularity and historical retrospection are unassailable, and they have manifestly led to superb interpretations in the fields of historiography, historical criticism, ethnography, anthropology, and sociology. But they do not go very far at all in some directions, and it is in those other directions that cognitive science has insights to offer.

First, particularity. While it is true that every particular is strictly unique, no particular is isolated. It is instead intelligible only because we bring to bear on it more general operations and knowledge, not to isolate it but to connect it with wide, sometimes very wide, mental arrays. We see an individual cockfight, but to see it, or know that it is a cockfight, or understand anything about it, we must use conventional conceptual frames—that is, conventional schematic packets of shared knowledge—concerning such things as public events, cocks, money, and anxiety; and we must also use very general cognitive operations ranging from vision to categorization. To recognize a particular speckled hen as a speckled hen is not a matter of particularity but rather of connection. To interpret, as an everyday matter, a particular symbolic act as an act, as symbolic, and as having an interpretation is not a matter of particularity but rather of connection.

Second, historical retrospection. The future of human action and meaning is not at all random, and it is therefore misleading to say that we live it forward but understand it only backward. In real senses, we already understand what lies ahead of us and we can make that understanding much more precise and scientific. We understand that what lies ahead of us must start from here and must develop through the neurocognitive processes that human beings have. We know that what can follow from our present point in the historical path depends strongly on the point, on the path, and on human cognitive nature. We want to know not only about particular past events but also about today and tomorrow. What is meaning and how is it constructed and how can meanings that have arisen be further developed? How can meanings interact to give birth to new, descendent meanings? What mental equipment do we have that provides the potential for creating new meaning out of old? The cognitive operations we will use tomorrow and probably twenty thousand years from now are the same as those we used yesterday, a hundred years ago, and probably twenty thousand years ago. We want to know not only the intricacies of the previous products of those cognitive operations but also what those cognitive operations in fact are and what our prospects are.

Geertz's article, while apparently dedicated to the retrospective interpretation of a highly particular sociological entity—the Balinese cockfight—struggles, just below the surface but not therefore any less powerfully, to discern the basic cognitive operations that make the invention of the cockfight possible. These basic cognitive operations, I will argue, are universal among human beings, fundamental to cognition, and indispensable to reason, inference, and invention. They are also imaginative and creative.

I will take one of these basic cognitive operations—conceptual integration, also known as "blending"—as my exemplary offering from cognitive science to social science. My demonstrations will all for the most part be displays of what happens when something like the cognitive science of conceptual integration is brought to bear on central themes in the social sciences. My hope is that these topical sketches will give representative pictures of what cognitive social science could be.

Conceptual integration—blending—is a basic mental operation. It is at the very center of what it means to have a human mind. It plays a profound role in all areas of thought and action, including deciding, judging, reasoning, and inventing. It is dynamic, supple, and active in the moment of thinking. It yields products that frequently become entrenched in conceptual structure and in grammar. It often performs new work on its previously entrenched products. For the most part, it is a routine, workaday process that escapes detection except on technical analysis. It is not reserved for special purposes, and is not costly. As we will see, some researchers have proposed that the development of this cognitive capacity for conceptual integration was the most important event in human evolution, the evolutionary leap that separated cognitively modern human beings from other species, and in particular from merely anatomically modern human beings. Conceptual integration, in this view, is the basic cognitive operation that makes human culture, science, and art possible—indeed, the one that makes us possible.

The early theoretical work on conceptual integration was done jointly by Gilles Fauconnier and me, and presented in various publications: Fauconnier and Turner (1994, 1996, 1998a, 1998b, and in preparation), Turner and Fauconnier (1995, 1998, and 1999), Fauconnier (1997), and Turner (1996a and 1996b). The model we offered—the "network model of conceptual integration"—has additionally played a role in Collier and Levitsky (1997), Coulson (1995, 1996, and 1997), Grush & Mandelblit (1997), Mandelblit (1996, 1997), Mandelblit and Zachar (1998), Oakley (1995), Ramey (1997), Sun (1994), Veale (1996), Zbikowski (in press), and many others. This work is presented on a website dedicated to conceptual integration: it is available by visiting *classicprose.com* and following the links to "Mark Turner" and then to "Blending."

A conceptual blend always has at least two conceptual influences, sometimes called its "contributors" or its "contributing spaces," sometimes called its "inputs," sometimes called its "parents," sometimes called its *espaces d'entrée*," depending on the culture of the audience. If we say, "This surgeon is a butcher," the influences are the prototypical notions of a surgeon and a butcher. If we say "front-loaded IRA," the influences are the notion of a conventional Individual Retirement Account and the notion of something's being "front-loaded."

Before conceptual integration can proceed, some provisional cross-space mapping must be constructed between the influences: the surgeon corresponds to the butcher; the conventional IRA corresponds to something that is "front-loaded." But the essence of conceptual integration is its creation of a new mental assembly, a blend, that is identical to neither of its influences and not merely a correspondence between them and usually not even an additive combination of some of their features, but is instead a third conceptual space, a child space, a blended space, with new meaning. This new meaning is "emergent" meaning, in the sense that it is not available in either of the influencing spaces but instead emerges in the blended space by means of blending those influencing spaces.

The blend inherits some of its elements and some of its meaning from the influencing spaces, and in this way it is the conceptual descendent of the influencing spaces, just as a child is the biological and cultural descendent of its parents. But like the child, the blend develops its own identity and is not merely a copy of its parents. It has meaning that is its own: "emergent" meaning.

The surgeon who is a butcher is a blended notion—neither a prototypical surgeon nor a prototypical butcher. *Incompetence* is the central feature of the butcher-surgeon even though *incompetence* belongs to neither the prototypical surgeon nor the prototypical butcher. The meaning *incompetence* emerges in the blend: it is not available from either of the influencing spaces, since neither the prototypical surgeon nor the prototypical butcher is at all incompetent. The blend, the "surgeon-butcher," is the descendent of the two influencing spaces *surgeon* and *butcher*, but it has its own "emergent" meaning possessed by neither of its influences: *incompetence*. By now in the history of the language, the word "butcher" can be used conventionally for anyone who does a sloppy job, but a new and unfamiliar blend that has not yet become conventional to us works in just the same way: "This surgeon is a lumberjack" can be interpreted as yielding *incompetence* for the blended lumberjack-surgeon even though *incompetence* belongs to neither the prototypical lumberjack nor the prototypical surgeon. "Lumberjack" could become conventional in the way "butcher" has. The surgeon-lumberjack is a blend, and while it is the conceptual descendent of *surgeon* and *lumberjack*, it has meaning of its own, new meaning that "emerges" only in the blend: *incompetence*.

An IRA—Individual Retirement Account—is a financial instrument for investing funds for retirement. It has (or had, until just now) an essential feature: the owner places untaxed income into it, hoping the investment will appreciate, and pays tax on amounts withdrawn later during retirement. It is thus "tax-deferred." "Front-loaded" suggests something whose load is by contrast at the front; metaphorically, with "front" referring to the earlier part of a time line and "load" referring to a burden, "front-loaded" suggests that the burden is suffered at first. So a "front-loaded IRA" is one whose tax burden is paid not at the end but at the beginning: one deposits taxed money into the front-loaded IRA and pays no tax on withdrawals made later in retirement. The emergent meaning here is obvious: one influence, "front-loaded," says nothing about IRAs; the other influence, the conventional IRA, is criterially a back-loaded *tax-deferred* investment account; but in the new blend, there is a new entity, with a new meaning that emerges only in the blend: an IRA that is not tax-deferred. The central feature of the category *IRA*—tax-deferral—is replaced in the blend by its opposite: tax up front. This emergent meaning is so profound as to count, in concepts of finance and in tax law, as a permanent revision of the category *IRA*. The emergence of this meaning has led to a revised set of meanings for *IRA* in which there are now two subcategories of *IRA*—"classic" IRAs are the original, back-loaded IRAs, while "Roth" IRAs are front-loaded, and all IRAs are investment accounts into which specifically limited amounts of money can be deposited for retirement.

We usually do not notice the work we are doing during conceptual integration. If we take "red ball" to mean a ball whose surface is permanently red, we must integrate the notion of a ball, which is a physical object with a surface that can be colored, and the notion of the color red, to produce a ball whose surface is red, and this is no trivial feat. But this product of blending is by now entirely conventional. If we take "red light" to mean a traffic sign that requires us to stop, we must integrate not only the notion of light and the notion of the color red, but we must additionally blend in the notion of traffic signs and the management of traffic. Yet in such a case the relevant meaning we need from the notion of traffic signs is usually indicated conventionally, either by the linguistic context ("Stop the car at the next red light") or by the nonlinguistic context (the red light is of a very special sort and form and hangs in exactly the conventional spot at a roadway intersection). Because of such conventional indication, we again do not notice that we are doing any mental work to make such a blend. It seems to us as if we are doing nothing, because all the work of blending in these cases happens below the horizon of observation, in robust but unconscious cognition, and only the product of all that work comes into consciousness: we recognize the red light or understand the use of the phrase "red light."

But a phrase like "left-handed pen" will seem mysterious to people who do not already know that it refers to any pen containing special ink that will neither smear nor stain. A "left-handed pen" thus causes no problems for the left-handed writer whose writing hand slides over the ink. When we learn the phrase "left-handed pen," we must integrate our conventional schematic knowledge of a left-hander with our conventional schematic knowledge of using a pen. That is, we must blend two frames. They are the influences that contribute to the blend. But the relevant structure we need to project from those frames to the blend may be hard to locate in memory or find in the context; we may have to ask for an explanation. In any event, as we build this blend, we are likely to notice that we are engaged in a mental act of blending. We have no such awareness when we hear "red light."

The basic cognitive operation of conceptual blending always establishes some set of connecting links, even a very minimal set, between elements in the two influencing spaces. This set of connecting links is called a "counterpart mapping between the influencing spaces." Conceptual blending also always projects structure *selectively* from the influences to the blended mental space. Through composition, completion, and elaboration, the blend develops structure not provided by the influencing spaces. Blending thus operates according to a set of uniform structural and dynamic principles.

There can be any number of influencing spaces projecting to a blend, and blending can happen repeatedly, so the array of mental spaces involved in any particular conceptual integration network can be quite elaborate. Moreover, blending is a dynamic activity, with spaces and connections formed and reformed as the network is forged. My diagram (figure 1.1) therefore presents only a poor suggestion of what is going on in conceptual integration.

In "Deep Play," Geertz provides a brilliant demonstration of the intricacy of conceptual blending, even though that is not at all his purpose. His purpose, at least his announced purpose, is instead to interpret, through historical retrospection, a fabulous, complex, particular sociological entity—the Balinese cockfight—and thereby to give us access to its local wonder, to make it intelligible to us who are not Balinese. Put generally, his guiding purpose is *historical retrospection* of a *narrow particularity*. What motivates his study is the mystery of the particular

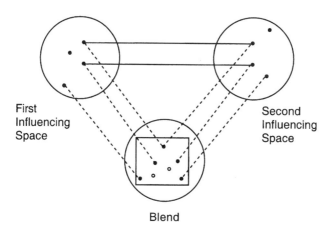

First Influencing Space

Second Influencing Space

Blend

Figure 1.1

sociological entity—the Balinese cockfight. What he offers to explain is the local meaning of that particular sociological entity.

My purpose, motivations, and goals are altogether different, but complementary, and that, I take it, is the general relationship of cognitive science to social science—cognitive science offers an altogether different but complementary line of analysis. What I mean to explain is how the Balinese cockfight and Geertz's interpretation of it arise from an underlying, general, basic mental operation—conceptual blending. What motivates my study is that basic mental operation. The Balinese cockfight—or rather the distributed conception of it that guides and makes intelligible its many enactments—follows the structural and dynamic properties of blending, and it conforms to the constraints on blending. I take the underlying mental operation rather than the particular sociological product as my subject of analysis.

Like the specific cockfight in April of 1958 during which Geertz and his wife were nearly caught in a police raid, the Balinese cockfight as a sociological entity is highly local, individual, and particular. Viewed as a bundle of past experience, surveyed in retrospect, it is an exotic and distant phenomenon, which Geertz, the anthropologist from the field, emerging with notes, finally makes sense of, after, like the elephant, it has disappeared from the scene. Geertz's work, after the fact, directed backward, tells us about something that does not properly belong to us.

But the same Balinese cockfight viewed as I view it is a recognizable product of a mental ability that is permanent, indispensable, and apparently universal to human beings, an ability that runs across all cultures, all histories, all languages, past, passing, and to come, a mental operation that no human being with a standard biological endowment raised in anything like a human environment can fail to develop and deploy widely and powerfully. Conceptual blending is, in this respect, part of human nature—controversial as that expression has become—a mental power characteristic of our species and, I think, the central cognitive characteristic of our species. Conceptual blending is like computation of color constancy in visual cortex (that is, the way we see an apple as red regardless of the fact that the light coming from it varies dramatically from pre-dawn to noon to dusk) or like categorization: just as human beings everywhere develop the intricate mechanisms for computing color constancy, just as they cannot fail to categorize perceptually and conceptually, and just as certain cognitive principles of categorization run across all of the many quite different category structures human beings have in fact constructed, so human beings cannot fail to do conceptual blending, and while the products of conceptual blending are impressively various and intricate, its cognitive principles are uniform.

The Balinese cockfight is local and past, but the mental operation that under-lies it is invariant over historical time and is the central engine of human mean-ing. It is part of us, where the "us" in this case is neither the Balinese of 1958 nor scholars in the year 2001, but all cognitively modern human beings, beginning very far before written history and stretching indefinitely into our phylogenetic future. Blending is basic, not exotic.

The idea of the Balinese cockfight is a conceptual blend. It begins from a conceptual connection between two very different kinds of things: cocks and men. As Geertz explains, "For it is only apparently cocks that are fighting there. Actu-ally, it is men" (1973a, p. 417). The outcome of the cockfight cannot alter the status of the men whose cocks are fighting, but the cockfight counts nonetheless as an action of their status rivalry. Geertz makes various attempts to say what kind of mental operation accounts for this conceptual connection—"An image, fiction, a model, a metaphor" (p. 444). The cockfight, he informs us at several points, is at once an act of nature involving cocks and an act of culture involving men. "This crosswise doubleness of an event which, taken as a fact of nature, is rage untram-meled, and taken as a fact of culture, is form perfected, defines the cockfight as a sociological entity" (p. 424).

Geertz's phrase—"crosswise doubleness"—for capturing the essence of the Balinese cockfight is in fact as perfectly descriptive a short name as could be devised for conceptual integration: "doubleness" for the two influencing spaces, "cross-wise" for the way in which their independent contributions come together in the blend.

Geertz works up to his magisterial interpretation of the Balinese cockfight blend by degrees, providing first a series of quick treatments of several other cock-based blends in Balinese culture. Here is one: "Even the very island itself is per-ceived from its shape as a small, proud cock, poised, neck extended, back taut, tail raised, in eternal challenge to large, feckless, shapeless Java" (1973a, p. 418). Some principles of conceptual blending can be seen from just this accessory blend, as follows.

The island of Bali, in this blend, is a fighting cock whose adversary is the island of Java. But, as everyone knows, the motivation for this blend comes not from ideas about islands as adversaries, but rather from ideas about the peoples on those islands as adversaries, and about the adversarial opposition of their cul-tures: Balinese versus Javanese, Balinese culture versus Javanese culture.

The island-cock in the blend is not just an island and not just a cock, or even just an island-cock; it is at once a cock, Bali, the Balinese, and their culture, and this multiple projection to a single element in the blend has many effects, includ-ing the feat of turning the Balinese into a single organism, the cock.

The blending of the Balinese with the cock arises, for us, against a background of some pre-existing templates for certain kinds of blending, all of them available as part of the standard mental furniture our culture provides: we can blend a people with an animal species (e.g., the English people with a bulldog); a group of people with a particular animal (the University of Georgia football team is a particular bulldog and is represented as such in cartoons in which the bulldog rips up the players of the opposing team); a national people with a particular person (French/Marianne; Americans/Uncle Sam); and a particular person with an individual animal of another species (my boss is a snake). Canonically for us, when a people is blended with an individual person, the blend has an element that is simultaneously both the "ethnic character" of the people and the individual character of the person (e.g., self-reliant Americans/Uncle Sam). Canonically for us, when a person is blended with an animal, the blend has an element that is simultaneously both the "character" of the person and the "instinctive nature" of the animal ("Bill is a fox"). Canonically for us, when a people is blended with an animal, the blend has an element that is both the "ethnic nature" of the people and the instinctive nature of the animal (indomitable bull dog/English). We also of course routinely blend animals and human beings: talking animals are the mainstay of children's literature.

All of these conventional templates for blending are guided by a much larger template used for blending an entity at one level (such as a person or a people) with an entity at another level (such as an animal or a plant or a physical object), on the constraining principle (first discussed in Lakoff and Turner, 1989) that, other things being equal, it is their "highest" natures that are to be fused. This is the principle that stops us from interpreting "My boss is a spider" to mean that my boss is black, although prototypical spiders are black. It stops us from interpreting "The legal profession is a disease" to mean that we could kill it off through poisons, although perhaps we could. Of course, the constraining principle can be overriden by other cues.

The Bali-as-cock blend has a single element that is a cock with an instinctive nature and a people with an ethnic character. This element also has some of the features of human individuality, since the behavior of the cock is not rigid instinctual behavior but instead something the cock has individually chosen and is to be admired for having chosen. Animals do not choose their instinctive natures.

It is important to see that blending is not just matching of structures that already exist in one influencing space (in this case, the animal cock) and the other influencing space (in this case, Bali and the Balinese). On the contrary, the Bali-Balinese-cock blend has crucial structure that is unavailable from the influencing spaces. In the influencing space with the actual cocks, the actual cocks fight; they engage, and the Balinese disrespect them if they do not engage; what they fight is other cocks. In the blend, the picture is very different: the cock does not fight but is rather frozen in eternal challenge—something entirely unsuiting to an actual cock—and is moreover admired for staying frozen. The object of its challenge is not a cock, is not even a recognizable animal, but is some shapeless and unrecognizable lump twenty or thirty times its size. The influencing space with the cocks cannot supply this structure because an actual cock could not behave this way. Moreover, an actual cock will fight any other cock regardless of its features, and with identical ferocity, but the cock in the blend is dedicated to a single adversary whose suitability depends upon certain features—namely, the fact that the geographical "head" of the island of Bali points at the island of Java and that the Javanese and the Balinese have lived as adversaries. This is a strange blended cock, who isn't interested in fighting either the cock to the east or the islanders to the east.

The conceit of Bali as a geographical and ethnic cock is a "double-scope" blend. The influencing spaces to a "double-scope" blend have conflicting organizing frames, and the frame developed for the blend draws on *both* of those organizing frames. The influencing spaces of the Bali-Balinese-cock blend certainly have strongly conflicting organizing frames—fighting cock versus geographical island. A cock is an animal and an agent, but a geographical island is not. In "double-scope " blends, the organizing frame of the blend borrows heavily from each of the two conflicting frames that organize the two influencing spaces. The more evenly the organizing frame of the blend borrows from the organizing frames of its influences, the more thoroughly "double-scope" it is.

We can see the way in which the Bali blend takes parts of each of the organizing frames of the influencing spaces. From the influencing space with the fighting cock, the blend takes the cock itself, its adversary, the moment of challenge before violence, and the fact that the cock has an instinctual, unchanging nature. However, there is crucial, indispensable organizing structure in that influencing space with the fighting cock that the blend does not take: the blend does not take the fighting cock's challenge as a punctual event that causes an immediate engagement; it does not take the status of its adversary as a cock or even a recognizable animal; it does not take the causal relationship between the extreme fighting spirit of the cock and its prospects of winning; it does not take the possibility that a spirited cock can win, or even that it can inflict serious damage on the adversary; it does not take the certainty that one way or the other, one of the adversaries, maybe both, will be eliminated completely and forever, probably sooner rather than later, or, alternatively, that the confrontation will be broken off and the adversaries will separate so as to have nothing more to do with each other.

Instead, the Bali-as-geographical-and-ethnic-cock blend takes considerable organizing structure from the influencing space with the Balinese people (as viewed by the Balinese people): the Balinese and the Javanese are two entirely different orders of being, and while the Balinese have a distinctive character, the Javanese are so indistinct and ill-defined as hardly to count as a people at all; the lack of spirit and vitality among the Javanese makes them no less inevitably dominant; the conflict between the Javanese and the Balinese is permanent, eternal; Balinese character partly derives from this relationship with the Javanese; and it would be best by far if the defiance deterred engagement, so that no fight ensued.

This blend of Bali-versus-Java also recruits structure from another conventional and abstract template for blending, in which personal character is fused with shapes of objects: we refer to a person's character as "distinct," "angular," "well-rounded," "smooth," "rough at the edges." In this way, character is conventionally understood as having form. In the Bali-versus-Java blend, the formlessness of the island of Java is blended with the character of the Javanese, to produce a character that is "indistinct, shapeless."

There is considerable emergent structure in this blend—that is, structure in the blend that is not available from either of its influencing spaces: in the blend, we have an entirely imaginary kind of cock, who fights on both the physical and spiritual planes, whose highest calling is eternal defiance, who is dedicated to a single adversary, who has human intentional structure and can know that it would lose any physical engagement even as it clearly wins on the spiritual plane.

The use of the island of Bali in the blend illustrates the nature of metonymy in blending. This is a complicated topic, which will take a few steps to introduce. By "metonymy," I mean an organizing relationship between one element in an integrated conceptual assembly and another: "all hands on deck" because *hands* are metonymically related to the *sailors* who have them. The hands are the relevant active part of the sailors. Such a part-to-whole relationship is a standard metonymy. Other common metonymic relationships are the relationship between a cause and an effect, between one stage in a transformation and another, between a location and the institution or activity located there.

Part of the goal of blending is to supply an integrated blended scene that is sufficiently intelligible, compressed, and memorable to be manipulated as a unit. This is a difficult goal to achieve: integrating all the important aspects of the influencing spaces into a unified and compressed blended scene takes imaginative work, not least because important things in the influencing spaces often are only distantly related. One of the great powers of conceptual integration lies in its ability to tighten those distant relations so they will fit into an intelligible, compressed, useful blended scene.

Consider an example of metonymy in blending to which we will return: in the conception of Death The Grim Reaper, there is a very long causal chain from Death as a general abstract cause applying to all living things, to the individual cause of death (cancer, accident, old age), to the death of the individual, to the corpse, the burial, the decay, the buried skeleton, and the exhumation that produces a visible skeleton. In the blend of Death The Grim Reaper, the skeleton becomes the *form* of Death. It is *part* of Death. Thus, in the blend, there is a very tight relation between Death and the skeleton: the skeleton is the *overall structuring part* of Death. In the blend, there is a tight Death-skeleton metonymy, a form-to-whole metonymy, in place of the very distant and many-step causal-chain metonymy in the influencing space that connects Death to the skeleton. In the blend, the cause (Death) and the effect (the skeleton) are combined, so that the effect (the skeleton) is now the most salient feature of the cause (Death). That is not at all the case in the influencing space. The blend also compresses time: something earlier in time (the advent of Death) and something much later in time (the existence of the skeleton) are collapsed into each other—that is, these two temporal stages now exist simultaneously. The blend also achieves compression of the process of change: the long process of change from *dying body* to *skeleton* is now, in the blend, manifest in the cause (Death) itself. This blend of Death The Grim Reaper thus tightens many related metonymies and fits all the elements they involve into a single intentional scene at human scale.

The Balinese cockfight blend uses metonymy compression in the same way. This metonymy compression may be a little harder to see because the compression in this case is maximal, reducing the metonymic relation to zero. That is, two things metonymically related in the influencing space become identical in the blend, as follows. In the influencing space having to do with Bali, there is Bali the island and the Balinese who live on the island of Bali, and there is a metonymic link between them. In this influencing space, Bali and the Balinese are not identical: the Balinese oppose the Javanese, but the island of Bali does not oppose the island of Java. In that influencing space, the Balinese *inhabit* Bali, and this is a metonymic relation. It is clear in this influencing space that Bali the island is not intentional and cannot attack or oppose.

But in the blend, Bali and the Balinese are fused. They become identical. Thus, in the blend, the opposition of the Balinese to the Javanese is an opposition of Bali the island to Java the island. In the blend, the island and the people are the identical element. And this Bali/Balinese single element is also blended with the cock, making Bali, the Balinese people, and the cock one element. Of course, this does not mean we are confused: when we achieve a blend, we do not (usually) lose the structure of the influencing spaces. In the influencing space with

Bali and Java, we maintain the distance and distinction between the geographical islands, their inhabitants, and cocks. But in the blend, we do not. We know what is in the influencing spaces, and we know what is in the blend, and we know the connections between them. Each of these spaces has its uses. One of the uses of the blend is to compress meanings that are diffuse in the influencing spaces.

This process of *metonymy compression* during blending operates under a constraint: other things being equal, when one element is projected from an influencing space into the blend and a second element in the same influencing space metonymically related to the first is also projected to the blend, it is better to shorten the metonymic distance between them. This shortening produces more compressed blends. In the Bali-as-cock blend, the metonymic distance between Bali and the Balinese is maximally compressed. In Death The Grim Reaper, Death and the skeleton are not compressed all the way to identity, but close: the skeleton becomes *part* of Death, the salient part.

Compressing a metonymic distance all the way to identity—that is, taking two elements at some metonymic distance from each other in an influencing space and fusing them in the blend—is relatively infrequent in blending since the accidental features that make it suitable or even possible are often lacking. But partial compression of metonymic distance is common in blending. Nearly every political cartoon, for example, involves some compression of metonymic distances to achieve a compressed blend, as when France in the blend is no different from Marianne (a French woman), or the United States is Uncle Sam (an American human being) or an automobile company becomes a particular car, or the "lobbying industry" becomes a single lobbyist and "Congress" becomes a single generic congressman, and so on.

Suppose, to choose one of these examples to dwell on, that one of three competing automakers is winning in its financial competition with the other two. To present this situation, the cartoonist might show a car race, in which one car is ahead of other two, where each car stands for the company that produces that car, and where each car is in fact the zippiest sports car made by that company. To help readers who don't know much about car models understand the cartoon, the cartoonist might label the cars, in standard cartoon fashion, with the names of the companies. These labels might be applied even if the sporty production model that supplies the image of the winning car is in fact losing money for its company, or even if the winning model car is selling less well than the two models it is beating in the race, because (in this particular cartoon) the cars stand not for the finances of their production models but instead for the finances of the larger corporations that produce those models. This is a severe compression of metonymic distance. In the influencing space with the automakers, there is a long metonymic distance from the finances of the company, to its operations, to its manufacturing, to its products, to the particular sports car. But in the blend, that metonymic distance is compressed to identity, and the financial aspect of the company is fused with the particular product of the company—indeed, more accurately, with a characteristic performance by that product.

This compression of metonymies is a standard instrument of advertisement. An advertisement for a lemon vodka cocktail using a particular brand of vodka consists of a metal lemon press (with crank and handle) whose top and bottom are simultaneously the top and bottom of the vodka bottle. The vodka and the lemon juice cocktail appear nowhere in the visual representation of the blend. Instead, the bottle, which is metonymically related to the brand of vodka it contains, and the lemon press, which is metonymically related to the lemon juice, are the content of the representation, and their compression into one unit signifies the combination of the vodka and the lemon juice into one cocktail. A different ad, this time for gin and tonic, consists of a bottle cap that is a fusing of one half of the gin bottle cap to one half of the tonic bottle cap.

The compactness of these blends satisfies the "integration" constraint on blending: other things being equal, the blend must constitute a tightly integrated scene that can be manipulated cognitively as a unit. The actual world in which the automakers operate—global finances and marketplaces—does not form a basic, distinct, perceptible, integrated human scene, but blending the automakers with the frame of competition gives some integration. Much greater integration comes from specifying the competition as racing—in fact automobile racing—and simultaneously exploiting the metonymy between the finances of the auto corporations and the sports cars they produce. This exploitation gives the blend a scene in which financial operation and car racing are fused, and the financial corporations and the individual cars are fused, and the financial corporations are instantly recognizable from the particular labeled cars that represent them. The result in the blend is a compressed, integrated, familiar, distinct human scene. In this case, compressing the metonymy has provided a way to help satisfy the integration constraint—that is, compressing the metonymy helps to make the blend more integrated.

The Bali-as-cock blend takes just this path of compressing a metonymy in an influencing space to achieve a tighter integration in the blend. While blending the Balinese people and the Javanese people with individual adversaries in a combat provides some integration, and yet greater integration comes from specifying the combat as a cockfight, there is additional integration to be had from compressing the metonymic relation between the Balinese, Bali, and the shape of Bali so that, in the blend, Bali, as the location of the Balinese, has the form of the cock. By this conceptual work the blend can compress the Balinese, Bali, and the cock into identity, giving a compressed, integrated, distinct scene that is culturally appropriate and, if you are Balinese, familiar: the moment of challenge in a cockfight. Again, compressing the relationship between two elements as they are projected to the blend provides a way to achieve greater integration in the blend.

There are other aspects of blending at work in the Bali-as-geographical-and-ethnic-cock blend. Most obviously, blending exploits accidents. It is merely accidental that the side of Bali lying toward Java juts to a point rather than, for example, curving along a concave crescent, and this accident makes it possible for Bali to be viewed as having a head jutting toward Java. Importantly, it is a general principle of blending that the accidental origins of a blend are no argument against its significance or profundity. Indeed, the most profound importance and essence can derive from the sheerest accident. In this way, the phylogeny of conceptual blends resembles the descent of species, in which accidents can set fundamental courses. Social science, not to mention human beings, might not exist had it not been for an accident roughly sixty-five million years ago in which a meteor struck the sea off Yucatán, giving mammals a lucky boost in their competition with reptiles.

The Bali-as-cock blend also shows that blending frequently requires us to reconceive and restructure the influencing spaces. I own a physical map of Bali, which I have presented to many people, including some people who are familiar with farm cocks and even some people who have seen cockfights in the Western Hemisphere. I have asked them what Bali looks like. Nobody has ever answered that it looks like a cock. But if you are disposed to think of Bali and Java as antagonists, and are steeped in cockfighting or otherwise primed to activate a frame for cocks, then, with a little work, the island of Bali is susceptible to being reframed as having the form of a fighting cock. Blending is an active process that can involve extensive work at any point in the conceptual array connected to the blend, including reconfiguration of the influencing spaces—in this case, of the influencing space with the island.

Geertz suggests that there is almost no end of blends in Bali involving cocks. For example, "A pompous man whose behavior presumes above his station is compared to a tailless cock who struts about as though he had a large, spectacular one" (1973a, p. 418). Other cock blends have to do with sex and dating, employment, desperation, stinginess, and morality.

The focal blend for Geertz, the one he takes as the subject of his after-the-fact, particular interpretation, the one whose interpretation by Geertz has become the canonical example of how to do interpretive social science, is a blend of fighting cock and social man. It creates the sociological entity that is the Balinese cockfight, which is not a natural event of the animal world at all but instead an intricate, imaginative, and highly sophisticated conceptual blend of cocks and people. Its emergent meaning forms and represents the Balinese.

We can begin to tease a fraction of this emergent meaning into view by looking at an ostensibly obvious, trivial, accessory fact: the fighting cocks wear sharp metal spurs. Cocks in nature have spurs that are natural equipment, but metal spurs exist only in the blend. In the influencing space with Balinese social men, men of prestige have assistants, and the projection of the role "assistant" from the influencing space into the cockfight blend creates a position for a technical helper who cultivates and enhances the natural equipment of the cock in whom the owner has an interest. The metal spurs in the cockfight blend—"razor-sharp, pointed steel swords, four or five inches long"—are the counterpart of the cock's natural spurs. But manufacturing these spurs, gracing them with ritual status, and affixing them to the cocks is the counterpart of performing a service for the owner, a human being. The metal spurs emerge from the blend of something having to do with cocks and something having to do with people. From one influence, the blend takes the fighting cocks; from the other, it takes human social purposive action and interaction. The metal spurs are one result.

The cockfight blend contains a wide variety of additional structure that has no place in a natural cockfight. Some of it is even antithetical to natural fighting. The blend has an audience, a handler for each cock, a context of previous engagements involving these owners and handlers as well as the cocks they have previously brought to the ring, cosmological indications for how and when to fight each kind of cock, a fifty-square-foot ring, a wicker cage under which to gather and infuriate the cocks when they are reluctant, and an umpire steeped in regulations written on palm-leaf manuscripts handed down through generations. The ritual of engagement includes precisely timed rounds and all-important intermissions:

> A coconut pierced with a small hole is placed in a pail of water, in which it takes about twenty-one seconds to sink. . . . During these twenty-one seconds, the handlers are not permitted to touch their roosters. . . . Within moments one or the other drives home a solid blow with his spur. The handler whose cock has delivered the blow immediately picks it up so that it will not get a return blow. . . . With the birds again in the hands of their handlers, the coconut is now sunk three times after which the cock which has landed the blow must be set down to show that he is firm, a fact he demonstrates by wandering idly around the ring for a coconut sink. The coconut is then sunk twice more and the fight must recommence. . . . In the climactic battle (if there is one; sometimes the

wounded cock simply expires in the handler's hands or immediately as it is placed down again), the cock who landed the first blow usually proceeds to finish off his weakened opponent. But this is far from an inevitable outcome. . . . (Geertz, 1973a, pp. 422–423)

Not even the motivation for the cockfight comes from the cocks—the Balinese decide that the cocks will fight, when they will fight, and which cocks are appropriate opponents. Bizarrely, but inevitably, the Balinese define "winning" and "losing" in the cockfight in a way that makes no sense for the cocks themselves. In natural cockfights, winning might mean ruling the roost or eating up the food or practically anything that increases fitness, but surely it does not mean falling down in the dust slaughtered alongside your opponent. In the cockfight blend, however, the winner is exactly whichever cock is left standing when the other drops, even if the winner "himself topples over an instant later." The winner wins no less absolutely if he expires immediately. The owner of the "winner" no less certainly takes the carcass of the "losing" cock home in order to eat it.

In the mental idea of the natural cockfight, there are of course two opposed cocks. If cocks did not fight on their own as a natural action, without human intervention, there would be no Balinese cockfight. In the quite different mental idea of Balinese society, there are two owners and the two cocks they own. These two owned cocks are not at all like natural cocks—they have a daily regimen of elaborate pampering that is invented, set, and supervised by human beings. Their breeding is at the pleasure of human beings. Never in their lives are they allowed to fight spontaneously. Nonetheless, different though wild and owned cocks be, they are connected; they are counterparts. In the cockfight blend, these two counterparts are fused: a single cock in the blend is simultaneously the prized and pampered property of a social man and a wild and violent autonomous animal.

This blending of natural and owned cock is merely a background achievement that invites the essential blending in the Balinese cockfight, a blending in which the owner is projected into his cock. The cocks in the Balinese cockfight are "surrogates for their owners' personalities, animal mirrors of psychic form" (Geertz, 1973a, p. 436). They include elements of their owners. Cocks "are symbolic expressions or magnifications of their owner's self, the narcissistic male ego writ out in Aesopian terms" (p. 419). Most important, the cock in the blend carries the owner's social status, making the cockfight blend, in a phrase Geertz borrows from Erving Goffman, "a status bloodbath" (p. 436).

This does not seem so remarkable until one recognizes that, in Balinese society, status is strictly inherited and cannot be changed, certainly not by a cockfight. The cockfight, says Geertz, makes nothing happen. "No one's status really changes. You cannot ascend the status ladder by winning cockfights; you cannot, as an individual, really ascend it at all. Nor can you descend it that way." But in the blend, you can. You can rise or fall, defeat or be defeated. In Balinese society, open altercation is impermissible and public display of social rivalry is so thoroughly masked as to be treated as if it never occurs. "The Balinese are shy to the point of obsessiveness of open conflict. Oblique, cautious, subdued, controlled, masters of indirection and dissimulation—what they call *alus*, 'polished,' 'smooth'—they rarely face what they can turn away from, rarely resist what they can evade" (Geertz, 1973a, p. 446).

But when men are cocks, which is to say, in the blend, they can attack each other furiously, and status can be gained or lost. "[H]ere they portray themselves as wild and murderous, with manic explosions of instinctual cruelty" (Geertz, 1973a, p. 446). Outside the blend, in the human social world and in the domain of natural cockfights, a man's status in society is entirely different from the status of a natural, autonomous cock in a fight. But inside the blend, the status of a man in Balinese society is blended with the performance of his cock, and this has psychosocial consequences: when his cock is victorious, his prestige is affirmed by the harmony between his status pride outside the blend and the status of his cock in the blend. Inversely, if his cock loses, his prestige is insulted by the discord between his status pride outside the blend and the status of his cock in the blend. The events in the cockfight blend thus have influence on the world of Balinese society. I will say that this is a "backward" influence, because usually the influence is from the influencing spaces to the blend, but in this case, meaning that develops in the blend has an influence on one of the original influencing spaces.

Crucially, inferences in the blend do not project back to Balinese society identically or even simply: the life or death of the cock in the blend does not entail the life or death of the social man outside the blend; the cock's gain or loss of status in the blend does not entail the gain or loss of social status for the social man; the fact that the cock cannot heal from death does not mean that the social man cannot recuperate from insult; the inability of the dead cock to get up ever again does not entail an inability of the social man to perform his roles. Yet inferences in the blend do project back powerfully, if temporarily, to the psychological uplifting or abasement of the social man. The Balinese compare heaven to the mood of a man whose cock has just won, and hell to the mood of a man whose cock has just lost. "A man who has lost an important fight is sometimes driven to wreck his family shrines and curse his gods, an act of metaphysical (and social) suicide" (Geertz, 1973a, p. 421).

The social man is of course a member of the social groups to which he belongs. By virtue of their metonymic link to him, they also project into the cock, so that the cockfight is—or more exactly, deliberately is made to be—a simulation of the social matrix, the involved system of cross-cutting, overlapping, highly corporate groups—villages, kingroups, irrigation societies, temple congregations, "castes"—in which its devotees live. And as prestige, the necessity to affirm it, defend it, celebrate it, justify it, and just plain bask in it (but not, given the strongly ascriptive character of Balinese stratification, to seek it), is perhaps the central driving force in the society, so also—ambulant penises, blood sacrifices, and monetary exchanges aside—is it of the cockfight. (p. 436)

The blend of social man and cock may look on first blush unusual, but it is, in the principles by which it arises, utterly familiar. The everyday mind has an effortless power to blend self and other. The man who says to a woman who earlier in her life declined to become pregnant, "If I were you, I would have done it," presents a mental blend that has impressive emergent structure: in the blend, which has the appropriate past time, there is a special blended person who has the capacities and situation and appearance and social identity of the woman but the judgment of the man, and this blended person becomes pregnant. The pregnancy is impossible for the two people involved in the influencing spaces: the man cannot do it; the woman did not do it. But the resolute counterfactuality of the blend does not at all suggest that it is an irrelevant fantasy. On the contrary, it is meant to illuminate the real world, the nature of the real man, the real woman, and real human life.

Such a blend creates a mental simulation, often extremely useful as a guide for potential enactments, judgments, and insights. Part of our ability to blend self and other is probably evolutionary: it is adaptive, in observing a predator or prey, to be able to make a blend that includes some of our reasoning and some of its situation and instincts. We can run a simulation to see what it might do. Certainly this is exceptionally useful in dealing with members of our own species, and in fact we blend ourselves and other people as a matter of routine interaction, a baseline capacity, part of what it means for a human being to be social.

Some of these blends of self and other involve what literary critics and psychologists call "identification." When we daydream that we are someone else, enacting what they have enacted, or what they might enact, and experiencing the emotional effects, we are creating an identification blend, a fictional simulation. Outside the blend, self and other remain perfectly distinct, unmistakably separate, not to mention unidentical, but in the blend, they join as a third person who is not merely a patchwork of some of their parts. The blend does not supplant or erase the spaces that influence it but rather exists with them inside a conceptual integration network. Like the influencing spaces from which it derives, the blend has its uses.

Blending offers the indispensable conceptual opportunity to disintegrate an integrated unit by projecting aspects of it to separate elements in the blend. This fission may seem schizophrenic, but it is only what we already do when we lament that our head is saying one thing and our heart another—in the blend, conflicted reason and emotion are separate people engaged in dispute. We can have three people in this blend if our judgment is made into a third person advised by reason and emotion: "my head is telling *me* one thing and my heart is telling *me* another." Like Faustus between the good and evil angels, our judgment receives conflicting lectures from the opposed advisors.

The Balinese social man, in exactly this way, is disintegrated in the blend. The status part of him, his psychological security, and his social "face" project from the influencing space with Balinese social man to the cock in the blend. His internal aggressiveness and his impulse to explicit social affront—completely inhibited in his life outside the blend—not only project into the cock but also leave their inhibitions behind as they go. The owner's virility and the virile activity of his penis also project into his cock. But other parts of him project to the owner in the blend, for the Balinese cockfight is a matter of human agency as much as animal action. The owner in the blend, if not the handler and spur expert himself, at least hires those people, discusses strategy with them, agrees to the terms of the fight, and speaks with the umpire. The owner's body and his speech, his power to own, and his normal social interaction all project to the owner in the blend. All the intentional actions that are permitted to him in society project to the owner in the blend; indeed, the only ones that project to the cock are those—some of them, anyway—forbidden to him in society. Last but not least, the owner's money in the influencing space projects to the owner in the blend: he places the (sometimes enormous) central bet. The owner outside the blend undergoes a disintegration as he is projected into the blend, since parts of him can now be found in two different places: the cock is more than a cock because it carries projections from the owner and is liberated in the blend to perform actions whose counterparts the man cannot perform outside the blend.

The Balinese cockfight blend has as its central purpose to comment on one of the influencing spaces—the men, not the cocks. It wants to say something about the space with the Balinese social men. It may be that the cockfight began originally as an entertainment, devoid of the blending that deliberately makes it into a "status bloodbath," but the Balinese cockfight of Geertz's interpretation exists to enact social aggression in a way that is impossible in Balinese society but vivid and pure in the blend, and to project consequences—slighting, affronting, insulting—back to the actual world of Balinese society, where those consequences are deeply felt even though the actions that create them are disallowed.

I will say that such a blend has as its purpose, or at least one of its important purposes, to "spotlight" or "solve for" or "say something about" one or both of its influencing spaces. As a consequence of this purpose, the blend must match the relevant influencing space in appropriate ways, for otherwise inferences that develop in the blend cannot be matched to counterpart inferences for that influencing space. Meaning that emerges in such a "spotlight" blend is meant to influence the influencing space, but the blend must "match" the influencing space in the relevant ways for this to happen. This "matching" has to do with relations between elements in a space. In general, other things being equal, when the purpose of a blend is to spotlight an influencing space, it is best if the *relations between elements in the blend* match the *relations between their counterparts in the influencing space from which they were projected*. Relations between elements in a space are referred to as "topology," and this constraint on building a blend is accordingly called the "topology constraint." The topology constraint is particularly weighty when the purpose of the blend is to "solve for" or "spotlight" or "say something about" an influencing space, because it is difficult to use the blend to say something about an influencing space if the relations in the influencing space are garbled as they are projected to the blend.

To be sure, blends can have many other purposes—among them humor, entertainment, heightened memorability, event integration—and for many of these purposes, backward projection to the influencing spaces is less important. For example, personal computers now standardly use the "desktop" interface, analyzed in Fauconnier and Turner (1998a), which is a blend of operations involving real desktops (opening and closing folders, putting files in folders, and so on), manipulation (moving a pointer around by hand, pressing buttons to lock and unlock), selecting from lists (pull-down menus), interpersonal commands (which the computer "executes"), and alphanumeric coding (programming languages). The purpose of the desktop blend, with its many influencing spaces, is to organize action—that is, the actual use of the computer—into a single integration; the purpose of the desktop blend is not to say something about desktops, manipulations, menus, commands, or programming. The desktop blend is not constructed in order to solve for, spotlight, or say something about its influences. Our integrated action in the desktop blend is meant to be guided by our intuitions projected from the influencing spaces, and that can happen only if the intuitions can flow into the blend, and *that* can happen only if the blend matches the influencing spaces in ways needed for the intuitions to survive and work appropriately in the blend.

Yet the desktop blend does not have as its purpose to project inferences and consequences back to the influencing spaces, so it need not match the influencing spaces on that account. For example, it is not important that the blend puts the trash can on the desktop instead of under it, or that its trash can never fills up, because we do not think the blend is trying to tell us something about how to deal with real trash cans. The purpose of the desktop blend is not to say something about actual desktops and trash cans, or menus, or manipulations, or commands, or coding languages.

But for the Balinese cockfight, the case is entirely different: consequences from the blend must project *back* to the actual social world. Accordingly, the blend must match the social world in certain ways. In cases of such backward projection, it is usually the structure of the *blend* that is manipulated to create the appropriate topological match between blend and influencing space; it is somewhat rarer that the influencing space is significantly altered to make the match.

To retreat and take up these complexities a little more slowly, let us consider a case in which we are *forbidden* to revise any of the established structure of one of the influencing spaces. This is the case in *reductio ad absurdum* arguments in mathematics (or logic). In such an argument, we prove that some assertion must be *false* by showing that a contradiction follows if we assume that it is true. These arguments proceed by blending. One influencing space has the established structure of the mathematical system with which we are working. The other has the assertion we think must be false. We keep the mathematical system, including its deduction procedures, intact, but blend some of it with the new and suspect assertion. We then run the blend according to the deduction procedures of the mathematical system until we derive something that conflicts with something else in the system.

Because the blend has been made to match the mathematical system perfectly except for the assumed hypothesis, we view the emergent contradiction in the blend as proof that the assumed hypothesis is false for the original mathematical system. (This view proceeds, of course, from the deeper assumption that the mathematical system itself is not internally contradicted.) Crucially, in setting up this *reductio ad absurdum* argument, *the influencing mathematical system is not at all adapted to match the blend*; rather, the blend is adapted, constructed, engineered so as to make an all-but-perfect match with the influencing mathematical system. At the outset of running the blend, the one imperfection in this match is exactly the assumed hypothesis.

Similarly, when a blend is constructed to solve a problem or riddle in the contributing spaces, preserving relevant matches between the blend and the contributing spaces is indispensable. Consider the riddle of the Buddhist monk, analyzed in Fauconnier and Turner (1998a): "A monk rises at dawn and begins to walk up a mountain path, which he reaches at sunset. He sits and meditates through the night, rises the next morning, and walks down the path, reaching the bottom at sunset. Prove that there is a place on the path that the monk inhabits at the same hour of the day on the two consecutive days." One interesting way to solve this riddle is to treat the ascent and descent as two influencing spaces and then to blend them, essentially by superimposition. Suppose you have a film of each monk on each day, beginning at dawn and ending at sunset, and you run the two films on two projectors simultaneously so the images superimpose on the same screen, making the two paths perfectly coincide. In the superimposed images, which combine the ascent and the descent, we will see at dawn two monks (that is, two instances of the same monk), one of them at the top of the path and one of them at the bottom of the path, who begin to traverse the path in opposite directions, each completing the journey at sunset. If one of them starts at the bottom at dawn and the other starts at the top at dawn, and by sunset they have switched places by walking along the same path, then they must have come together at some point. The monk must have met himself someplace, and that is exactly the place we seek.

There is an emergent event in the blend: the two monks meet. In the space with the ascent there is no meeting, and in the space with the descent there is no meeting. This emergent, inferential event of meeting in the blend projects back to give correlative inferences for the influencing spaces: now we know that in each influencing space, there exists some location on the path that the monk occupies at the same hour of the day in the two spaces, the ascent and the descent. The blend is able to deliver this solution only because, as the blend runs, the clocks in the three spaces match each other exactly, and, for each of the monks in the blend, his location and clock time match exactly the location and clock time of his counterpart in the relevant influencing space. In sum, the location and the clock time in the influencing space are projected *identically* into the blend: the location and the clock time for a monk in an influencing space match *exactly* the location and the clock time for his counterpart monk in the blend. If the blend were not engineered to preserve these exact relations from the influencing spaces, the inference of the encounter in the blend would not have clear counterpart inferences for the influencing spaces, and we would therefore not be able to solve the puzzle posed for those influencing space ;. In this case, where the blend is obviously built to "say something about the influencing spaces," matching the relations between influencing spaces and blend is achieved by engineering the blend in the right ways. This is the typical strategy.

Certainly the cockfight blend follows this typical strategy: the blend is manipulated to achieve relation matches between the blend and the contributing space of Balinese man. To begin with, Balinese society is finely governed by traditional conventions, and so the cockfight blend is engineered to be governed in this way, even though such traditions would be meaningless, unintelligible, and alien in a natural cockfight. Traditional governance is manufactured inside the blend for the purpose of increasing the match between the blend and Balinese society.

But what I want to focus on now is the conceptual engineering in the *opposite* direction—that is, changing the influencing space so it matches the blend better. This, as I say, is not the usual strategy for satisfying the topology constraint—that is, "Other things being equal, if two elements from an influencing space are projected to a blend, it is better if their relationship in the blend aligns with their relationship in the influencing space."

Remarkably, the influencing space with the Balinese men is *itself* changed to achieve a better match between the two influencing spaces and a better match between the influencing space with the men and the blend. It is changed in two ways. The first way arises as an attempt to fix a profound mismatch between the Balinese social matrix and natural cockfights. The Balinese social matrix is manifold, multivariate, and nonlinear. A single man is at once a member of several interacting social groups, some of them partially allied, some of them overlapping, some of them opposed, thus giving any particular social action significance simultaneously in many of these groups and making social life far more complicated than a sum of discrete and punctual face-to-face encounters. Cocks, on the other hand, engage in just these punctual face-to-face encounters. To make the match between men and cocks better, the influencing space with the men is engineered so as to select two men, two owners, and to make them stand out against the backdrop of the Balinese social matrix, to profile them against their full social context. For a moment, their one-on-oneness is cast into relief in the influencing space. This is a perfectly acceptable casting of particular social relations in Balinese society, and this casting of the influencing space makes it easier to match that influencing space with the other influencing space and with the blend. The inaccuracy of this profiling as a picture of the Balinese social matrix is softened, remedied by having each man backed up, as it were, by his social groups when he is involved in a cockfight. It is also remedied by some direct engineering of the blend: Balinese cockfights are scheduled one after another, so that the suite of cockfights gives us not a single sharp profiling of one-on-one opposition but instead many different oppositions, and this multiplicity of oppositions gives us a much fuller set of snapshots of the social matrix, from which we can deduce a larger and more nuanced system of relationships. For example, two men who take opposing sides in one Balinese cockfight might take the same side in a subsequent cockfight. The picture we get of allegiance in one cockfight is thus clarified, nuanced, and specified by situating it in the context of several other cockfights and the various allegiances they present.

The second manipulation of the influencing space to improve the match with the blend is the essential one, the one Geertz analyzes thoroughly and brilliantly—namely, the betting. Through wagering, which brings real consequences to the real social men, the psychological reality in the influencing space with the social men is altered so that it matches the blend better. This introduction of wagering is prompted by the central problem that the cockfight, being just a cockfight, does not have direct natural significance for the state of mind and prestige of the two owners and their groups. The cockfight has, after all, no actual effect on status. To be sure, ritual representation can be powerful, but its power in this case comes partly from strong engineering that makes the cockfight heavily consequential *in social reality* for the principals, since they bet (and must bet) heavily on their own cocks, and it is real money—not just funny "blend" money—that they really lose or really win through this betting.

Geertz explains the gradient between "shallow" cockfights, in which the principals have relatively low social status, bet little money, and may be most interested in the money gambling, and "deep" cockfights, the ones that are the prototypes of the game, that everyone takes seriously, and that Geertz is interested to interpret. In "deep" cockfights, the principals have high social status, bet enormous sums, and are engaged mostly in status gambling. "Deep play" refers to these deep cockfights; it is a term Geertz borrows from Jeremy Bentham, who uses it, Geertz explains, to mean

> play in which the stakes are so high that it is, from his [Bentham's] utilitarian standpoint, irrational for men to engage in it at all. If a man whose fortune is a thousand pounds (or ringgits) wages five hundred of it on an even bet, the marginal utility of the pound he stands to win is clearly less than the marginal disutility of the one he stands to lose. In genuine deep play, this is the case for both parties. They are both in over their heads. (Geertz, 1973, pp. 432–433)

Winning or losing a relatively large amount of money is a real social event. In Balinese society, wealth correlates with status, and a change of wealth powerfully represents a change in status without actually entailing it. Since, in the Balinese cockfight, the "house" does not bet, and excises only a ten percent vigorish to cover the cost of the event, and since winners can never get out of the game for long, since cockfighting is, for people of high status, an obligatory part of cultural life, this dramatic, sudden change of wealth is, for all but irrational bettors, only temporary. The invention of the betting is a manipulation of the social world to improve the match between the cockfight blend and the influencing space with the Balinese social men: the cockfight is no longer just a cockfight, not even just a cockfight with strong ritual connotations, but instead the cause of impressive and visible, thrilling and disturbing, changes in wealth for the Balinese social men.

Geertz (1973a), in so many words, provides a superb analysis of the way in which the betting serves to make a better match between the relations in the blend and the relations in the influencing space that has Balinese society:

> But for the Balinese, although naturally they do not formulate it in so many words, the explanation lies in the fact that in such play, money is less a measure of utility, had or expected, than it is a symbol of moral import, perceived or imposed . . . (p. 433). It is because money *does*, in this hardly unmaterialistic society, matter and matter very much that the more of it one risks, the more of a lot of other things, such as one's pride, one's poise, one's dispassion, one's masculinity, one also risks, again only momentarily but again very publicly as well. In deep cockfights an owner and his collaborators, and, as we shall see, to a lesser but still quite real extent also their backers on the outside, put their money where their status is.
>
> It is in large part *because* the marginal disutility of loss is so great at the higher levels of betting that to engage in such betting is to lay one's public self, allusively and metaphorically, through the medium of one's cock, on the line. . . . (p. 434)
>
> What makes Balinese cockfighting deep is thus not money in itself, but what, the more of it that is involved the more so, money causes to happen: the migration of the Balinese status hierarchy into the body of the cockfight. (p. 436)

Much of the power of Geertz's analysis comes from his elaborate "theory which sees cockfight wagering as the link connecting the fight to the wider world of Balinese culture," or, as I would put it, his explanation of the way in which the betting system changes Balinese social reality (one influencing space) so as to make a better match between relations in that influencing space and relations in the cockfight blend.

I have mentioned only the rudiments of Geertz's analysis. I have also skipped entirely his discussion of the principles according to which the center bet is made up of funds pooled by the owner and his social associates, and skipped his thorough analysis of the extraordinarily complicated system of side betting, which is not, in its appearance or financial structure, anything like the central betting, and which allows those not participating in the central bet to make public announcements—in the form of shouted bids—not of their evaluations of the cocks but rather of their allegiances to those engaged in the central betting. Geertz explains the complicated interaction between these two formally asymmetric kinds of betting as aspects of a larger nonlinear cultural system of signification.

Bettors in the cockfight blend are guided by this strong match between the social matrix and the cockfight blend. Placing any bet prefers one cock over another, and, via the match between the blend and the Balinese social matrix, it prefers one man over another. This presents an impossible situation to a bettor whose loyalties are evenly divided between the two men. A participant caught in this bind simply ejects himself from the blend: "where a man is caught between two more or less equally balanced loyalties, he tends to wander off for a cup of coffee or something to avoid having to bet" (Geertz, 1973a, p. 439). Because there is a strong match between betting on a cock and preferring its owner, a change in social allegiance can be signaled by placing a certain bet: "There is a special word for betting against the grain. . . . The institutionalized hostility relation, *puik*, is often formally initiated (though its causes always lie elsewhere) by such a 'pardon me' bet in a deep fight, putting the symbolic fat in the fire." Conversely, the cessation of hostility is signaled when one man bets on his previous enemy's bird.

But using betting to make a better match between Balinese society and the blend—so that which cock wins and which loses has immediate and large financial consequences for the actual Balinese men—creates a dicey problem. Social man must avoid open altercation, even confrontation. To be sure, the Balinese cockfight very nicely solves the problem by projecting the social aggression into the blend, where it is the cocks, not the men, who do the work. But this partitioning, while highly satisfying, cannot be entirely successful because the betting—the central mechanism for making events in the blend consequential for prestige and status in the society—actually has another consequence: it creates confrontational roles for the actual men *inside the blend*. Inside the blend, the men must confront, in some fashion, if they are to make a match, place bets, or collect winnings, and these are the very men who are socially constrained to avoid open, face-to-face confrontation.

Therefore, the blend is engineered as much as possible to deal with the sticky but unavoidable problem of confrontational roles for men who are supposed to avoid open confrontation. For example, while in many cultures it is common in betting for a neutral party to hold the stakes to make sure that the bets are actually paid, in the case of the Balinese cockfight there is an additional motivation for the umpire's holding the stakes in the central bet and awarding them to the winner: to make it possible for the two opponents to be completely disengaged at the moment of payment. This disengagement avoids, among other things, "the intense embarrassment both winner and loser would feel if the latter had to pay off personally following his defeat" (p. 439). The procedure for making the match and placing the central bet is designed to export as far as possible all the confrontation to the cocks:

> After a fight has ended and the emotional debris is cleaned away—the bets have been paid, the curses cursed, the carcasses possessed—seven, eight, perhaps even a dozen men slip negligently into the ring with a cock and seek to find there a logical opponent for it. This process, which rarely takes less than ten minutes, and often a good deal longer, is conducted in a very subdued, oblique, even dissembling manner. Those not immediately involved give it at best but disguised, sidelong attention; those who, embarrassedly, are, attempt to pretend somehow that the whole thing is not really happening. A match made, the other hopefuls retire with the same deliberate indifference. . . . (p. 421)
>
> The center bet . . . is thus the most direct and open expression of social opposition, which is one of the reasons why both it and matchmaking are surrounded by such an air of unease, furtiveness, embarrassment, and so on. (p. 439)

Even side bets are paid hurriedly, furtively, with embarrassment.

The umpire is an index of this structural problem, which arises because men socially constrained to avoid confrontation are inserted into a blend where the central act is pure, violent, punctual slaughter and where they bet in a pattern that cannot be leeched of all its confrontation. Uninhibited, overt, bloody confrontation can be left to the cocks, but the cocks cannot set rules or enforce them, keep time or hand over money, nor, for example, can two dead cocks decide which of them has won. The role of umpire is created in the blend to handle all of these potential sources of open conflict and thus to remove them as points of tension between two men who would, to decide them, have to confront face-to-face. The umpire's role is created in the blend by projecting to it all of the strong constraints against altercation that prevail in society. It is not just that the umpire's official authority is absolute; no one even protests or reacts to it:

> I have never seen an umpire's judgment questioned on any subject, even by the more despondent losers, nor have I ever heard, even in private, a charge of unfairness directed against one, or, for that matter, complaints about umpires in general. . . . In the dozens of cockfights I saw in Bali, I never once saw an altercation about rules. Indeed, I never saw an open altercation, other than those between cocks, at all. (pp. 424–425)

At the same time, and in the same way, the umpire indexes another fascinating aspect of the Balinese cockfight blend—namely, that the governing structure of the Balinese cockfight blend has been negotiated by many social actors over generations. This elaborate negotiation by many social agents is unusual, or at least, it marks the Balinese cockfight as a certain kind of blend, because other kinds of blends are not governed in this way. A daydream or thought experiment blend, for example, of course arises according to structural and dynamic principles of blending and is governed by the set of competing guiding principles, but the mind doing the blending is free to try various projections without consulting the entire tribe about their acceptability. In the Balinese cockfight blend, however, there is a lot at stake; there will be a winner and a loser, so naturally, everything from making the match to engaging the cocks is governed by traditional negotiated rules. The carrier of this tradition of distributed negotiation, and the enforcer of its rules, is the umpire. His role requires exceptional authority of every kind, and predictably is created by blending together as many pre-existing authorities as the Balinese can find: "Likened to a judge, a king, a priest, and a policeman, he is all of these, and under his assured direction the animal passion of the fight proceeds within the civic certainty of the law" (p. 424). The holder of the role must be suitable for this authority, and so "Only exceptionally well trusted, solid, and given the complexity of the code, knowledgeable citizens perform this job, and in fact men will bring their cocks only to fights presided over by such men" (p. 424).

Again, not to belabor the obvious point, the Balinese social matrix has no role for "umpire," and certainly the domain of natural cockfights has no role for "umpire." The role of umpire, launched by the blending of "judge, king, priest, and policeman," is a new pivotal and indispensable role that arises in the cockfight blend as emergent conceptual structure. The meaning of the space with the Balinese men and the meaning of the space with the autonomous, natural cocks descend into the blend and create a new descendent, the Balinese cockfight blend, which has new, emergent meaning, including the new role for an umpire.

HAVING IT BOTH WAYS

The Balinese cockfight blend has peaceful social men and violent animal cocks blended into a contradictory package that may seem at first impossible or at least anthropologically exotic but that, in its principles, is normal and universal for human beings. When we daydream about being another person, or imagine ourselves better or worse, or wonder whether we would be happy doing this or successful doing that, or speak from our experience to advise a child, we are running a mental simulation in which, inside the blend, there is an element that is both us and not us. When we think about how things might be if only a particular event had not occurred, or had occurred, we are running a mental simulation in which, inside the blend, we have our life but do not have our life. In the blend, we have it both ways. If someone says, "Why don't you have a fax machine at home? I do. You could be reading my paper now," we are prompted to construct a "crosswise doubleness"—"doubleness" for the two influencing spaces, "crosswise" for the intersection of some of their meaning in the blend. We are asked to construct a conceptual integration network, a having-it-both-ways no different, in its mental operation, from the Balinese cockfight.

Of course, there are always astounding examples of any mental operation, blending included, and having it both ways can produce some hilarious scenarios. At a cocktail party following a presentation I gave on blending, a professor revealed that he had once, as a graduate student, returned to his apartment building so drunk that he could not get his key into the door, and despaired, but in a flash realized that he could solve the problem by pushing the buzzer for his apartment, thereby alerting himself that he needed to be buzzed in—an admirable blending of two scenes (himself at the door and himself inside his apartment) with a beautiful logic that indeed solves the problem because it replaces a difficult, precise action (insert key) with two easy, gross actions (push big buttons), yet which happens to fail in practice fails because its particular impossibility stops it from applying in a useful way to reality. You can't be both downstairs at the door to the building and inside your apartment. Blending in a goofy case like this does not differ as an operation from blending in "Paul believes he'll get his daughter admitted to Princeton because he thinks Mary is the dean of admissions," which prompts for a blend of some of what we believe to be true about Paul, his daughter, Mary, and admission to Princeton, but with emergent structure, true only in the blend, that Mary is dean of admissions and Paul's daughter is admitted. The falsity, perhaps even impossibility (Mary could be dead, for example), of this blend is now not funny, not even a hilarious mistake on Paul's part, but instead an explanation of his dispositions and actions contingent upon his beliefs and desires. "I wish I'd had your house; I'd still be living here," said a speaker to a listener as they viewed the remains of the speaker's home, which had been burned to the ground, both knowing that the listener owns an adobe home four hundred miles away, virtually fireproof but completely impossible for the speaker's lot.

All of these examples and, in fact, much of what we think, say, and do in an ordinary day require intricate, orderly, and impressive conceptual blending. Mundane blends are often as intricate in their conception as angels, marionettes, and the Balinese cockfight.

The Balinese cockfight has it both ways (slaughter and peace, cock and man) in the blend, but it also, like all conceptual integration networks, has it both ways in another sense: it allows us to think both inside and outside the blend. The blend does not eliminate the influencing spaces. On the contrary, the blend exists inside a conceptual integration network of different and interacting mental spaces, all of them with their uses. We can work inside the blend, or outside the blend, or in both simultaneously and interactingly. This having-it-both-ways by being both inside and outside the blend is recognized by the Balinese and analyzed by Geertz (1973a):

> Fighting cocks, almost every Balinese I have ever discussed the subject with has said, is like playing with fire only not getting burned. You activate village and kingroup rivalries and hostilities, but in "play" form, coming dangerously and entrancingly close to the expression of open and direct interpersonal and intergroup aggression (something which, again, almost never happens in the normal course of ordinary life), but not quite, because, after all, it is "only a cockfight." (p. 440)

Operating at the same time in different mental spaces, inside the blend and outside the blend, is not irrational, not even unusual. The person cursing the spare tire, or the telephone, for refusing to comply with her wishes is not deluded. Although she finds it useful to have emotions and actions that make sense inside the blend, in which the phone or tire is intentional, she will, if asked whether she believes the object is literally refusing to comply, find it hard to take the question seriously. Working inside the blended space does not preclude working with the entire integration network, including of course the space in which it is "only" a tire or a telephone. We create mental blends to see whether we want to make them real, or to create emotional states, or to draw inferences that impinge upon reality, or to solve problems, or to achieve a compressed version of more diffuse knowledge, or to supply a global insight into diffuse knowledge, or to create new meaning, or to help us reason to choices, or for other purposes, and in doing so we often work inevitably, simultaneously, having it both ways, with a blend and an influencing space that are incompatible or even, sometimes, centrally opposed.

Blends let you do what you cannot do, be what you cannot be, not always so you can escape your situation, but instead, often, so you can learn about, make decisions about, and develop consequences for your situation, especially your mental and social reality, through events in a blend that, sometimes, for one reason or another, cannot or will not in fact be real. The Balinese, for example, when they are working outside the blend, enforce the sharpest possible distinction between man and animal: "The Balinese revulsion against any behavior regarded as animal-like can hardly be overstressed," writes Geertz. "Babies are not allowed to crawl for that reason." Even eating is regarded as disgusting, "to be conducted hurriedly and privately, because of its association with animality" (1973a, p. 420). And yet, in the blend, men can be animals:

> In identifying with his cock, the Balinese man is identifying not just with his ideal self, or even his penis, but also, and at the same time, with what he most fears, hates, and ambivalence being what it is, is fascinated by—"The Powers of Darkness." . . . In the cockfight, man and beast, good and evil, ego and id, the creative power of aroused masculinity and the destructive power of loosened animality fuse in a bloody drama of hatred, cruelty, violence, and death. It is little wonder that when, as is the invariable rule, the owner of the winning cock takes the carcass of the loser—often torn limb from limb by its enraged owner—home to eat, he does so with a mixture of social embarrassment, moral satisfaction, aesthetic disgust, and cannibal joy. (pp. 420–421)

REPRESENTATIONS AND INSTANCES

The cognitive features of the Balinese cockfight blend I have run through so far—influencing spaces, counterpart mappings, partial projection to the blend, emergent structure in the blend, possibilities for backward projection so that inferences and emotions developed in the blend can influence the original influencing spaces, and competing guiding principles like topology, integration, and metonymy compression—apply to all instances of conceptual integration, but the Balinese cockfight blend has an arresting exceptional feature that, however common, is not at all required for blending: it has an external, material representation or anchor.

My using the word "external" with the connotation "exceptional" conjures up for me, unbidden, a vivid blend in which Clifford Geertz, reading my prose, shakes his head in slow dismay. Geertz has spent a lifetime arguing that meaning is public. He has attacked cognitivist, behaviorist, and idealist "fallacies" for their misconceptions of culture. He has argued that "thinking as an overt, public act, involving the purposeful manipulation of objective materials, is probably fundamental to human beings; and thinking as a covert, private act, and without recourse to such materials, a derived, though not unuseful, capability" (Geertz, 1973a, p. 439).

Modern cognitive science, far from recycling the simplistic views Geertz has attacked, instead provides the best argument for the complex interactions upon which he has insisted. Human capacities result from interacting suites of genetic mechanisms, cellular mechanisms, developmental programs, physical environments, and social, cultural, and intentional environments. Cognitive science has generally recognized and demonstrated that only through empirical investigation can we come to know which suites and interactions actually make human beings what they are. The role of bodily, interpersonal, and public action in the development of minds that are able to engage in covert thinking is a common issue in cognitive science, from developmental psychology to cognitive linguistics. Cognitive scientists who study "distributed cognition" have shown the ways in which successful cognition often requires many functionally interacting agents and instruments, no one of whom conducts the thinking entirely or even mostly, as is the case when an aircraft carrier is successfully and coherently navigated by rotating teams of navigators, some of whom interact with other people and instruments on the ship. Edwin Hutchins's "How a Cockpit Remembers Its Speeds" is a fine, short study in this tradition. Cognitive science routinely explores the ways in which bodily states influence thinking, environments influence thinking, and human beings arrange their environments to serve, extend, and alter their thinking, or, metaphorically, rely on their environments to do some of their thinking for them.

"Public" and "distributed" are compatible with "mental" and "neurobiological." The natural conjunction of these terms, which have often been used as if they were antithetical, is part of what cognitive science has to say to social science. Meaning, attributed by intentional beings—indeed, by the brains of those intentional beings (in bodies, in environments, in cultures)—can be crucially public, distributed, and indispensably dependent upon objects and situations, but it is still the people, not the tools or the spaces, who find things meaningful.

In the case of the Balinese cockfight, one can have the mental blend without having ever seen or engaged in the overt, public acts of its representation. Indeed, anyone reading this chapter has by now developed a mental blend of men and cocks, but Geertz is probably the only reader among them who has ever had the chance to develop some of that blend by learning it from its public representation in the fifty-square-foot ring in a Balinese village. And most of the very many mental blends a human being constructs in a day have no external representation at all. For example, I can have my blended Geertz—which, interestingly, is not my image of how Geertz responds to my assertions but instead my image of how other people's mistaken conception of Geertz responds—without anyone's being aware of the blend except me and without there being any perceptible mark of it and without there being any perceptible text of any sort that serves to prompt others to construct it and without my developing it through public, overt action.

But, by contrast, the Balinese cockfight blend does have a representation, or rather, particular instances of it have representations, with particular people and cocks in its various roles, and particular events that happen in and around the fifty-square-foot ring, events understood by everybody as a representation of the particular mental blend of these owners and these cocks.

It is characteristic of Geertz that he would select for analysis a blend with an external representation that is maximally public and maximally populated by an anthropological group, and that moreover, in its serial instances, involves the entire community. It is also characteristic of Geertz's preferences that the representation would, on its surface, look exotic to his scholarly audience, and that he would investigate it as a matter of historical retrospection, emphasizing its particularity. Interpretive social science does its work on this plane of historical retrospection and particularity, of overt public acts, of cultural meanings on their face inscrutable. But Geertz's analysis is compatible with working on a different scientific plane, one in which it is natural to see the Balinese cockfight as a product of a universal, common, routine mental operation that only exceptionally pivots on external representation, public performance, or group involvement. Blending these two planes gives us a fuller story of human meaning.

Geertz emphasizes that some of the purposes of the cockfight representation are shared in general by representational art, from *Macbeth* to *David Copperfield*. If your purpose is to prompt someone to construct a mental blend, then there has to be a prompt, perhaps a representation, and the prompting must be effective. What is most remarkable in the case of the Balinese cockfight—something that separates it from *Macbeth* and *David Copperfield*—is that it makes no sense to ask what "the inventor" of the Balinese cockfight hoped to prompt the audience to construct (in the way we can intelligibly ask, using the traditional principles of historical criticism, what the author of *Macbeth* might reasonably have hoped the mental reception of its performance would be). There was no inventor or author of the Balinese cockfight representation in the canonical sense. It seems instead to have developed by gradual accretion and refinement into a representation that prompts for a cultural conceptual integration network and that educates the community in its intricacy, without having anything in its history that resembles an intentional author. If that is the case, then the selection of the Balinese cockfight is in another way appropriate to Geertz's tastes: it shows not only maximal distributed cognition in the moment of the cockfight but also maximal distributed invention over its history.

Even more, it is a case where aspects of the representation (cocks fighting) existed before they were a "representation"—that is, before they had been given a constructed significance inside the conceptual integration network of the Balinese cockfight. The notion of the Balinese cockfight could have come up quite incrementally—all that is needed to start it is some minimal conceptual conjunction of social man and cock. After that point, any knowledge or fact having to do with cocks and their fights becomes a potential carrier of meaning in the blend. Whatever belongs to the representation tends to acquire conceptual significance: we are disposed to take elements of representations as prompting us to construct some counterpart structure for the conceptual blend, and to take structure in the blend as connected to the influencing spaces. This makes the Balinese cockfight a particularly fine example of the way in which the public actions of an artform can be prior to their significance, prior even to their status as artforms. The Balinese cockfight, historically and developmentally, begins where Geertz prefers, in the public and distributed arena.

Much of the ingenuity and appeal of the cockfight arises from an unusual feature: the representation deploys realities to which its influencing spaces refer. Specifically, one of the influencing spaces has cocks (as mental elements, of course) and refers to real cocks; the other influencing space has social men (again, as mental elements, of course) and refers to real social men. But the representation has real cocks and real social men.

To see how strange that is, consider a cartoon representation of a politician as a spider. The representation—the physical cartoon itself, printed on the page—does not deploy a real flesh-and-blood politician-spider (an element to which the blend refers), nor does it deploy a real flesh-and-blood politician or a real flesh-and-blood spider (elements to which the influencing spaces refer). Representations typically do not deploy real elements to which the influencing spaces refer. Consider, for example, the central panel of Rogier van der Weyden's *Altarpiece of the Seven Sacraments*, which naturally shows the Eucharist as located inside the church, but through a double representation: the first, minor representation of the Eucharist in the painting is the mass that is being celebrated inside the church, at the altar, in the background of the painting, by the priest who is raising a consecrated host; the other, theological representation of the Eucharist in the picture is Christ crucified, attended by the Virgin, Saint John, and the Holy Women, who are reacting to crucifixion as an immediate event, and who are located inside the church, in the foreground of the painting. We are to understand that the consecrated host is a blend of the object of transubstantiation and the body of Christ: as wafer, it has a human manufacture, and, as body of Christ, it has a divine origin. But Rogier van der Weyden's double representation *does not deploy the real elements to which the blend refers or to which the influencing spaces refer—* simply, the physical painting (paint, frame, etc.) does not use wafer, Eucharist, something transubstantiated, something edible, the mouth of a communicant, something of divine origin, and so on. (It does use something of human manufacture, but not the human manufacture referred to by the influencing space with the wafer.)

Similarly, if we survey high canon representations of the Annunciation, we "see" the Virgin holding, anachronistically, a lectionary, opened to the narrative of the Annunciation. We have no trouble interpreting this representation as evoking a blend of a young girl and the Mother of God. The Virgin's bedroom may additionally have features of a church—the lectionary stand and veil that are part of the furniture of an altar, trinitarian tracery windows in Broederlam's version, a full Gothic church interior as in one of Jan van Eyck's versions. Annunciations may have a representation of God in the upper left, although we do not interpret this to mean that God was just up and to the left of the bedroom. They may also have lines interpreted as the "breath" of God, even though breath is invisible and the substance issuing from God's mouth is not only breath but also spirit and the creation of life. This inspiration may carry a dove that is simultaneously the Holy Spirit, or perhaps, as in the Mérode Altarpiece, a homunculus already tolerating his own miniature cross. There are lilies, a fountain (or kettle or pitcher and bowl), the snuffed candle, and, always, scenery familiar to the artist. The representation evokes a blend of girl with Mother of God (itself a blend, of course), bedroom with church, breath with life, and so on, but the physical painting (paint, frame, etc.) that is the representation does not use a real girl, her real bedroom, a real church, God, or the Mother of God, nor does it use real breath, real lilies, a real dove, and so on. No doubt, the representation of the Annunciation represents elements to which the blend and the contributing spaces refer, but it does not actually use those real elements.

The Balinese cockfight blend, by contrast, has a representation that does use elements to which the influencing spaces refer. It uses real cocks. It has particular, real owners placing a particular, real central bet in a particular, real village on a particular, real day, and particular, real cocks who really fight, with a particular, real outcome. What all this reality represents is the particular mental blend of these particular owners and these particular cocks. That particular mental blend is of course an instance of the general Balinese cockfight blend, which has roles for owner-cocks and outcomes but no values in those roles. The general Balinese cockfight blend is the one we have been discussing all along, since we have made no mention of particular owners, particular cocks, or particular outcomes. But an enacted Balinese cockfight is always a representation of a specific instance of that mental blend, and—the surprising part—it always has real cocks that really fight. It is as if Rogier's representation of the Eucharist used a real crucifixion. It is as if the Mérode representation of the Annunciation somehow used a real dove, or, odder still, used real elements from Mary's real bedroom and a real church. The representation of a particular Balinese cockfight blend is of course quite real—real things really happen in the real fifty-square-foot ring. That reality always includes real elements—cocks—that are referred to by one of the influencing spaces.

This reality—real, particular cocks really fighting—has a dynamic structure all its own. Cocks are live tactical agents. Deploying them in the representation has the amazing consequence that the central event in the representation is not scripted; instead, it is handed over largely to the unpredictable actions of real cocks. The general Balinese cockfight blend comes with structure, as Geertz puts it, "joining pride to selfhood, selfhood to cocks, and cocks to destruction" (Geertz, 1973a, p. 444), and this structure is entirely inherited by any particular instance of the Balinese cockfight blend, but in the particular instance, what gets destroyed and by whom is largely a matter for the real birds to settle. It is essentially the real cocks in the representation that are in charge of how the representation plays out, and how it plays out has strong influence on the structure evoked for the conceptual blend. In turn, the structure it evokes for the conceptual blend has effect for the actual pride of the actual men in the influencing space. Through this chain, the unpredictable dynamism of the representation has a profound effect on the influencing space that has the particular social men (as mental elements, of course), and, indeed, on the real psychology of the real men to whom that space refers. This makes the Balinese cockfight appropriate in yet another way for Geertz's tastes, since it portrays meaning, even the most vital understandings of self and other and society, as induced through public action whose root causality—which cock's spur bolts into which cock's body—is beyond covert thought, and certainly beyond individually controlled covert thought. Individual inner meaning having to do with selfhood is, in this case, brought on by the actions of other agents in public.

Actually, blends that are set up like this, to be driven by their representations, are not all that rare. A particular Tarot reading of a deck of cards, for example, evokes the blending of elements of a life story with elements of a deck of cards. The representation—that is, the real turning over of the particular cards in a particular sequence—includes something referred to by one of the influencing spaces, namely the real deck of cards and its order. How that representation plays out is a matter largely of the accidental facts of that particular deck of cards—some cards will come up, in some order. These accidents in the representation evoke specifications of the blend, which in turn can induce revision of the influencing space with the person whose life is being read. Astrology is another case in which fate, the universe, chance, and systems beyond human control are allowed to have their say about human reality, through blending, and in which elements referred to by an influencing space—that is, the heavenly bodies and their dynamics—are actually deployed in the representation.

Leaving aside the possibility that various match sports are already blends of combat and cooperation, enemies and friends, and looking at only those cases where the matched teams are additionally national—America's Cup sailing, World Cup soccer—we again have a representation of the blend (in this case, a blend of national status and sports-team status) that includes real agents whose actions drive the specifics of the representation, thereby evoking structure in the blend, thereby affecting the influencing spaces. I was once surprised to find myself a little unsettled when it became evident that "we"—Americans in this case—were going to lose the America's Cup. I had thought I was interested exclusively in the sailing, and until that moment had been certain I wanted the Kiwis to win, so the next Cup could be held in the Hauraki Gulf in Auckland. I have been in European countries where the entire population has seemed to go into a psychological subduction near mourning because a few random guys—"their" soccer team—lost to a few other random guys "representing" a neighboring country. All of this makes more believable historical accounts of, as Geertz might put it, "the thrill of risk, the despair of loss, the pleasure of triumph" attendant upon a medieval joust. Battle by champion, if it ever in fact happened, would be an even more dramatic case in which the blend of political competition with man-to-man combat had a representation that used elements referred to by an influencing space, and whose dynamics actually altered the reality referred to by the political influencing space.

Geertz especially emphasizes the way in which a representation can give a public revelation of meanings otherwise veiled. In the case of the Balinese cockfight blend, the representation publicizes a set of social attitudes and dispositions that are otherwise strongly masked and never directly enacted: "The slaughter in the cock ring is not a depiction of how things literally are among men, but, what is almost worse, of how, from a particular angle, they imaginatively are" (1973a, p. 446). Public revelation is a medium of education:

> Attending cockfights and participating in them is, for the Balinese, a kind of sentimental education. What he learns there is what his culture's ethos and his private sensibility (or, anyway, certain aspects of them) look like when spelled out externally in a collective text; that the two are near enough alike to be articulated in the symbolics of a single such text; and—the disquieting part—that the text in which this revelation is accomplished consists of a chicken hacking another mindlessly to bits. (1973a, p. 449)

Although some blends can be realized ("If he goes to the plastic surgeon in Rio, you won't recognize him"), the Balinese cockfight blend cannot be fully realized, not least because a single organism cannot be both man and cock, but also because the Balinese do not want their social ethos and private sensibilities enacted as confrontation. Yet its representation can make some of the elements of the blend real and can also make some symbols connected to other elements of the blend real, and this is important, for powerful as mental simulation is, it does not have the same force as perception and action. The reality of the representation gives a taste of an imaginative domain that the Balinese do not want realized. Having a bit of something, especially if we have it regularly, can be enough to let us see that (and why) we want only that much.

THE HUMAN MIND

In analyzing the Balinese cockfight as a cultural text, Geertz has equally exposed it as a product of a basic mental operation. That basic mental operation is universal to all cognitively modern human beings, everywhere, in all cultures, past, passing, and to come.

This claim, unbearably broad no doubt for the typical interpretive social scientist, understates what Fauconnier and I have argued since 1995, that conceptual integration, especially conceptual integration of the double-scope sort evident in the Balinese cockfight, is the mental capacity that makes human beings human, the one that separates them, and phylogenetically did separate them, from other species and from earlier anatomically modern human beings. Some species appear to be perfectly capable of perceptual and conceptual categorization, short- and long-term and episodic memory, social and natural intelligence, framing of even novel situations according to existing frames, and the adjustment, tuning, and refinement of frames. What they do not appear to be able to do with facility is double-scope blending. Fauconnier and I have proposed, for example, that double-scope blending was indispensable for the development of language or any systematic and flexible symbolism.

In 1994, Fauconnier and I published a technical report on blending, followed by some articles, and two years later, we each published a book—mine was *The Literary Mind: The Origins of Thought and Language*; his was *Mappings in Thought and Language*—presenting the elements of the theory. At nearly the same time, other scholars, working independently of us, began to advance similar claims emphasizing the singular importance of these integrations. In 1996, Steven Mithen, a cognitive archeologist, published *The Prehistory of the Mind: The Cognitive Origins of Art, Religion, and Science*, in which he argues that our species did not come into its own, did not invent what we think of as culture, until our ancestors developed a sophisticated ability to blend together structure from different conceptual domains. He calls this ability "cognitive fluidity" rather than "blending," and the flavor of his work is quite different from ours in its focus on archeology and the stages of hominid evolution, but it still offers an unmistakable and arresting overlap with our claims that double-scope blending was, as Mithen puts it, "the big bang" of human evolution. Even his diagrams and his examples are congenial with ours: he discusses people-animals in totemism, animal-people in anthropomorphism, animals with human social behavior in jokes ("A kangaroo walked into a bar and asked for a scotch and soda . . ."), people as objects to be manipulated, and dining as a blend of eating and social communication.

Also in 1996, Terrence Deacon, a comparative neuroscientist and evolutionary anthropologist, published *The Symbolic Species: The Co-evolution of Language and the Brain*. Without explicitly addressing conceptual blending, Deacon argues that the essential leap for human culture and the human brain was the development of an ability to forge relational networks of symbols that hold together other relational networks, in a cascade, thus making it possible for human beings to draw together elements from many different domains. This evolutionary leap was hard. The incremental transition to nascent symbolic culture was made possible by the invention of ritual, which, in Deacon's view, is a pedagogical device for supporting the difficult learning of cross-domain associations and suppressing the disposition to attend exclusively to immediate tokens. The cognitive power of ritual lies in its public repetition—over and over again in the same scene, immediate and memorable—of prompts to forge and hold a specific set of cross-domain conceptual blends. In fact, his analysis of ritual is almost exactly parallel to the one Geertz gave in "Religion as a Cultural System":

> In a ritual, the world as lived and the world as imagined, fused under the agency of a single set of symbolic forms, turn out to be the same world, producing [a] transformation in one's sense of reality. . . . (1973a, p. 112)

Mithen and Deacon disagree on so many points that they might be surprised to see themselves shaking hands here in my text, but it is intriguing that such different thinkers, coming from such different fields, have proposed that the defining story for our species—culturally, intellectually, and neurobiologically— is the story of how we came to develop the ability to forge conceptual integration networks.

This story is neither triumphal nor joyful. Double-scope blending carries grave pain, not for genes but for the emotional human minds routinely obliterated when human bodies die. A human mind lives in a dynamically shifting weave of many blends and through them constitutes its existence and imposes meaning, not always pleasant, on its life. A child who died horribly a decade ago is still with us, never leaves, is always there to cast his shadow on the day, even though our days have changed radically over the decade. In the blend, we can imagine him living and appropriately aged, and we do. We can cringe or smile at what we imagine to be our dead grandmother's reactions to our daughter's decisions, although in life our grandmother never met our daughter. We often take our cues for action, feeling, or belief from these blends. We assemble blended futures and choose between them, or blended counterfactual presents and grieve at their counterfactuality.

"Who has twisted us like this?" asks Rilke (1961/1922, p. 65), "*Wer hat uns also umgedreht?*"

> . . . the shrewd animals
> notice that we're not very much at home
> in the world we've expounded.
> und die findigen Tiere merken es schon,
> daß wir nich sehr verläßlich zu Haus sind
> in der gedeuteten Welt. (p. 2)

No person, thing, idiosyncratic culture, or local event has twisted us like this, but rather our common phylogenetic development for a mental capacity that brings unprecedented power but no guarantee of pleasure—blending.

Blending is the deepest play of all. What I mean by "deep play" is the mental operation that makes us distinctively human. What Geertz means by "deep play" is a particular historical, and fairly bizarre-looking, sociological entity, optional, punctual, and relatively infrequent, somewhere on an island in Indonesia. But Geertz's Balinese deep play is a product of cognitive deep play, the mental operation of blending, which is neither particular nor past, neither punctual nor infrequent, neither bizarre nor optional, but constant, the working web of the human mind, the phenomenon that distinguishes the human mind from minds in other species. It is special to no culture and no epoch. It is universal, as old as cognitively modern human beings, and must continue to be characteristic of human beings for as long as the species exists. While its operation can be altered by conditions—during dreams and meditations, for example, blends are completely decoupled from bodily action, and especially during dreams their governing principles seem to be relaxed—yet blending operates by the same structural and dynamic principles in art, science, religion, and everyday thought, consciously, unconsciously, during sleep, in covert contemplation and in public action.

To make such a claim is to take an intellectual flight away from Geertz's analysis of the Balinese cockfight. Yet in his own analysis Geertz does claim that many of the representational functions of the Balinese cockfight are shared by representation across cultures, and it may seem to some who have studied Geertz as if my claims are already implicit in his work. It sometimes seems that way to me. If Fauconnier and I had not spent four years hatching the theory of conceptual integration and making our way through technical analyses of its operation and principles before I encountered Geertz's article, it seems to me that his article should have provided me immediately and easily with many of the discoveries Fauconnier and I had managed to uncover only through great mental labor, often after many stages of reflection and revision. It is curious that in 1994, twenty-two years after the publication of "Deep Play: Notes on the Balinese Cockfight," when Fauconnier and I first published our work on conceptual integration, there was no prior theory of conceptual integration, not even a recognition of the mental phenomenon, for us to use as a springboard. Hadn't Geertz already laid it out in 1972?

But then, I feel the same way when I read *The Runaway Bunny*, published in 1942, one of the two most popular and successful picturebooks for two-year-olds. In *The Runaway Bunny*, a bunny talks with his mother (already a blend, if one of the most routine). He says that he is going to run away, and the mother says she is going to come after him. He says, "If you run after me, I will become a fish in a trout stream and I will swim away from you." His mother responds, "If you become a fish in a trout stream, I will become a fisherman and I will fish for you." Some of the blends are highly intricate, and depend on previous blends. An especially complex blend occurs when the little bunny says, "I will become a little boy and run into a house," and his mother says, "If you become a little boy and run into a house, I will become your mother." Two-year-olds have not the slightest difficulty putting together the blends and drawing the appropriate inferences. If a two-year-old who knows that fishermen use hooks and bait to fool fish, to snag them, to hurt them, to haul them in, and to eat them is looking at the illustration of the mother-bunny-fisherman fishing for the baby-bunny-fish with a carrot-hook on the end of the line, and you begin to ask questions, the dialogue goes like this: "What is this?" "A carrot." "What is it for?" "To catch the baby bunny." "What will the baby bunny do?" "Bite the carrot." "Will he swim away down the river." "No. He bites the carrot." "What is the mommy bunny doing?" "Fishing for the baby bunny." "What is she?" "She's a fisherman." "Does the baby bunny know his mommy is fishing for him." "No. He wants the carrot." "Can the baby bunny swim?" "Yes. He's a fishie." "Does he have a fishie tail." "No. He's a bunny." "Will the carrot hurt the baby bunny?" "No! The mommy doesn't hurt the bunny!" "What will happen when the baby bunny bites the carrot?" "The mommy bunny will pull him in and hug him and kiss him." "Will he smell like a fish?" "No! He's a baby bunny!" The two-year-olds effortlessly conceive one amazing blend after another and project the relevant inferences back to the influencing space of mothers and toddlers, of which of course they and their own mothers are an instance. Perhaps this is why the book speaks profoundly and memorably to two-year-olds, and why many thousands of copies of this book are sold every year. An analysis of *The Runaway Bunny* reveals the operation of conceptual blending in much the same way an analysis of the Balinese cockfight blend does.

Unlike *The Runaway Bunny*, however, Geertz's article has explicit commentary in nearly every paragraph, about "crossed conceptual wires," "joining *w* to *x*, *x* to *y*, and *y* to *z*," and the disarrangement of "semantic contexts in such a way that properties conventionally ascribed to certain things are unconventionally ascribed to others, which are then seen actually to possess them" (1973a, p. 447). This is the Geertz who has argued in support of the hypothesis of "the psychic unity of mankind"—that is, the proposition "that there are no essential differences in the fundamental nature of thought processes" (a noun phrase that presupposes that there is such a fundamental nature of thought processes) "among the various living races of man" (p. 62), and who, in what may be the most famous and influential essay of the second half of the twentieth century, "Thick Description," writes:

> What, in a place like Morocco, most prevents those of us who grew up winking other winks or attending other sheep from grasping what people are up to is not ignorance as to how cognition works (though, especially as, one assumes, it works the same among them as it does among us, it would greatly help to have less of that too). . . . (1973a, p. 13)

Not, I grant, a ringing endorsement. Geertz has said of the Balinese that they "never do anything in a simple way that they can contrive to do in a complicated one," and that preference for complication graces Geertz's sentence. He does not say that *knowledge* about how cognition works would "greatly help," but rather that *less ignorance* would greatly help. His endorsement of cognitive science, or at least what I take to be cognitive science, is buried in a parenthesis, and I had to look hard through Geertz's works to find even a parenthesis this clear. Most damaging, his backhanded endorsement is set in the context of telling us that what we most of all need is *not* an understanding of universal human cognition.

Nonetheless, and I hold onto this, it does say clearly, and Geertz maintains this clarity in some other places, that cognition—by which I take it he means basic mental operations—works the same in us and in Moroccans, and, by implication, in all human beings.

How then do we account for the fact that interpretive social science and cognitive science have not yet enthusiastically joined forces to study human meaning? The impediments between them seem to me to be not matters of scientific principle but instead matters of aesthetics and ritual, vocabulary and emphasis. The cognitive scientist does not emphasize retrospective interpretation of historical particulars, after the fact, for their own sakes, yet the interpretive social scientist is strongly disposed by temperament to do exactly that: he "strains to read" cultural texts "over the shoulders of those to whom they properly belong" (Geertz, 1973a, p. 452). The cognitive scientist tries to explain the mental operations that underlie those texts and those readings, but the accomplishments of cognitive science remain unfulfilling to the interpretive social scientist because they are not interpretations of specific subjects of the sort the interpretive social scientist is trained to give and wants to give.

To be specific, the interpretive social scientist may remark that the theory of conceptual integration, in itself, does not even begin to constitute an interpretation of the Balinese cockfight. That is quite true, in exactly the same way, and for exactly the same reason, that the theory of evolution does not, in itself, even begin to constitute an explanation of the wild cherry tree outside my window, or even distinguish it from the dogwood, the cedar, the pine, the yew, the Japanese maple, the oak, and the locust, or for that matter, distinguish the trees from the Salvadoreans, the African Americans, or the Armenians I can see in the three houses beyond the trees. To explain species requires retrospective investigation into the actual historical paths of evolution—over niches, under accidents, through divisions now irreversibly entrenched—the many paths where reproduction developed its bag of tricks, and the human mind formed its dispositions.

But the theory of evolution is indeed part of the explanation of each of these things; it helps explain the wild cherry tree in explaining the dynamic biological principles according to which it came to exist. The theory of evolution allows us to connect this particular tree to another of its same kind, and one kind of tree to another kind, and trees to other species, not for purposes of simplifying but because, as a matter of fact, in their process and in their descent, they are connected to one another.

In the identical way, the theory of conceptual integration is part of the explanation of the Balinese cockfight. The theory of blending attempts to explain the nature of the basic cognitive operation by which the Balinese cockfight blend arose and descended. The theory of blending additionally lets us connect the Balinese cockfight to a vast set of other products in other cultures, and thus—perhaps countervailing the preferences of interpretive social scientists—to show the ways in which the Balinese cockfight is not at all exotic but instead shares a category with various other conceptual meanings, some of which belong properly to us.

Consider, for example, the current American infatuation with playing the stock market for the ostensible purpose of "wealth accumulation." The mood of the country has changed in the last thirty years, and many people who in the 1960s and 1970s either despised capitalism outright or threw a social cordon around it as vulgar, tedious, and above all to be prevented from sullying their personal identity, now invest themselves proudly and publicly in following the daily ups and downs of their equity portfolios. Sometimes they do this hourly. They digest quick news reports on financial matters, follow the ticker, keep an eye on foreign markets tied to U.S. markets. Once in a while, they even make a trade. Their roller-coaster emotional reactions in a single day, and their reactions to the end-of-the-day closing stock prices, are frequently entirely irrational by their own standards. These investors are not day traders; they do not strap on the seat belt and forbid themselves lunch to stay on top of puts and calls; they are not engaged in market arbitrage. Instead, they have bought securities they mean to hold for a long time, and they know that the prices of these securities must wiggle around, insignificantly, inside trading ranges; they know that they haven't made or lost any money until they actually execute a trade; and they know that the closing price has no special significance as long as nothing interesting happens overnight. Yet slight and insignificant changes in prices that are quite unlikely to signify gain or loss in the long term can make an investor feel, at the end of the day, subdued and anxious, or, in the other direction, elated, eager to dine out and brag. If some of these investors are attaching pride to selfhood, selfhood to stock picks, and stock picks to market prices, then we have a blend that not only in its operations but also in some of its content is similar to the Balinese cockfight blend. As the *Wall Street Journal* put it on March 30, 1999:

> With its unpredictable movements, second-to-second pulse and, lately, air of invincibility, the stock market has become a living entity for many of the 80 million or so Americans who own equities. It's there ticking away, at the breakfast table, the gym, the office. Sweeping indicators like market shifts and hot stocks somehow connect to the intensely personal—the retirement account, the college fund—as calculations of net worth blend into notions of self-worth. (Suskind, 1999)

So, yes, I claim that there are basic mental operations that unite the yuppie investor in 2001 with the Balinese cockfight participant in 1958, and that those basic mental operations have intricate systematic and dynamic principles. But, no, I do not claim that investing and cockfighting reduce to blending or to each other. That would be absurd. The theory of blending is by no means a reductive formula professing to explain the products of blending, any more than the theory of evolution is a reductive formula professing to explain frogs, toads, and salamanders.

"Man," writes Geertz, in his most famous phrase, "is an animal suspended in webs of significance he has spun" (1973a, p. 5). Yes, and blending is his main way of spinning them. Blending is to human beings what web-spinning is to spiders. To analyze individual webs, each tailored to its local situation, is of course indispensable and illuminating, but particular, retrospective, local analysis of individual webs should be combined with the study of what makes web-spinning possible, a theory of the nature of web-spinning. Interpretation shows us the web; cognitive study connects past webs to each other and to future webs in its attempt to explain the underlying capacities that make all of those webs possible. It is only a natural widening or narrowing of our focus, not a toggle between opposites, when we move back and forth between the study of the Balinese and the study of human beings. With enough of this back-and-forth, the two varieties of research may grow together.

"I take culture," Geertz continues, "to be those webs, and the analysis of it to be therefore not an experimental science in search of law but an interpretive one in search of meaning." Here, at last, Geertz and I part ways, or apparently so, depending on how heavily he means to emphasize "search for law," since cognitive science does not search for law either, in the senses that physics and chemistry do. Cognitive science is at once an interpretive science in search of meaning and an experimental science weighing linguistic, behavioral, genetic, sensory, and neurobiological data, making hypotheses, building models, offering explanations, sometimes offering even predictions or tactics for intervention. Interpretive science and experimental science are, for Geertz, a dichotomy. For me, they are compatible and mated parents only occasionally at one another's throats, with a baby called "cognitive social science."

At the conference at the Institute for Advanced Study on "25 Years of Social Science," in May 1997, during the intellectual stock-taking about the future of social science, I offered the view that the future of social science lies in the blend of cognitive science and social science. Where exactly do we stand? Between two different research agendas, our focus divided between them. Where do we go from here? Toward bringing them together as sharing the identical object of study. What kind of work do we want to sponsor? The integrative kind, finding ways in which cognitive science and social science supplement each other. What kinds of problems should we be addressing, with what kinds of approaches and arguments? The integrative problems, with whatever approaches and arguments from cognitive science and social science look as if they might be useful.

What should the School of Social Science in the Institute for Advanced Study do? That seems clear. It should find a way to support this integration. I even bet—here comes the blend—that the Luce Foundation would put up some of the money.

⚘ 2 ⚘

REASON

AT THE May 1997 conference on the future of social science held in the Institute for Advanced Study's Wolfensohn Hall, a sociologist from Harvard, Orlando Patterson, while reading his paper (all of the conference presentations, three days of them, consisted of scholars reading papers from a podium onstage) remarked pointedly that he would like to present some socioeconomic evidence but could not, because to do so would require "the use of"—he paused to get our attention, then finished with ironic disdain—"an overhead projector."

His message was unmistakable. The conference, in its style, was a living display of interpretive social science's rejection of the trappings, and maybe some of the principles, of science—graphs, charts, statistics, regression analysis, theorems. When Albert O. Hirschman, the economist in the School of Social Science, spoke in Wolfensohn Hall as part of a faculty lecture series, he stood at the podium and read a paper on commensality. When, in the same series, Edward Witten, a mathematical physicist, gave his lecture on string theory, he worked through an exhaustive set of overhead projections, each filled with diagrams and equations.

At my afternoon seminar in the School of Social Science a few days before the conference, there were no overhead projectors, diagrams, charts, or theorems, only a paper which the participants had read and were prepared to discuss as we sat in "the U. N. room" of the library, at an enormous oval wooden table, taking coffee from a discreet service, looking out at the serene Institute pond. My presentations at Princeton University, by contrast, only a mile away, had one diagram after another, sometimes with iota subscripts, presented by means of overhead projectors, under fluorescent lights in windowless rooms.

Different kinds of scholars who study human beings—what human beings are, what they do—hold quite different expectations about the nature of scholarly presentation. In some fora, it goes without saying that I will give a lecture deploying special vocabulary and bookishness while pretending—pretense being an admired component of the obligation—that I always talk this way. In other fora, it goes without saying that I will put up a diagram, example, or even a theorem for people to scrutinize while they listen in on my commentary. *The Literary Mind* contains not a single diagram, and only one illustration, at the very opening, before the book begins, of a parable from the *Thousand and One Nights*. An eminent scholar congratulated me on the "intellectual rigor" of keeping all those "silly" diagrams out of the book. Language, she offered, is a tool of infinite nuance and clarity, while charts, diagrams, and tables are the plumage of a bad scholar, or anyway one who has lost analytic focus and hopes to distract the audience from his deficiencies. Predictably, an equally eminent scholar, grinning, chastised me in assured moral tones for failing to include the essential diagrams in the book. My technical articles were, he said, as one could see just by skimming the graphics, certain to be more precise than any "monotonous string of mere paragraphs." The present book must disappoint both of them: it does have diagrams, but they are simple.

These anecdotes illustrate a persistent and intriguing anthropological division inside the academic professions dedicated to the study of human beings. The strength of these aesthetic preferences makes me wonder whether the main impediment to integrating these various branches of study is not so much ideas and principles as conflicting ritual appearances. The intellectual body of cognitive social science is one, but there are disagreements about the wardrobe. Economists for the most part want a costume of theorems and graphs and nodes, a fashion increasingly influential in other areas of social science, notably in rational choice theory and positive political science. If birds of a feather flock together, it is no surprise that interpretive social scientists on the one hand and positive, experimental, or evolutionary social scientists on the other mainly ignore each other.

Inconveniently for me, this dodge of ignoring outsiders is unavailable to the analyst of cognition, from whose viewpoint all these social scientists are talking about the same thing, often in the same ways, however different their appearances. They are talking about basic cognitive operations that run across not only their subjects of study but also their scholarly methods.

In the preceding chapter, I focused on interpretive social science. I turn now to the kinds of social sciences that go under the name of "qualitative research," which aspire to be, and are, sciency, often self-consciously concerned about their methodologies. I hope to show in this chapter and in the next that qualitative social science relies on unrecognized cognitive dimensions just as interpretive social science does, and that qualitative research stands to gain equally from integration with cognitive science. We have seen conceptual integration at work in interpretive social science. In this chapter and the next, I turn to its fundamental role in qualitative social science, first in counterfactual reasoning and then in "rational choice" by agents.

It is easy to show the centrality of counterfactual reasoning in the social sciences. Consider *The Pity of War*, one of the most widely discussed books of 1999. Its author, Niall Ferguson, is an Oxford don. Ferguson's fundamental method of social scientific inquiry and argument is counterfactual reasoning, as this snapshot from a profile published in *The New Yorker* shows:

> Rather than joining the Allied war effort [in World War I], he said, Britain should have maintained its neutrality and allowed the Germans to win a limited Continental war against the French and the Russians. In that event, he postulated, Germany, whose war aims in 1914 were relatively modest, would have respected the territorial integrity of Belgium, France, and Holland and settled for a German-led European federation. Had Britain "stood aside," he continued, it is likely that the century would have been spared the Bolshevik Revolution, the Second World War, and perhaps even the Holocaust. He concluded, "With the Kaiser triumphant, Adolf Hitler could have eked out his life as a mediocre postcard painter, and Lenin could have carried on his splenetic scribbling in Zurich, forever waiting for capitalism to collapse."
>
> The import of the speech was stunning. That Ferguson was assigning Britain the role of villain in a story in which it had always viewed itself as the savior of Europe was heretical. That Britain was somehow accountable for the century's subsequent catastrophes was unthinkable. (Boynton, 1999, p. 43)

We are asked to blend together the state of Europe in 1914 with a scenario of "standing aside," to create a counterfactual blend that, when elaborated, has no Hitlerian Germany, no Russian Revolution, no World War II, maybe no Holocaust. The rhetorical effect of making that counterfactual blend is to lay immense blame on Britain for having caused its counterfactuality. Ferguson's book-length counterfactual blend provoked a firestorm of controversy among British and American social scientists, which spilled over into the popular press.

To explore how counterfactual reasoning as a method of social science operates, I begin with a smaller example that nonetheless involved a major corporation, an advertising agency, a lot of money, an audience of at least several million consumers, and an article in the *New York Times* that surveyed the damage. Its aggressive and pyrotechnic presentation makes its use of conceptual blending unmistakable and shows us some of the cognitive mechanisms and principles at work in counterfactual reasoning.

COME FLY WITH ME

In 1996, at a cost of fifteen million dollars, British Airways presented a suite of printed advertisements in newspapers and magazines. Each had a big photograph, a small inset photograph, and a few words to help us integrate the two photographs. The big photograph in one of these ads depicted a dove in a bird bath, and its small inset photograph depicted the head of a grinning man in a shower. Its text announced that British Airways provides private showers for its customers at its arrival lounges at Heathrow and Gatwick airports in London.

The inset photograph in these ads is always an intrusion. Like the big photograph, it has sharp rectangular boundaries. The two photographs are distinguished by technical features of photography and have content taken from different conceptual domains. But the ads typically suggest some morphological continuity between key elements of the two photographs. For example, the head of the man in the shower rests on the body of the dove in the bird bath.

The ad I want to talk about presents a big black-and-white photograph printed in a style taken from the 1940s. It has low contrast, ambient lighting, and a hint of brownish coloring. It depicts an attractive young mother with wavy hair, a simple string of pearls around her neck. She wears a short-sleeve knit top and a woven skirt, and sits cradling her infant in her arms so it reclines on its back, its head elevated and its knees slightly elevated, its legs sprawled in enviable comfort over her forearm, its outer thigh additionally supported by her left hand, on which she wears a set of wedding bands. She smiles at the face of her sleeping child, who wears a cloth diaper in a period style.

But the head of the infant is occluded by an inset photograph, in color, with relatively high contrast and strong directional lighting, depicting a smiling, sleeping businessman who is balding. He is reclined in an airline seat. The scale of the photographs has been chosen to make the shoulders of the businessman fit the shoulders of the infant and to locate his head where the infant's head would be if his weren't in the way. The text above the photograph reads, "The new Club World cradle seat. Lullaby not included." The text beneath reads, "Introducing the unique new business class cradle seat. It doesn't simply recline but tilts as a whole, raising your knees and relieving your body of stress and pressure. Pity you may not be awake to enjoy all the other changes on new Club World."

Obviously, even obtrusively, the ad represents a blended scene that the reader of the ad is expected to connect to different mental spaces. We cobble these mental spaces together as we look at the blend. They are the conceptual influences to the blend. The first conceptual influence to the blend I will call the "business flight" space—it has a businessman in a business class cradle seat on a British Airways airplane. The second conceptual influence to the blend I will call the "mother-child" space—it has a child cradled in the arms of its mother. Thinking and talking always involve the construction of such conceptual packets for purposes of local understanding and action. "Mental spaces" is the term Gilles Fauconnier uses to refer to such conceptual packets. Mental spaces are interconnected, and can be modified as thought and discourse unfold. Blending—of the sort we see in the British Airways ad—is an operation over mental spaces.

The reader of the ad is prompted to construct a *counterpart mapping* between some elements of the two spaces—the business flight space and the mother-child space: the cradle seat is the counterpart of the mother's cradling arms, and the businessman is the counterpart of the infant. These counterparts are projected to the blend: in the blend, the man is the baby and the seat is the mother's arms.

There is *selective projection* from the influencing spaces to the blend: from the mother-child space we are to project comfort and happiness but not the baby's incompetence at business, speech, and dining; from the business flight space we project his reclining position but not our certainty that he would prefer to be someplace else.

There is *emergent structure* in the blend: in the blend, one can have the power, benefits, and responsibilities of advanced professional maturity and yet the comforts of infant dependency and irresponsibility.

There is also *projection back to the influencing space*: the unruffled comfort of the man-baby in the blend is to be projected back to the business flight space. Regardless of our experience of airplane travel, the passenger in business class on British Airways is blissfully content.

Considerable work has been done to make it possible for the reader of the ad to establish even more elaborate counterpart connections between the two conceptual influences, thereby increasing the match of relations between the blended space and its influences. The posture of the baby in the mother's arms looks entirely natural but has been carefully posed to emphasize the raising of the knees and the tilting of the body and so to make the baby's posture blend more easily with the posture of the businessman in the cradle seat. The disparity in period styles of the photographs can be read as signifying temporal distance between the two influencing spaces—the business flight space and the mother-child space— inviting the reader to frame the businessman as the grown-up infant. This makes the woman in the blend his actual mother as she appeared and as she nurtured him when he was an infant. Projecting these identities to the blend gives features of happiness and comfort there that come from being cradled not only like an infant but also by one's own mother, who adores her child and cares for it. The mother-child influence can now be further framed as something remembered fondly if unconsciously by the businessman as he reclines. His comfort in the cradle seat brings back to him, effectively if indistinctly, the pleasure of being in his mother's arms.

Actually, in the business flight space, the businessman's mother may be dead or otherwise incapable of holding him in this way, and if she is living and tried it, the result would be uncomfortable and possibly injurious. The businessman cannot have in reality what he remembers so fondly. But in the blend, the businessman can have again what he can no longer have, he can have it both ways—he can be an adult who is a sleeping infant cradled in his mother's arms. Who would not want to fly with British Airways on these terms?

The advertising agency that developed this ad presented it to focus groups, whose members assured the agency that its meaning was unmistakable.

But as the *New York Times* reported in an article that reproduced the advertisement and analyzed it, actual readers often objected to it (Bryant, 1996). "Many have written the airline to say they think the ad is Freudian, sexist, and even demeaning to flight attendants, who in the eyes of some beholders are represented by the mother in the ads."

The ad agency should not have been surprised. Conceptual blending is a quick, powerful, and inventive cognitive operation. A reader who interprets a representation by coming up with a blend and its accompanying influencing spaces typically regards the interpretation as natural and inevitable, hardly an "interpretation" at all. In the case of the British Airways ad, whether we like it or not, we all possess the cultural frame in which an attractive young stewardess attends gently to the physical and psychological comfort of the older businessman. In this publicly-shared conceptual frame, it is understood that part of what the airline is selling is the attention of such a woman. Despite the elimination of the most suggestive uses of this conceptual frame in airline advertising, it is still routinely used in print and video advertisements, in which an attractive stewardess, although her uniform is more conservative than the once-stereotypical short skirt, stockings, and pumps, and although she additionally now shares the screen in alternation with an attractive steward, nonetheless gazes at the potential customer with an altogether attentive and pleasing look as if to suggest the prospect of her personal service. Once we have a young, attractive woman in the blend taking care of the businessman, it is straightforward for readers to recruit the frame of a stewardess and use it to structure both the blend and the business flight space, forming a connection between the stewardess in the business flight space and the woman in the blend. In the blend, the stewardess is a young, attractive, attentive mother, and the inference projected back to the business flight influencing space is that on British Airways, you can expect a stewardess who treats you in a similar fashion.

According to the *New York Times*, the ad agency tried to dismiss these complaints by explaining that "People thought way too much about this," but that seems unlikely: people did not think they were "interpreting" at all; they thought they were responding to what was "there." In the blend, the woman is attractive, however proper. She caresses the businessman intimately, holding him against her full bosom, gazing down at him lovingly. Readers know the standard cultural frame of Oedipal sexual attachment to the mother, and the father is conveniently out of the picture. Given the ways in which conceptual integration operates, it is natural for readers to interpret these features of the blend as prompts to create corresponding elements in the business flight space.

Conceptual integration is path-dependent: the knowledge we use to construct the blend and to connect it to influencing spaces depends crucially on the conceptual path we have mentally traveled. At any moment in the path of our conceptual life we will have particular concerns and emphases, and we will have a greater or a lesser reliance on one or another set of conceptual connections. Knowledge that is highly charged at any moment in that path has a lower threshold for activation. Therefore, readers can be expected to bring their politically and ideologically charged conceptual structures to bear whenever possible in the construction of integration networks. In doing so, they will no more imagine that they are "reading meaning into" the blend than will the biophysics engineer who sees this ad and interprets it as a straightforward display of the posture achieved in the new cradle seat on British Airways.

For many readers of the ad, recruiting these politically and ideologically charged conceptual structures had a basic effect on their choice: the ad, which was intended to offer them incentives of personal comfort, thereby leading them to reason to a commercial choice, instead led them to align commercial choice with political choice and so to scorn a corporation they judged to be sexist.

This example suggests two points about political persuasion. First, the British Airways ad suggests an answer to the abiding question, Why do politicians stick with hackneyed presentations of their positions and policies—new bridge, new deal, rebuilding the infrastructure, land of opportunity, new day, dawn in America, drawing us together, closer to the people, a stronger America—despite pleas in every forum that they offer something new? Perhaps the politicians lack invention, but alternatively, perhaps they know intuitively that offering a new blend runs the risk that members of their audience will bring to its interpretation highly charged conceptual frames, causing some of them to interpret it in a way that will hurt the politician, who will then have to back-peddle. In a climate of negative political attack, where a politician's utterances are read by opponents with an eye toward making them sound evil, the prudent politician will prefer clichés. When George Bush, as president of the United States, proposed an international "New

World Order," it wasn't meant to evoke Hitler, but Bush's opponents lost no time in reminding their audiences that Hitler used the phrase first—thereby inviting their audiences to blend Hitler and Bush so Bush becomes a perhaps mild but still threatening proponent of an oppressive global political system.

Second, it's nice to have your cake and eat it, too. I do not at all suggest that the ad agency (or anyone else) behind the British Airways blend thought this way, but imagine that market research had shown that the important audience for these ads is senior male businessmen and that they love the sensual, Oedipal connotations of the ad. In such a situation, a marketing executive, calculating payoffs and costs in different audiences, might conclude that the payoff from stimulating the businessmen far outweighs the cost of angering those who will find the ad both sexist and offensive, on the condition that the accusation of sexism can be plausibly denied. The marketing executive would then have incentive to approve a blend that prompts for a persuasive interpretation strongly enough to induce it but tangentially enough, or with enough distraction, to make it deniable. This ploy is a standard weapon in the everyday political arsenal: offer a presentation sufficiently new and sufficiently nuanced to suggest a persuasive interpretation that the politician can then ignore, neglect, or disavow. But this is risky business.

BACKSTAGE COGNITION

The British Airways ad shows us in obvious form the basic cognitive operation of conceptual integration. Conceptual integration creates conceptual blends. The inventors of the ad used conceptual integration as a tool for guiding readers to reason toward a commercial choice. To the surprise and regret of British Airways, some readers connected that commercial choice to a political choice.

Conceptual integration is related to conceptual framing. A "frame" is a conventional schematic bundle of knowledge. For example, we have a frame for "air travel." A frame typically has roles (passenger, pilot, course, airplane, departure airport, arrival airport, and so on) and relations between those roles (the pilot flies the plane, the plane is a vehicle for the traveling passenger, the plane follows the course, and so on). We are mentally "framing" a situation whenever we take it to be an instance of a general, schematic, conventional conceptual frame. For example, if I am flying tomorrow from Los Angeles to New York, I use my "frame" of "flying on an airplane" to structure my thoughts about that event.

Frames come in various levels of specificity. For example, I and several people I know have a lot of experience flying from San Francisco to Washington, D.C. My frame for that knowledge is a special instance of my frame for "air travel," in the sense that "air travel" is the skeleton for "flying from San Francisco to Washington, D.C." But the frame for "travel" is more general than the frame for "air travel," and the frame for "motion along a path" is more general still. Frames are used to organize and structure more specific arrays of knowledge. For this reason, "framing" is often referred to as a kind of "schematic cognition." For example, we might have a schematic frame for *government of a Western democracy*. We use it to "frame" the person Jacques Chirac by considering him to be the *value* of the role *head of state* in the frame *government of a Western democracy*.

Framing is one type, a minimal type, of conceptual blending. In this type, one of the input spaces is a schematic frame (*government of a Western democracy*) and the other has specific elements (*Chirac, France*). In this integration network, there is cross-space mapping of counterparts: *head of state* in the frame is the counterpart of *Chirac* in the other input; *Western democracy* in the frame is the counterpart of *France* in the other input. The cross-space connectors between these counterparts are, in this kind of blending, role-value connectors. *Chirac* and *head of state* are both projected to the blend, as are *France* and *Western democracy*. In the blend, there is important if nearly invisible emergent structure: we create the role *head of state of the nation of France*, which is not in either of the inputs. These "simplex" blends are often skeletal, and often provide structures that become new conventional frames: blending *France* and *head of state of a Western democracy* provides *head of state of France*, which can (and of course has) become a frame. People with yet more knowledge will have even more intricate blends, such as *president of the Fifth French Republic*.

Blends can themselves be blended. For example, we can first blend the two frames *secretary* and *exchequer* to create the blended frame *secretary to the exchequer*. We can also create the blend of *exchequer of an organization* with *Brunei* to produce *exchequer of Brunei*. But then we can blend the two frames *secretary to the exchequer* and *exchequer of Brunei* to create the frame *secretary to the exchequer of Brunei*. This blend could of course become a conventional role. And we could blend it with a specific element to place a particular person in the role of *secretary to the exchequer of Brunei*.

The influencing spaces for the British Airways blend are organized by skeletal frames like *cradling* and *flying*, but the influencing spaces themselves are more specific than those abstract frames, and each of those spaces is in fact organized by more than one abstract frame. For example, the business flight space is organized by both the frame for *air travel* and the frame for *businessman*, and it has a fixed value—British Airways—in the role of *airline company*. Its organizing frame is *business air travel on British Airways*.

In interpreting the British Airways ad, we use framing and blending. These basic cognitive operations are part of the "backstage cognition" that is involved in making sense of the ad. Reason, judgment, and choice always depend profoundly upon systematic and highly intricate operations of backstage cognition, but we usually fail to notice that dependence because backstage cognition happens quickly, in ways too intricate for consciousness to handle, and with powers of access and recognition not typically available outside of backstage cognition. This combination of features—speed, intricacy, and deft access and recognition—is partly responsible for the power of these operations, but also partly responsible for the notorious difficulty of recognizing their existence, or the greater difficulty of noticing them as they operate, or the yet greater difficulty of analyzing what it is they do when they operate. It is typical for social scientists to skip lightly over the backstage cognition that takes place in the thinking of the subjects they analyze and in the thinking of the social scientists doing the analysis.

There are several basic mental operations of backstage cognition: focal point reasoning (as when we structure knowledge with respect to a particular reference point, such as the number 100 or the city of Paris, or a particular viewpoint, and so on); categorization; schematic cognition; grammar; prototyping; memory; the assembly and connection of mental spaces; conceptual projection; conceptual integration; narrative; and others.

Gilles Fauconnier coined the term "backstage cognition" for the ensemble of these mental operations that are involved in interpretation and inference (Fauconnier 1997). The British Airways ad helps me drag evidence of backstage cognition onstage because, quite exceptionally, the inventors of the British Airways blend recognize that it is a blend, mean the audience to recognize that it is a blend, and succeed in that intention. It is good as an introduction, bad as a prototype, since most blending escapes notice.

COUNTERFACTUAL REASONING

The blend in the British Airways ad is profoundly counterfactual with respect to reality—a seat is not really mother's arms and a businessman is not really a baby—and could have been suggested by any number of explicitly counterfactual statements, such as, "If our British Airways cradle seat were your mother's arms, it could not be more comfortable." In the counterfactual blend, the seat is your mother's arms. The influencing spaces for this counterfactual blend are (1) "you" as an adult in the airplane seat; (2) "you" as an infant in your mother's arms. Actually, identifying the influencing spaces in this case can be quite complicated. The influencing spaces could differ even across readers who achieve essentially the same blend. For example, people who were never cradled by their own mothers could still construct the intended counterfactual blend by using an abstract "Mother Cradling Child" scenario. The blend would in that case take a specific "you" and a specific "mother" from the specific influencing space, but it would take cradling from the abstract "Mother Cradling Child" influencing space. In the blend, the specific "you" would be cradled in a way that had no biographical referent. It is even possible for a reader to interpret the two "you's" in the two influencing spaces as entirely abstract and so to construct a blend that applies to most people but not to the reader—perhaps the reader has some medical condition that prevents both being cradled and reclining in seats. Such a reader could even resent the blend.

A moment's thought shows that even in the relatively uncomplicated interpretation in which one influencing space is just "you" as an adult in the airplane seat and the other is just "you" as an infant in your mother's arms, the projections from those influencing spaces to the counterfactual blend are highly selective. For example, we do not interpret the counterfactual assertion as meaning that the seat is as short as your mother's arms, or that your mother could hold you comfortably for twelve hours. We do not interpret it as meaning that a passenger in a British Airways cradle seat must wear a diaper, or that infants are in fact permitted to use these cradle seats.

Counterfactual reasoning, which is made possible by conceptual integration, is an indispensable element of political reasoning. Consider a prototypical counterfactual assertion of the kind much discussed in methodological studies of qualitative research:

> If Churchill had been prime minister in 1938 instead of Neville Chamberlain, Hitler would have been deposed and World War II averted.

This counterfactual assertion asks us to blend conceptual structure from different mental spaces to create a separate, counterfactual mental space. The influencing spaces include (1) Churchill in 1938 as outspoken opponent of Germany; and (2) Neville Chamberlain in 1938 as prime minister facing the threat from Germany. To construct the blend, we project parts of each of these spaces to it and develop emergent structure there.

From the first mental space, the blend takes Churchill. From the second mental space, the blend takes the role *prime minister*. In the blend, Churchill is prime minister by 1938. The blend is contrary to fact with respect to both of its influencing spaces. The antecedent and the consequent exist in the blended space; neither exists in either of the influencing spaces (see Figure 2.1).

Because the process of blending is largely unconscious, it seems easy, but it is in fact complex. It has many standard features that can be illustrated from the Churchill example.

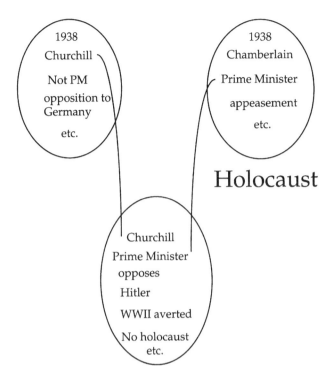

Figure 2.1

• *Blends exploit and develop counterpart connections between influencing spaces.* The space with Churchill and the space with Chamberlain share many identity counterparts, such as date, England, Germany, Hitler, and international tension. Churchill and Chamberlain are additionally frame counterparts—that is, they are values of the same role in the same frame: each is an English political figure, holding a political office, with views about Germany.

• *Counterparts may or may not both be brought into the blend, and may or may not be fused in the blend.* Many paired counterparts are brought into the blend as fused units: Hitler in the blend is a single fused entity corresponding to Hitler in each of the influences but not equal to them—the Hitler in the blend has a different life. Churchill is brought into the blend but not Chamberlain. Chamberlain's political office is brought in but not Churchill's.

• *The projection from the influencing spaces is selective.* The blend takes from the space with Churchill his opposition to Germany but not his political office or his reputation in 1938 as having poor judgment of the sort that would prevent him from obtaining a position of leadership. The blend takes from the space with Chamberlain the role *prime minister* and the situation faced by the prime minister in 1938, but not Chamberlain himself or the default knowledge attached to *prime minister* that world leaders facing aggression are concerned greatly to avoid unnecessary war. We frame Chamberlain according to this default knowledge but keep it out of the blend, where we need a prime minister who views conflict as inevitable.

• *Blends recruit a great range of conceptual structure and knowledge without our recognizing it.* Very little of the structure needed for the contrary-to-fact blended space is mentioned. The Churchill blend recruits conceptual frames of world leaders, political aggression, and wars. It recruits the relevant history of Germany and England. These recruitments are needed for the reasoning to work properly in the blend. Academic theories may also be recruited to the blend—game-theoretic interaction during political aggression or deterrence by "power-maximizing" actors. These recruitments may drive the elaboration of the blend in one direction or another.

• *Blending is a process that can be applied repeatedly, and blends themselves can be inputs to other blends.* Someone might respond to the Churchill counterfactual, "That's only because Hitler was irrational: a more rational Hitler would have seen that his strategic chances were still excellent, and would not have backed down." This new counterfactual blend takes part but not all of the original Churchill blend, and additionally takes part but not all of the characteristics of Hitler from spaces that refer to actual situations. In the new counterfactual hyper-blend, World War II is not averted.

Former prime minister Margaret Thatcher created just such a hyper-blend when she argued that, as leaders of Britain, France, and the United States should have refused to appease Hitler, so Western leaders should refuse to appease aggressors in the war in Bosnia. Thatcher asked members of her audience to take two spaces—the space referring to the situation in Bosnia and the counterfactual blend in which Hitler was opposed and the atrocities were averted—as inputs to the construction of a third, blended space in which the Western leaders oppose the aggressors in Bosnia and atrocities are thereby averted. Her policy—"Not Again!"—is anchored in what she takes to be the persuasiveness of the original counterfactual blend (see Figure 2.2).

Of course, Thatcher implicitly invited her audience to imagine the counterfactual blend in which Margaret Thatcher is still prime minister during the period in which war breaks out in Bosnia, and the further counterfactual blend in which Margaret Thatcher is prime minister in 1938 and opposes Hitler. In both of these counterfactual blends, the aggressors back down and the atrocities are averted or ended. These two counterfactual blends can be made stronger if they receive projections from the space that contains (a Tory view of what the British call) the "Falklands" war, in which Margaret Thatcher is prime minister, "The

Iron Lady," war victor, courageous adversary of aggressors, enforcer of Britain's policy over vast geographical distances, staunch in her defense of honor regardless of the considerable practical difficulties. Thatcher need not refer to the Falklands space; her identity evokes it, perhaps more effectively than any mention could.

The Falklands space and the two counterfactual blends in which Thatcher faces down (a) Hitler and (b) the aggressors in Bosnia are available to serve as reinforcing inputs to the Not Again! space, which offers Thatcher's policy toward Bosnia. Projections of this sort demonstrate the remarkable way in which character—once it has been connected to a specific actor in a space that we take to apply to reality—can be projected to blends in which that specific actor faces past or hypothetical situations. In fact, character can be projected to *other* counterfactual blends having to do with what *other* actors might do or might have done if they possessed that character.

• *Blends develop structure not provided by the influencing spaces.* Typically, the blend is not a simple cut-and-paste reassembly of elements to be found in the influencing spaces but instead resembles what Kahneman (1995) calls a "mental simulation," in which it develops considerable emergent structure. Usually, we

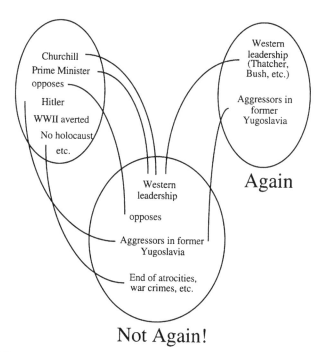

Figure 2.2

focus on this additional emergent structure. For example, in the Churchill blend, but not in any of its influences, Hitler backs down and World War II is averted.

• *Inferences, arguments, and ideas developed in the blend can have effect in cognition, leading us to modify the initial influences and to change our view of the corresponding situations.* A student of large and systematic historical patterns, transcending mere individuals, that supposedly led to World War II might know Churchill's personality well but not have brought what she knows to bear on her conception of appeasement in 1938. The Churchill blend might challenge her to reconsider the causal weight of personality. Thatcher's blend might lead someone to rethink the situation in Bosnia and even to choose to intervene.

• *Selectivity of projection and variability of recruitment can lead to different constructions and inferences.* We saw in the British Airways blend a classic case in which activating different influencing spaces for the blend led to different reasoning and different choices. Many people, hearing the Not Again! blend proposed by Thatcher, which asks us to compose a scene in which Western powers intervene in a distant country, will complete that blend with structure from a Vietnam frame. Thatcher's blend will then include disaster for the intervening Western powers.[1] Thatcher's blend is meant to lead people to reason to one political choice, but it can lead them to reason to the opposite choice if it is completed and elaborated differently.

How does structure develop in a counterfactual blend? How does structure that has been developed in a blend lead us to reconsider the influencing spaces?

Blends develop by three mechanisms: composition, completion, and elaboration. We selectively project meaning from input spaces to the blend and thus *compose* in the blend meaning that is not composed in the inputs. This partial composition often provides a working blend that will host further compositions as the blend is developed. The Churchill blend composes Churchill and Hitler as heads of state. *Completion* provides additional structure once a few elements have been brought in. A minimal framing of Churchill and Hitler as adversarial heads of state invites us to complete that structure by recruiting any amount of specific or general knowledge we have about personal opposition, international relations, negotiation, and so on. *Elaboration* develops the blend through imaginative mental simulation according to principles, logic, and dynamic patterns in the blend. Some of these principles, logic, and dynamic patterns will have been brought to the blend by completion. Continued development of the blend by further completion can recruit new principles and logic. But new principles and logic may also arise through elaboration itself.

Composition and completion often draw together conceptual structures usually kept apart. As a consequence, the blend can reveal latent contradictions and coherences between previously separated elements. It can show us problems and lacunae in what we had previously taken for granted. It can equally show us un-recognized strengths and complementarity. In this way, blends yield insight into the conceptual structures from which they arise.

Composition, completion, and elaboration all recruit selectively from our most favored patterns of knowing and thinking. Consequently, blending is very power-ful, but also heavily subject to bias. It is hard to evaluate bias in blends, for two reasons. First, for the most part, composition, completion, and elaboration oper-ate automatically and below the horizon of conscious observation. Therefore, we rarely detect consciously the infrastructure in the blend that makes it effective. Second, since the emergent structure in the blend comes from our favored pat-terns of knowing and thinking, we are likely to regard biased infrastructure in the blend as unobjectionable even if we somehow manage to detect it.

For example, in trying to reason about a blend on the basis of only its proper historical structure, we may unwittingly complete the blend with evidence from a later historical moment. In the Churchill counterfactual, we use what we know of 1938. But once we have Churchill as prime minister in the blend, it is impossible to prevent completion from another (covert) influencing space—Churchill as prime minister later in time. The counterfactual blend in which Churchill opposes Hitler in 1938 is plausible only because we can recruit to it Churchill's strength of character in opposing Hitler during World War II, and we can know about that character only because World War II was not averted. Our reasoning in the blend—that World War II might have been averted—depends on its counter-factuality: paradoxically, the blend seems plausible to us only because it did not happen. In this way, our *ex post* knowledge can affect our supposed *ex ante* reason-ing in ways detectable only on analysis. Even the selection of objects of *ex ante* reasoning can be influenced by *ex post* knowledge: Had Churchill never been prime minister, it is unlikely that we would think of constructing a blend in which he was prime minister in 1938.[2] *Ex post* input spaces seep into *ex ante* counterfactual blended spaces, and in fact prompt us covertly to construct them.

CONSTITUTIVE PRINCIPLES, GOVERNING PRINCIPLES, AND PURPOSES

The theory of conceptual blending posits a set of principles that constitute the phenomena it treats: a conceptual integration network must have mapping be-tween the influencing spaces, selective projection from the influencing spaces to the blend, and so on. There are also governing principles that pressure blends in one direction or another, as discussed in Fauconnier and Turner (1998a). They compete and often conflict, and so are called "optimality" principles. The *inte-gration constraint* is a governing principle: it requires that a blend constitute a tightly integrated scene that can be manipulated as a unit. The *web constraint* is another: it requires that the manipulation of the blend as a unit maintain the web of appropriate connections to the input spaces easily and without continued rejuggling and recomputation. The *unpacking constraint* is a third: it requires that the blend alone enable the understander to unpack it to reconstruct the influencing spaces and the connections between them. The *topology constraint* is a fourth: it requires that any element in a blend that has been projected from an influencing space have relations in the blend that match the relations of its corresponding element in the influencing space.

The weight of any one of these governing principles varies with the purpose of the blend. When blending is used to conceive of a new policy, model, or activity (as when we use the "desktop" interface as a basis for interacting with a computer), the integration constraint may play a dominant role for the blend, since the blend is meant to provide the mental basis for extended integrated activity. In such cases, we usually minimize the projections from the blend back to the influencing spaces since the blend usually does not have among its purposes either to help us reconceive the influencing spaces or to help us discover something about them. Other things being equal, *web* and *topology* may be relaxed in these cases, since we are less concerned with connections back to the input spaces.

But we can easily see that a different purpose may in fact require a stricter adherence to *web* and *topology*. An attempt to construct a new consensual policy that is a blend of conflicting policies supported by conflicting parties may require strong *web* and *topology* over just those parts of the influencing spaces cherished by each party, since neither party wishes to yield on central points. For example, suppose management and labor are trying to settle on a retirement package. Each side will have a proposal, and in blending those proposals, the essential goal is not to achieve efficiency or simplicity, for example, but instead to achieve agreement to the policy by both sides, and this may require including many elements from both proposals that otherwise have no particular merit. Where achieving consensus is a purpose, we may even weaken integration in the blend—producing, for example, a retirement policy more diffuse, less thrifty, or even less financially wise than is possible—in order to get the conflicting parties to accept it.

In cases where the blend has been constructed with the purpose of casting light on one of the influencing spaces ("spotlight blends"), *web* and *topology* are likely to dominate, since abandoning relevant connections to the influences and altering relations between elements may make the blend less useful as a spotlight for analyzing the influence.

Casting light on an influence is the principal purpose of counterfactual blends in the social sciences. Pascal's counterfactual argument, *If Cleopatra's nose had been an inch longer, Antony might not have been so infatuated, and the history of Rome and the West might have been entirely different*, is meant to spotlight the potential effect of specific private and personal affairs on large impersonal public political events. The Churchill counterfactual is meant to spotlight the causal role of the leader's personality. Neither is concerned with determining all the changes from our world that would have been necessary to make the counterfactual world possible.

Let us contrast such spotlight counterfactual blends in the social sciences with *reductio ad absurdum* blends, often found in math or physics, in which the purpose is to prove that a blend *must be* counterfactual because of internal disintegration, usually with the further purpose of projecting some inference back to one of the influencing spaces. In a *reductio ad absurdum* blend, the blend is required to match topologically all of the logic and known structure of some influencing space A except for some hypothetical structure X not known to be in A. A and X are blended. The resulting blend is tested to see whether it meets the *integration* constraint absolutely. The logician demonstrates that the blend is disintegrated by finding a contradiction in the blend. Finding such a contradiction allows her to project an inference to input A, namely that X cannot be in A unless A is itself already disintegrated. Mathematical examples are prototypical, but *reductio* of this sort is also common in everyday reasoning, as when we ask ourselves whether it could have been Grace who telephoned a few minutes ago, check the clock to determine that Grace would now be driving on the freeway and so would have to have called from her mobile telephone, observe that she has left her mobile telephone on the table, and so conclude that it was not Grace who called. In this case, blending some of what we know of the world with the hypothesis that Grace called leads us to develop emergent structure in the blend—Grace's having her mobile telephone with her—that is contradicted by other structure in the blend. The blend is therefore disintegrated, and the hypothesis is ruled out.

THE FUNDAMENTAL PROBLEM OF CAUSAL INFERENCE IN THE SOCIAL SCIENCES IS COUNTERFACTUAL REASONING THROUGH CONCEPTUAL INTEGRATION

As we have seen, counterfactual reasoning, a prime tool of social scientific research, arises by means of the essential cognitive operation of conceptual integration, which is much more complicated and systematic than is suspected, and whose operation occurs for the most part below the horizon of conscious observation. Counterfactual reasoning is part of the routine mental operation of political agents and political scientists. Its scope is much wider than might be apparent—counterfactual reasoning, as a basis for choice, is only very rarely flagged by an "if-then" linguistic form whose first half has a verb in the past perfect. Grammatical hints of counterfactual thinking are often subtle. As Gilles Fauconnier (1994) observes, they include subjunctivity, main verbs like *wish* or *prevent*, modal verbs like *could*, and adverbs like *not*. Linguistic form often provides no test at all, since the same form can express counterfactuality in one case and not in another: "The President could hold your opinion, instead of the one he takes" evokes a counterfactual blend; "The President could hold your opinion. Have you asked him?" does not.

In fact, there seems to be *no form of causal inference in the social sciences* that does not depend upon counterfactual reasoning and hence upon conceptual blending. Gary King, Robert O. Keohane, and Sidney Verba, in their influential *Designing Social Inquiry: Scientific Inference in Qualitative Research* (1994), provide a definition of causality in the social sciences in a section titled "Defining Causality" (pp. 77–79). They instruct us to consider an election in a specific congressional district: the Democratic incumbent runs against one Republican (nonincumbent) challenger and receives fraction x of the vote. We are to "imagine that we go back in time to the start of the election campaign and everything remains the same, except that the Democratic incumbent decides not to run for re-election and the Democratic Party nominates another candidate," who receives fraction y of the vote. King, Keohane, and Verba are seeking to give a precise definition of the effect of the cause on the relevant scenario. The cause they are considering in their illustrative example is the incumbency of the Democratic nominee; the effect is the difference in the vote produced by that incumbency. King, Keohane, and Verba call this effect the "causal effect" and define it for this case as the quantity $x - y$—that is, the difference between the vote the Democratic incumbent did actually receive and the vote a nonincumbent Democratic candidate would have received. Of course, this means that investigating causality requires constructing counterfactual blends. In this example, the influencing spaces are the space with the congressional election as it did happen and the space with an abstract role for a Democratic nonincumbent candidate. These two spaces are blended to create an imaginary scenario. In that blended scenario, a Democratic nonincumbent runs and receives fraction y of the vote. King, Keohane, and Verba are entirely clear on the necessity and importance of the counterfactual blend. They write:

> This *counterfactual* condition is the essence behind this definition of causality, and the difference between the actual vote [x] and the likely vote in the counterfactual situation [y] is the causal effect. . . . Of course, this effect is defined only in theory since in any one real election we might observe either [x] or [y] or neither, but never both. Thus, this simple

definition of causality demonstrates that we can never hope to know a causal effect for certain. Holland (1986) refers to this as *the fundamental problem of causal inference*, and it is indeed a *fundamental* problem since no matter how perfect the research design, no matter how much data we collect, no matter how perceptive the observers, no matter how diligent the research assistants, and no matter how much experimental control we have, we will never know a causal inference for certain.

Methodologists in qualitative research, concerned with the widespread (and apparently indispensable) use of counterfactual blends in social scientific argument, have proposed criteria for regulating their acceptable use. A survey can be found in Philip Tetlock and Aaron Belkin's introduction to their edited volume, *Counterfactual Thought Experiments in World Politics* (1996).

These criteria have been developed in the hope of using counterfactual spaces to substitute for controlled laboratory experiments. In some sciences, it is possible to design two situations that vary only on the independent variable, to run the two situations experimentally, and to contrast the effects in the two cases. For example, one lab rat (the control) may receive a normal diet while a genetically identical lab rat receives a diet in which fructose has been replaced by glucose. In the social sciences, and especially in reasoning about world events, it is usually impossible to run two such situations as an experiment. The methodological substitute for doing so is to contrast the actual situation with an imagined counterfactual situation.

To prevent imagination from running wild in the construction of these counterfactuals, the methodologists have proposed, for example, that counterfactual spaces must be thoroughly specified in their details, especially the details of their causal antecedents and consequents; that they must be consistent with well-established historical facts (for example, they should require minimal rewriting of the original influencing spaces; the antecedent should have been recognized historically as a possibility and should additionally have been possible to bring about; and the antecedents and consequences should be close in time); that they must be consistent with well-established theoretical laws and statistical generalizations; that they must be parsimonious (explain as much as possible with as few assumptions as possible); and so on.

But in fact creators of spotlight counterfactual blends are typically indifferent to these kinds of criteria, because these creators want to cast a spotlight on an influencing space rather than to build a full and detailed simulation of a possible situation. This is very clear even in an example that does not involve human reason and choice, such as the following:

If the Earth were as close to the sun as Venus, life as we know it never would have evolved on our planet.

This counterfactual blend conforms very badly to the criteria summarized in Tetlock and Belkin. Imagining the Earth as forming in the orbit of Venus violates the laws of astrophysics and the history of our solar system, according to which a planet in the orbit of Venus must have the size and mineral composition of Venus. The only planet that could be as close to the sun as Venus is one essentially identical to Venus. For the Earth to form in the orbit of Venus would require violating so many fundamental theoretical laws as to render the solar system unrecognizable to us. Alternatively, if we image the Earth as having been formed in its own orbit but then moving to the orbit of Venus before the origin of life, we must have magical ways for transporting it and keeping it there. This have-it-both-ways counterfactual blend (an Earth-like planet in the orbit of Venus) has not only unimaginable physics but also unspecifiable consequents and antecedents.

Yet it is an excellent conceptual instrument. The blend is conceptually coherent and easy to build. Mentally, it is easy to move the Earth at the right moment in its planetary history to the orbit of Venus, provided we have mentally scaled the solar system down to human spatial scale. We all have experience in moving objects from one place to another at that human scale. The mental space containing Earth and the mental space containing Venus already share elaborate counterpart structure because they are both instances of the frame of a planet in our solar system. Earth and Venus are of course counterparts in those mental spaces. To construct the blend, we need only take partial structure from each of the already highly matched counterparts in the highly matched influencing spaces, and develop an Earth-as-Venus. It is additionally easy for us to conceive that the sun is a powerful source of heat, and that something a lot closer to a powerful source of heat becomes a lot hotter very quickly. The reasoning works fluidly and properly in the blend. In the orbit of Venus, everything near the Earth's surface would be subjected to extremely high temperatures; yet all forms of terrestrial life known to us die at only marginally higher temperatures; the result is the absence of life. Given the right audience, this spotlight can illuminate something interesting in the influencing space that contains the Earth: life as we know it may seem marvelously flexible in its adaptation to widely varying terrestrial environments, but it requires extremely narrow specifications, relative to the scales of variation that obtain in our solar system.

Spotlight counterfactual blends are indeed subject to the governing principles that are relevant to their purpose. Since they are constructed to pick out important features—often causal—in an influencing space, they must obey *unpacking* very well, or the relevant influencing space may not even be accessible. They must obey *web* and *topology* well enough that the structure in the blend can be connected back to the structure we want to spotlight; but they may purposely violate *topology* where it is the notable difference between the blend and the input that signals the interesting structure in the influencing space, as when Hitler *backs down* in the blend. A spotlight counterfactual blend must obey *integration* over relevant structure, but it can ignore integration for peripheral or subtle structure in the blend that is inconsequential for its spotlight function. In general, a governing principle has effect only to the extent that it is needed for accomplishing the purpose of the blend.

Completely impossible have-it-both-ways blends often guide our real actions, and are offered as arguments in deliberative rhetoric: the attested sentence "If Bosnian Muslims were Christians (or bottle-nosed dolphins), the West Europeans and Americans would never have allowed the slaughter of innocents to go on as long as they did." This blend has unclear specification of antecedents and consequents, and violates many well-established facts, laws, and generalizations: it would require drastic rewriting of centuries of Mediterranean history to keep Islam out of the relevant geographical area; dolphins live in water and have social organization very far removed from anything underlying human political organization.

But it is potentially a superb conceptual instrument. Although the blending requires intricate unconscious conceptual work involving wild departures from actuality, that work is well within our competence. Consider the dolphins: we know that fishers are actually harvesting fish, have no animosity toward dolphins, and are killing the dolphins only incidentally, but they have been framed as wanton slaughterers of dolphins. We project only a small part of that frame to the blend, bringing along the associated moral judgments, including the judgment that we, the audience, have a responsibility to act. By means of the blend, aspects of the "environmental responsibility" frame come to be projected back onto the "foreign policy" frame. In the blend, the dolphins are fused with the Muslims and the fishers with the killers of Muslims. Suppose the audience actually feels, in the blend, some responsibility for taking action, and therefore recognizes that its sense of responsibility varies with the identity of the victims—human versus ocean mammal (or Muslim versus Christian)—and feels ethically uncomfortable that its sympathies depend upon the identity of the "victims." Then the blend has led the audience to see something about the causality involved in its attitude, to reconsider its position, perhaps to change the normative frame that motivates and shapes policy, perhaps even to do something. The blend flatters the audience, for a rhetorical purpose, by assuming that the members of the audience are moral, responsible, and active in most cases but have, atypically, been neglectful in this one isolated case.

The great danger for the qualitative social scientist who uses counterfactual reasoning, or who studies it, lies in assuming that we already understand how counterfactual reasoning works merely because we are so good at it, or, worse, assuming that the mechanisms of counterfactual reasoning are visible and open to conscious manipulation and control. The danger is easily overlooked: King, Keohane, and Verba, for example, nonchalantly slip into their description of the counterfactual blend a requirement that "everything remains the same, except" for a single explicit change. But the counterfactual space in a thought experiment involving the real political world is almost never a mere copy of one of its influencing spaces (in this case, the real election) with one explicit change. On the contrary, the projection to the counterfactual space is typically highly selective. Moreover, the counterfactual space develops emergent structure. Even if it could be argued that some counterfactual spaces can be found that are copies of an influencing space with one explicit change, this is a shaky requirement to impose on all counterfactual reasoning and hence on all causal reasoning.

Conceptual integration in reasoning and choice is useful, indispensable, systematic, and intricate, but it does not in general accord with the criteria summarized by Tetlock and Belkin or required by King, Keohane, and Verba. It is largely invisible to the kind of conscious management implied by such criteria. For example, strong biases are likely to influence which counterfactual blends will spring to life. We invent one counterfactual blend but not another. These biases governing which spaces spring to mental life may have much greater influence on the construction of any particular counterfactual argument than do the kinds of biases social science methodologists have so far discussed.

ESCAPE THROUGH SMALL-N AND LARGE-N?

The social scientist who argues that, in an actual case, "C was a cause of event E" can compare the actual case to either (1) a counterfactual case in which C is absent or (2) other actual cases. Using a small number of contrasting actual cases and analyzing them qualitatively is called "small-N" analysis or "comparative" analysis. Using a large number of contrasting actual cases and analyzing them using quasi-experimental regression analysis is called "large-N" analysis. All three strategies—using explicit counterfactuals, small-N comparisons, or large-N comparisons—attempt to solve the same statistical problem, of finding more cases so the analysis will have positive degrees of freedom (that is, more cases than explanatory variables).

Can the problems of conceptual integration, counterfactual reasoning, and causal inference in the social sciences be evaded by turning to small-N methodology or even away from qualitative methods altogether to the statistical methods used in large-N analyses? Maybe not. As James D. Fearon (1991) has shown in "Counterfactuals and Hypothesis Testing in Political Science," small-N and large-N analysis *also* depend in essential ways upon counterfactual reasoning. Fearon begins,

> If there are other causes of the phenomenon in question that are not considered explicitly in the analysis, and if any of these are in fact systematically related to the causes explicitly considered, then effects of the other causes will be wrongly attributed to those of the causes that are being evaluated. Simply put, estimates of the effects of the proposed causes will be biased. (1991, pp. 173–174)

To dispense with this problem, the analyst of actual cases must assume that if the actual cases had looked different on the independent variables not considered in the analysis, there would have been no systematic difference in the observed effects of the causes the analysis does consider. But this assumption, of course, is a counterfactual blend. Fearon writes,

> In statistics this is the familiar problem of whether any independent variables are correlated with the contents of the error term (which contains the effect of all unspecified, unmeasured "other causes"). (pp. 173–174)

As Fearon observes, in the case of the analyst using statistical methods on actual cases, the analyst must make an assumption that is equivalent to the following counterfactual assertion about the statistics: "If the cases in the sample had assumed different values on the independent variables, the contents of the error term would not have differed systematically" (p. 174). In sum, Fearon points to the fact that the analyst of actual cases must make an assumption that fundamentally involves counterfactual reasoning. This danger of hidden but essential counterfactual reasoning presents a risk so severe that "some analysts tend to be skeptical of large-N or comparative historical work; they prefer case studies in which the risks of (an often implicit) counterfactual strategy may seem intuitively less serious" (p. 174).

COGNITIVE ANALYSIS OF SOCIAL SCIENTIFIC METHODS

I began with Niall Ferguson's alternative history of World War I in *The Pity of War* and an exotic British Airways advertisement for its Club World business cradle seat to demonstrate the power and complexity of backstage cognition, which, for all its importance, remains largely undetected and unanalyzed. Only a specialist is likely to recognize backstage cognition, much less examine it. Yet intricate, systematic, complex, biased, in many ways mysterious operations of backstage cognition lie at the basis of methods of counterfactual reasoning and hence of causal reasoning in qualitative social science. Counterfactual reasoning involves all the structural and dynamic principles, governing principles, and biases of conceptual blending. Blending drives a great deal of social science research, but its influence has gone largely unrecognized by social scientists.

Methods of social science are able to exist because they borrow the seemingly effortless but highly complex power of backstage cognition. Social science, its methods, and individual social scientists have a deep if unrecognized cognitive debt to backstage cognition. That debt carries with it profound and systematic if equally unrecognized cognitive influences and biases. Backstage cognition channels and conditions social science, but how it does so is an area we have only begun to explore.

✣ 3 ✣

CHOICE

Cognitive science, allied with precursor and tributary traditions—psychology, philosophy of mind, interpretive anthropology, rhetoric—thinks it has something to say, useful if embryonic, about principles of human reason and choice. So, too, do economics and political science, lately with increased confidence. The rise in economics and political science of research programs for modeling decision and judgment—viewed as causes of action, on the assumptions of greed, rationality, and equilibrium—has created a social scientific armada parallel to cognitive science in its interest in reason and choice.

"Cognitive" studies are on one side, preference and judgment and "positive" studies are on the other. They often talk about identical patterns of human reason and choice. But until recently they did not converse. Exceptions are impressive but out on the border, and the great initial exception, Herbert Simon, may have inadvertently done harm to the development of the conversation, because his work has come to be summarized by the slogan "bounded rationality," interpreted to mean that human reason and choice, dragged down by cognitive limits and mental dispositions toward illusion, are a collapsed and partial version of an ideal rationality whose principles we already understand. "Bounded rationality" means, colloquially, "what rational choice theorists already propose, but adulterated." Economists and political scientists have, it seems, heard as much talk about "bounded rationality" as they can stomach, and the phrase leads anyway to the conclusion that they can proceed with all legitimacy as they have done, so long as, at the end of the day, they concede that actual human beings have a handicap.

My subject here is not bounded rationality. My subject is instead how human beings actually do reason, judge, and choose; and I propose, first, that some of the most important mental work they do is not a bounded form of "rational

85

choice," and, second, that their performance is often spectacularly good, indeed sometimes better than it might be if they executed rational choice mechanisms perfectly.

Herbert Simon's original comment on the interaction of cognitive science, political science, and economics stressed the general indispensability of cognitive science to economics and political science. His remarkable 1986 essay, "Rationality in Psychology and Economics," began with an inspiring assumption—"economic actors use the same basic processes in making their decisions as have been observed in other human cognitive activities" (1986, p. 39)—a crucial perspective—"The emerging laws of procedural rationality have much more the complexity of molecular biology than the simplicity of classical mechanics. As a consequence, they call for a very high ratio of empirical investigation to theory building. They require painstaking factual study of the decision-making process itself" (p. 39)—and an invaluable prescription:

> Economics without psychological and sociological research to determine the givens of the decision-making situation, the focus of attention, the problem representation [i.e., the framing of the problem in context], and the processes used to identify alternatives, estimate consequences, and choose among possibilities—such economics is a one-bladed scissors. Let us replace it with an instrument capable of cutting through our ignorance about rational human behavior. (pp. 39–40)

Simon's call for a conversation between cognitive science and social science has had little effect, despite work by brilliant and, lately, powerful dignitaries like Kahneman and Tversky (1979), Kahneman, Slovic, and Tversky (1982), and Thaler (1991). The persistence of the divide between cognitive science on one hand and economic and political science on the other is reviewed in Hogarth and Reder (1987), Smith (1991), and Lewin (1996). Lewin's summary paints the scene: "the 'declaration of independence' from psychology remain[s], and it haunts economics to this day" (p. 1295).

I have the impression that virtually everyone recognizes that this division is bizarre and that it must end, but the institutional and professional barriers to pulling it down seem to be strong and high.

TWO EXAMPLES

To begin to discuss how we might get over the division, I introduce two examples, one from political science and the other from economics. Both concern choice and preference. The first appears in a technical article from *American Political*

Science Review, titled "The Nature of Utility Functions in Mass Publics," by Henry Brady and Stephen Ansolabehere. Brady and Ansolabehere begin from the simple notion that people choose among alternatives according to their preferences, and that the standard method in political science of modeling this kind of reasoning makes two necessary assumptions: "First, preferences must be transitive. If an individual prefers *j* to *k* and *k* to *m* then the individual must prefer *j* to *m*. Second, indifference must be transitive. If an individual is indifferent between the pair *j* and *k* and between the pair *k* and *m*, then the person must be indifferent between *j* and *m*" (1989, p. 144). Working from data on presidential primaries, the authors found that transitivity of indifference did not hold: in its simplest form, voters who claim to be indifferent between candidates A and B and indifferent between candidates B and C might say they prefer candidate C to A. The authors conducted elaborate tests on voluminous survey data to test a basic tenet of "rational choice theory," found that it fails, and then tried to account for the failure.

The second example is a chestnut case from economics, first brought to my attention by Gilles Fauconnier. It is discussed thoroughly by Colman (1995), Binmore and Brandenburger (1990), and many others. It consists of a schematic situation I call "Watch It Grow" and which economists call "Centipede."

Consider, as an example, a game with two players, Angela and Tom. But wait—this game will make no sense to you whatever unless you first commit yourself to a form of extreme social blindness that violates not only the elements of rational common sense but also every iota of your lived experience: you must not ask who or what is providing the money (it is not the players!), or why anyone would be willing to provide the money, or how, in real life, this game could possibly exist, because it probably could not. If you ask such questions, Watch It Grow will seem like science fiction, because it is.

Anyway, back to Angela and Tom, who have somehow ended up in this mind-bogglingly eccentric situation. (Remember: don't ask how.) They take turns, Angela first, then Tom. A turn consists of picking up the money on the table or passing. They begin the game with one dollar on the table. Every time Tom passes, the money on the table is increased by a multiple of 10. Picking up the money ends the game. The player who picks it up keeps 95 percent of the money and hands the remaining 5 percent over to the other player, and that's that. If Tom passes 100 times, the game ends and neither player keeps any money. Begin by considering Tom's turn in round 100, the last turn of the game. Tom will of course pick up the money, since otherwise neither he nor Angela receives any money at all. Angela knows that Tom will pick up the money, so she will pick it up on the previous turn, to get 95 percent rather than 5 percent. But since 95 percent of x is greater than 5 percent of $10x$, Tom will pick up the money on Tom's turn in round 99. Working backward by induction in this manner leads to the conclusion that Angela will settle for 95¢ in round 1, even though the worst payoff for Angela in round 100 is $(.05)(10^{99})$ = a ton of money, with Tom's payoff being 19 such tons.

Notoriously, real players (that is, real people imagining themselves in this situation or pretending to be in this situation, who, I grant, are not actually real players) never take the 95¢. They fail to conform to what seems to be the indisputable logic, and they resist that logic when it is explained to them. Their resistance is interpreted as presenting a problem for rational choice theory since the players reject what appears to be "rational play." Accordingly, some rational choice theorists have made adjustments to their models to get the models to fit the data better. Later, we will explore how cognitive science might shed light on these efforts.

A PICTURE OF THE PRINCIPLES OF HUMAN CHOICE

These two examples—transitivity of indifference, backward induction along a sequence of economic decisions—offer, implicitly, a picture of the principles of human choice and preference that is quite familiar because it comes from philosophical systems of logical implication. I will go through some of its general principles and then say why they are suspicious as a picture of human choice.

• *Propositions are derived by implication from other propositions (often through very long chains).* How the voter feels about candidate A versus candidate C, how Angela and Tom act in the first round of "Watch It Grow," are not observed actual events, studied and explained, but rather propositions, evaluations, that are computed hypothetically by derivation from other propositions. From the propositions that the voter is indifferent between A and B and between B and C, we *derive* the proposition that the voter is indifferent between A and C. From what is stipulated to happen at the termination of round 100 we *derive* what Tom does just before, in the last turn of round 100, and so on back to Angela's first turn. Angela's reasoning in the initial situation of rational play consists of her coming to hold a proposition that motivates action—"It is optimal for me to pick up this dollar bill, so I choose to do so"—and it arises not by consideration of the situation directly but by derivation back over a long chain of implications from propositions that are temporally and epistemologically distant, out on a horizon of action that is in principle at least as many serial steps away as necessary.

• *The principles of implication are themselves each simple, even commonsensical, almost tautological: reasoning (about preferences) is not inconsistent.* These features are hallmarks of principles of implication in technical logical systems. Examples include the logical principles of "the excluded middle," namely, Either p or *not-p* (Either *2 and 2 are four* or *2 and 2 are not four*); "modus ponens," namely, p and *if p then q*, taken together, imply *q* (*the cube is green* and *if the cube is green, then it is hollow* imply *the cube is hollow*); and transitivity of implication, namely, *p implies q* and *q implies r* imply *p implies r*. And so on.

• *The derivation of propositions is additive.* We know some propositions, and we add other derived propositions to them, but we never lose any of them. As we run the implication engine, we do not change the proposition that the voter prefers A to B or the proposition that on his last turn, it is optimal for Tom to pick up the money. (Technically, there are cases in implicational logic when a proposition is eliminated, as in *reductio ad absurdum* arguments, but that is only because the proposition was marked as assumptive to begin with, and the purpose of running the implication was to test the assumption. In short, the proposition eliminated was from the outset explicitly marked as not knowledge or truth.)

• *The implication runs over all possibilities.* At each turn of Watch It Grow, all possibilities are relevant. There is infinite look-ahead to a horizon of outcomes whose distance from the moment of action can in principle be indefinitely far, limited only by the number of rounds stipulated for the game. It just happens, as an accident, that in this case the possibilities are artificially sharply limited. Similarly, in the derivation of preference and indifference by transitivity, any chain of any length over any combination of preferences and indifferences produces a conclusion as legitimate as any other. For example, if *aPb* means "*a* is preferred to *b*" and *aIb* means "neither *a* nor *b* is preferred," then *aPb* & *bPc* & *cId* & *dIe* & *ePf* & *fPg* & *gIh* & *hIj* & *jPk* imply that *aPk*. There is nothing within the system of implication to indicate which are the interesting or relevant implications.

• *The principles of implication run over all conceptual domains.* For example, transitivity of preference and indifference apply, as principles of reasoning, equally across voting, dining, mating, traveling, swimming, education, medicine, and dressing, equally across choosing a charity and choosing a murder weapon, because they take no account of the content of the preferences and indifferences, looking only to the formal existence of preferences and indifferences. The principles for deriving implications in Watch It Grow do not depend on the context, on the fact that money is involved, and so on. Rather, they apply uniformly across rational choice in any domain—war, teaching, progeneration. They are purely formal principles. In any case where Angela's evaluations of final possible outcomes indicate that Tom, given the chance, will chose an alternative that leaves Angela with a deal that is worse than she could have had by making a different choice in her turn before his, she must prefer that choice, regardless of the conceptual domain they are working in and regardless of what is at stake. In any such case, since the implication spreads over all possibilities, this elimination of "downstream" choices can, if the numbers work out that way, iterate all the way back to the initial turn and tell her what to do at the beginning. This principle of reason does not depend at all on the conceptual content over which it operates. Stated a little hyperbolically, in this view, meaning does not matter.

WHY THIS PICTURE OF HUMAN CHOICE IS SUSPICIOUS

Not surprisingly, the picture I have just sketched of principles of choice and preference will look suspicious to nearly anyone caught up in cognitive science because it runs up against some prejudices widely shared in cognitive science, prejudices so uncontroversially and routinely deployed as to make their threshold of activation nearly zero. Not everyone holds all of them, but most cognitive scientists hold most of them. They are in the wings. They go without saying.

I think there are five basic prejudices that are likely to come to the mind of cognitive scientists looking at the picture of human choice implicit in my two examples.

The first prejudice concerns conflating implication and inference, two things that in cognitive science are sharply distinguished. (By "implication" I mean not everyday "logic" or "common sense" or "reason" but instead the technical deduction of propositions by means of formal implication of the sort familiar since Aristotle's analysis of syllogisms. For example, it is a formal implication that if all elements of set M are in set N and m is in M, then m is in N. Meaning does not matter in these operations. That is why they are called "formal.") The prejudice in cognitive science is that implication of the derivational and additive sort familiar in technical deductive systems of logic is one thing, but how people actually make inferences is another. Stated a little more strongly, implication is a bad model for actual human inference, not because human beings are irrational, but because implication (of the formal, deductive sort, of course) is, mostly, except for some rarified scenarios, unsuited to actual human conditions.

Consider, as one example, Gilbert Harmon's comment in *Change in View* on the status of modus ponens in human reasoning (1986, pp. 3–10). Modus ponens is the principle that, taken together, p and *if p then q* imply q. Consider Mary, who believes that if she looks in the cupboard she will see cereal, and who then looks in the cupboard and of course believes she is looking in the cupboard. Under implication according to modus ponens, she does not need to see the cereal in the cupboard to know that she is seeing it; her seeing it is already implied. It is impossible under implication that she not see it, but it would be a routine affair in human action for her to look in the cupboard and fail to see the cereal, because in human action inference is not necessarily additive—that is, we often delete some of what we knew to be true rather than only add to it.

If Mary were to reason by implication, she must conclude that she faces a logical contradiction. This is terrible, since logical contradiction, inside an implicational system, logically implies anything inside that system. At the moment of recognizing inconsistent beliefs, she must, according to implication, believe everything, including that the moon is made of green cheese and that it is not made of green cheese. In actual human reasoning, of course, she might unconsciously zero out her thinking about cereal when she sees none—after all, she is probably thinking consciously about something else—and soft-boil an egg for breakfast instead, returning as is her habit tomorrow morning to look again in the cupboard and unremarkably see cereal there (she expects to) because the efficient daily routine of shopping has replenished the standard supply.

As a matter of implicational logic, Mary could eliminate the problem by concluding that her perception must be wrong: she is indeed seeing the cereal. Alternatively, she could take her action and experience as a reductio experiment, which would involve viewing one of the two propositions as not a belief but only an assumption, and therefore a possible cause of the contradiction. In that case, Mary might conclude that she is not looking in the cupboard. In human inference, these are not at all the mental strategies she is likely to pursue or the beliefs she is likely to develop, and a good thing, too.

Under formal logical implication, there are indefinitely many propositions implied by the two propositions that if Mary looks in the cupboard, she will see cereal and that she is looking in the cupboard. These implications include that she is either looking in the cupboard or she is herself the cupboard; that it is not the case that she is both looking in the cupboard and not looking in the cupboard; and so on. But in human reasoning, only relatively narrow bands of inference will have any warrant to be developed, and it is typically a big job to explain what those warranting principles might be. Principles of inference include, crucially, principles of inhibiting inference.

As Harmon, summarizing decades of work in cognitive science, explains, it may be a mistake to expect principles of reasoning and choice to take the form of a logic (1986, p. 6). He does not mean that human beings are illogical or that human choice and preference do not operate according to principles that are intricate and orderly and that we might call "logical" in the everyday sense (blending is eminently logical in that sense), or that we cannot investigate, discover, and admire those eminently "logical" principles, but instead that it may be a mistake to expect human reason and choice to operate the way formal implication operates in deductive systems of philosophical logic.

The second prejudice of cognitive science evoked by my examples of choice has to do with the apparent extreme complexity of actual mental operation. It is a commonplace in cognitive science that even when people are doing mental work whose products are apparently so simple as to make them think they are doing no mental work at all—work like seeing red, seeing a ball, needing something and reaching for it, understanding an extremely simple sentence—they are in fact likely to be doing it in a completely unpredictable way far more complicated than anything anyone but the specialist has imagined.

Consider vision and language. It may seem obvious that the appearance of a spot in the visual field is determined by the light coming to our eye from it, but that is false. The amount of light reflected to our eye from a *black* letter in a newspaper headline outside in the sun is about twice the amount of light coming from the *white* paper in a dimly lit office, but we still see the letter as black and the paper as white under both conditions. Another interesting example is that a large spot of uniform illumination seems uniformly vivid, but ganglion cells are in fact reporting information from only its border, making the vividness of the interior, no matter how apparently real, a downstream cerebral computation. Something that looks red under one unexceptional illumination of the visual field and something that looks green under a different unexceptional illumination can in fact be reflecting the *identical* light in the relevant bands of the visual spectrum.

In the cognitive scientific study of language, the results are even more dramatic. Regardless of one's allegiances as a linguist, there is no dispute that human mental operations in dealing with apparently simple language are highly complex and often quite unlike what anyone had assumed or predicted.

In principle, it is not actually impossible that human beings in ecologically normal situations operate by simple and predictable mechanisms like ordinal ranking of alternatives and backward induction to eliminate the strategies that give them the worse outcomes, but if they do, and if that can be proved rather than assumed, it would be big news to cognitive scientists.

The third prejudice evoked by my two examples of choice and preference has to do with their assumption that principles of choice are independent of content and context. It is a commonplace in cognitive science that the basic human developmental path—the developmental interaction of inevitable human biology and (except in nearly unthinkable cases) inevitable human experience—produces human beings who are extremely good at operating in a number of different basic domains, but that there may be substantial differences in the principles of their operation from domain to domain. How we choose when faced with a predator, when choosing a friend, when selecting a destination, when making a tool, when forming conversational alliances, when sharing, and so on, may exhibit substantial differences.

These differences often have to do with possible paths of reasoning. Often, recognizing a situation brings immediately with it a drastic operational narrowing of the alternatives to be considered. In some cases, as neuroscientist Antonio

Damasio discusses in *Descartes' Error*, a very low-level, unconscious recognition of a situation (appearance of a predator, proximity to someone who might do harm, physical environment that puts us at risk, prospect of a certain pleasure, etc.) induces a body state, and we choose action based not on computing various outcomes but instead on our simple awareness that our body is in that state. We may *decide* that a particular situation is bad not through computing and comparing various possible outcomes of various lines of action or inaction but instead through direct, narrow, and simple awareness that we have a *bodily disposition* to keep away from it. These low-level, unconscious recognitions carry, at the neurocognitive level, what Damasio calls *somatic markers*. Somatic markers can, among other things, force attention on a negative outcome of a possible action and so force immediate, uncalculated, underived rejection of that choice, protecting us against loss by reducing, sometimes to exactly one, the number of alternatives we consider. To be sure, in one sense, evolution may have "calculated" the utility of this somatic marker. But the human being who reacts to the somatic marker is not calculating over the space of possible outcomes to arrive at the choice; on the contrary, any such elaborate calculating is, according to Damasio, shut down from the outset, and that is the main worth of the somatic marker. Such a view of choice is consistent with studies by Tversky and Kahneman (1986) showing that framing a situation one way to highlight risk of loss and framing it in a contrasting way to highlight risk of gain lead to different choices by subjects, who generally avoid risk in the first case but seek it in the second, even though the different framings make no difference to the mathematical analysis of gain and loss in the situation.

There is a principle of practical rationality in economics that has been called the "Choice Function Assumption." It provides another example of reason by implication—additive, derivational, at first blush entirely commonsensical—that in fact may turn out in practice to depend on the conceptual domain to which it is applied. The Choice Function Assumption is: if someone is choosing alternatives from any subset J of all the alternatives M, the elements j in J that will be chosen are all those for which there is no k in J such that k is preferred to j.[1] This abstract assumption might be regarded as very weak, perhaps the minimum that we can demand of a rational agent, since it requires only that the chooser choose with a minimal consistency as feasible sets change.

The Choice Function Assumption often looks indisputable. Suppose, for example, that of ten paths from Rome to Paris by car, seven are open, and of those seven, you prefer one. It seems nonsensical to imagine that there could be some different road in the seven that you prefer to the one you chose, for if you preferred it, why didn't you choose it? Similarly, it seems nonsensical to imagine that if you are suddenly informed of the closing of two more roads, but not the one you chose, you could now prefer a different road among the five remaining open roads to the one you originally chose, for again, if you preferred that other road, why wouldn't you have chosen it in the first place?

But the Choice Function Assumption looks quite different if we apply it to a conceptual domain that can involve social or strategic interaction, such as a presidential primary. Suppose you must vote for Tom, Dick, or Mary. You choose to vote for Tom. Now Dick withdraws from the race, and you switch your preference to Mary. Perhaps you always preferred Mary to Tom but thought she had no chance of winning while Dick was in the race. Or perhaps you thought Dick himself could not win now but would become vice-president under Tom and then succeed Tom as president, and you liked that possible future best.

Whatever your reasons, in your choosing of Mary you have, in the strict sense, violated the Choice Function Assumption by choosing Tom from a set of three candidates, even though, one against one, you preferred Mary to Tom. When Dick withdraws, the feasible set changes, and according to the Choice Function Assumption, you are showing inconsistency of choice as the feasible set changes. Similarly, suppose Catherine could marry any of three brothers—Paul, Bill, and James. She prefers Paul. But now Bill dies. She decides she prefers James, perhaps because she thought Paul's superiority depended upon the support, guidance, and wisdom of Bill, or perhaps because Paul and Bill are identical twins, Catherine and Bill were once intimate, and Bill's death so traumatizes Catherine that she concludes she cannot spend her life seeing Bill in Paul's features. Whatever Catherine's reasons, she has violated the Choice Function Assumption.

Rational choice theorists fully recognize such violations and have ways of dealing with them. When the chooser takes into account strategic aspects such as a candidate's chances of winning, rational choice theorists redefine the situation as a problem of choice under uncertainty, and the chooser is said to choose the alternative with the highest expected utility. When the chooser takes into account the contribution of the choices not chosen—such as Bill's guidance of Paul—the rational choice theorist might require us to redefine the choices so that Catherine is choosing not Paul but instead Paul plus Bill. In the case of Catherine's not wanting to see the ghost of Bill in Paul's face, I do not know what the rational choice theorist would say. Before Bill's death, Catherine might have preferred Paul to his brothers without taking into account interactions or interdependencies among Paul, Bill, and James, but Bill's death has changed her preferences. In this case, the chooser's preferences change as a direct consequence of the changing of the feasible set. Perhaps the rational choice theorist might propose that there was actually a hidden interdependency between Paul and Bill that had influenced Catherine without her realizing it.

What these methods of salvation for the Choice Function Assumption show is exactly that it is not a formal principle of implication applying identically over all conceptual domains but instead an abstracted, tidied-up, evocative rubric that can apply differently in different domains, depending on the possibilities for interdependency, and the kinds of interdependency, that happen to come into play in specific domains of application. Any straightforward choice of A over B—Mary over Tom, or James over Paul—looks as if it reveals a preference, but when technical analysis shows that the choice violates the Choice Function Assumption, it is a tip to the rational choice theorist to take up the hunt, to inspect and reconsider the specific conceptual domain of application, to locate some features of interdependency there that might cause the violation, and, in a manner, explain the violation away.

In sum, if something like the Choice Function Assumption operates in actual human inference, it seems plausible that its operation varies across conceptual domains.

The fourth prejudice evoked by my two examples is historical, and it partially subsumes the first three. For roughly a quarter of a century, beginning in the mid-1950s, the study of artificial intelligence employed an army of researchers, very many of them exceptionally talented and trained in formal analysis, in its attempt to model reason as propositional implication—derivational, additive, spreading over branching trees of alternatives, formal, symbolic, and independent of conceptual content. Artificial intelligence of this sort had legendary successes in areas like expert systems, but its central attempt to produce a model of ecologically valid human reason and choice was a flop, and everyone in cognitive science is thoroughly aware of the nature of that failure. No one familiar with the intellectual quality of the personnel involved in this effort can suppose that the failure came from lack of talent, and anyone who wishes success to the modeling paradigm in economics and political science, as I do, is bound to observe, not uncharitably I hope, that it shares much of its style, assumptions, and methods with the earliest stages of artificial intelligence, which were, indeed, centrally concerned with theorem-proving, calculation over alternatives, optimal paths through trees of possibilities, dangers of becoming stuck at a local maximum ("hill-climbing"), elimination of inferior branches, and formal principles that applied over seemingly diverse content.

Artificial intelligence had considerable early success in the modeling of what are now called "mini-worlds"—small universes with limited elements and relations and a prescribed list of possible actions, universes like chess, stacking and unstacking blocks, minimal and artificial adversarial interactions. The great hope of early artificial intelligence was that these small-scale autonomous models would, with much more work and detail, scale up appropriately to models of plausible situations. That is the dashed hope of artificial intelligence. The world is exceptionally rich, and so is the brain, and that is the baseline from which human cognition operates.

The fifth prejudice evoked by my two examples is easily stated and is perhaps somewhat less widely shared among cognitive scientists: experience, and analogy based on experience, seem to be crucial elements in human reasoning, but they do not seem to be given a role in the picture of human reason offered by my two examples.

RATIONAL CHOICE

The study of rational play has various names—game theory, rational choice theory, theory of rational expectations, theory of interdependent decision making, positive political theory, the new institutionalism, economic theory of politics, and so on. It attempts to extract formal aspects of how interdependent actors make reasoned choices with the goal of maximizing their profit, or, more accurately, their subjective expected utility. The backward-induction analysis of Watch It Grow, which leads to the conclusion that Angela should settle for 95¢ on her first turn, is a straightforward example of the way rational choice theory works.

A better example, which I will use to illustrate some of the principles of rational choice theory, is "The Battle of the Bismarck Sea." An admiral must transport troops by ship. He can select the shorter northern route or the longer southern route. An enemy admiral must try to bomb them. He can send his planes either north or south to look for the targets. (Many restrictions are quietly assumed; we are not to ask entirely appropriate questions about, e.g., whether the enemy admiral might send half of his planes in each direction, and so on.) There are (artificially, of course) exactly four sets of possible choices, since each player has (artificially, of course) two choices. Values are assigned for each player to each of the four outcomes. We then inspect the mathematics of the game tree to see which choice is better for each player.

This extremely simple example already has most of the features of game-theoretic, rational choice analysis. The choosing is interdependent and the players act on their choices. A choice in a situation leads to yet another situation in which various choices are possible, until at last we reach a final outcome. We can think of any situation in which a player must choose as a "node," and of a choice as carrying the players from one node to another, and of the final outcome as an "end node" where no further choices are to be made. Then all the possible paths of choosing form a branching tree of nodes. We can compare all the possible outcomes and assign them values for each player. For example, if the admiral sends his ships north and the enemy admiral sends his planes north, the outcome is that the ships are bombed, which has low value for the admiral whose ships are bombed and high value for the enemy admiral.

In simple examples of this sort, these values might be given in number of ships bombed or number of troops lost or dollar amounts or percentages of market share or years in jail or number of fatalities or some other unit, but in principle all such values are really subjective values assigned by the players to the outcomes, relative to other outcomes. Players are always trying to enhance what they perceive to be their welfare by achieving higher subjective relative utilities. The values are arrayed into a matrix of payoffs of outcomes for players. Game theory is the study of arithmetic conditions that arise in the tree of nodes leading to the outcome numbers, on the view that the arithmetic drives or should drive choices at each node.

Inevitably, rational choice theory has taken fire for making simplistic assumptions. For the most part, the game theorists appear to be well aware that these games are cartoons of reality—"parsimonious models" rather than "thick descriptions." Not without reason, they are proud that their mathematically encrypted but conceptually simple analyses nonetheless show something about interdependent decision making. Something is already a lot in the analysis of reason and choice.

Moreover, game theory has made rudimentary attempts to acknowledge some of the complexity of interdependent decision making. For example, a preliminary attempt has been made to recognize some gross distinctions in the extent and kinds of knowledge about the game possessed by the players (games of perfect, certain, symmetric, or complete information). An attempt has also been made to recognize the role of conceptual focal points (e.g., the number 100 rather than 99) in decision making.

What I offer is not an attack on rational choice theory but a demonstration of how it might be made less implausible and more adequate by being integrated with cognitive science. There are many avenues that could be taken to a "cognitive theory of choice." Some of them are quite well-known:

- The world is rich, and in the typical situation, actors are engaged in simultaneous games that overlap. In life, any action is usually a move in many different games. Strategies to maximize expected utility over all these games are typically nonlinear. In principle, the output of any subgame of any game can be input to any subgame of any other game. It would be quite a challenge to develop rational choice theory to take account of this richness of the world.
- In the typical situation, actors are adaptive: their first and strongest disposition is often not to play the game but to reinvent it, change it. Rational choice theory does not typically take account of this cognitive reinvention.

- Strategies for doing well in these simultaneous games include leaving some of them and relinquishing hope of gain from them. Exiting the game is a very common part of real choice by real human beings engaged in real complex life in the richness of the world.
- In the typical situation, actors work at conceptual reinterpretation of the history of play, so as to persuade other actors that the value and status of a past action must be changed, and further, to persuade them that the action led to nodes different from those to which it was once thought to lead. Conceptually, which is what counts, the history of the game is not fixed.
- Actors must operate in general without knowing what game they are in, and the question always arises, who has the authority to recognize and establish the game being played? Actors attempt to influence other actors' thoughts about the game being played.

Comments like these, common in discussions of rational choice theory, underscore the ways in which actual human choice typically requires elaborate and complex cognitive work of sorts that rational choice theory does not at present take into account.

I will focus for the rest of this chapter on a major challenge for rational choice theory, the fact that actual human choice during complex life in our rich world depends upon elaborate conceptual blending. How can we begin to develop models that could embrace the insights of both conceptual blending theory and rational choice theory?

First let us consider the hidden role of conceptual integration in rational choice theory, beginning with what game theorists call "an off-the-equilibrium-path node." This is jargon for a possibility that is considered while we are thinking about choices to be made but that is prevented from becoming real. Suppose Alice is thinking about a path of choices through a "tree of nodes" (e.g., if I do P, he might do Q, then I might do R, then he might . . .). Suppose she is thinking about one of the "nodes" or scenarios that arises along that path of choices (e.g., If I have done P, and he has then done Q, and I have done R, then we would be at situation S, and how do I like S?). She thinks about S and above all about where S might ultimately lead, and she decides that S is bad, or at least relatively unattractive. She would rather be at some node other than S, and she has the power to stop S from becoming real. She therefore decides to avoid the choices that would lead to S. As a result, the choices made by the players never lead to S: S is imaginary but never real. A path of nodes that the players might agree to make real is an "equilibrium path." S is not on the (or an) equilibrium path. It remains "off the equilibrium path" and never becomes real. It ends up, once the game as enacted goes past the level at which S was possible, being counterfactual with respect to reality.

Let us inspect the cognitive work involved in this thought experiment. Specifically, imagine that Alice (actor A) has the chance to choose to take action P but believes that, for the past, present, or future, if she does P, Bob (actor B) responds by doing Q, and this leads to situation S. Desiring to avoid S, A has never done P and plans never to do P. Translated into human language, this means that if A imagines doing P, she doesn't like the imagined consequences, so she doesn't do it.

Obviously, the off-the-equilibrium-path node S in the game tree that comes from A's doing P and then B's doing Q can be put together only through conceptual blending of specific knowledge and conventional schematic frames, because it does not refer to any actual situation, and no one has any memory of it. To arrive at a conception of that space, we must blend together concepts of real actors (A and B), real characteristics of those actors, unreal actions (P), and models of behavior, and, running the blend, we must develop hypothetical responses (Q). Importantly, this blended space is *causal* for the space of A's *actual* behavior: under game-theoretic assumptions of rationality, this imaginary space S, put together by blending, *causes* its own counterfactuality; it *causes* the player to make another choice. And so we see conceptual blending, its mechanisms, biases, and products, at the heart of rational choice.[2]

In fact, all nodes in a game must be constructed cognitively by conceptual integration, which is easiest to do for very simple games with two players, each of whom has a single move, and where the outcomes are relatively clear since some external agency imposes or provides payoffs in a single, monolithic, publicly recognized unit (yen, years in jail) and at a level that overshadows all other payoffs. This explains, I propose, why rational choice theory routinely uses simple games like The Battle of the Bismarck Sea or The Prisoner's Dilemma as its illustrations.

It becomes not only harder to do the requisite conceptual integration as the game becomes more complicated (as in, for example, what a game theorist would call a "highly iterated nonconstant sum game without a dominant strategy equilibrium but with many Nash equilibria"); it also becomes less defensible to rely on the product. Game-theoretic analysis of simple, encapsulated games like tic-tac-toe is partially justified because of the unusual conditions of play ("partially" because we still must ignore, e.g., all the social and psychological aspects of playing the game, even though these aspects influence choices involved in winning and losing the narrowly defined game, as when, for example, a player intends to use the game as a distraction, or as a pretext for holding a conversation, or as a way to engage a child, or . . .). For more complicated strips of rational play, game-theoretic analysis can be much less convincing, for the reason that conceptual blending is not a deterministic or algorithmic process, and, therefore, the more active and iterated the blending, the more alternative and imaginary developments there will be for the node one is trying to evaluate. If Alice does P, just how will B respond by doing Q, and what else will B do in the process of doing Q? This is a question that conceptual blending must decide, and, while the answers it gives are informative and principled, they are not determined by the influencing spaces, and can be elaborated in potentially many different directions.

There is another crucial way in which conceptual blending is fundamental to theory of rational choice. In game theory, in order for the decision making even to begin, values must be assigned to outcomes. Game-theoretic analysis begins by taking those values as *given*. In this way, the game theorist takes the payoff matrix as an *oracle*, in the technical sense: in mathematics, one way to attack a problem is to try to show that if there were an oracle that could supply the answer to some part of the problem, we could solve the entire problem; this shows that the larger problem reduces to the problem solved by the oracle.

But in reality, it turns out that this matrix of values comes not from an oracle but from conceptual integration. In rational play, a player who is trying to weigh a choice C somewhere along the path must connect it to outcomes, and assign values to those outcomes, and, working backward, make a judgment about C. But the world is rich, and in the real world, an outcome, like a choice, is typically part of many different "games" we are playing. To evaluate an outcome requires us to weigh the value of that outcome in all the "games" in which it has some role. If the value of an outcome (walking down the street) is just the simple sum of its values in all the "games" in which it has a role (the game of "going to the store," of "getting some exercise," of "enjoying the sunshine," of "learning whether the road crew has finished its work," of "flirting with the neighbor," . . .), then we say that its overall value in the big game of Life is the "linear sum" of its values in each of the games in which it plays a role, considered as if they had no relation to each other. But we typically cannot evaluate an outcome X by thinking of each game separately and then taking the linear sum of values. Instead, we typically must form a conceptual blend of all those games where they intersect at X in order to judge the global value of X. For example, suppose Sue believes that if she has a chance to tell a certain story in casual conversation in a group that includes Max, then telling it will prompt Max to begin to court her. She believes the same of Joe. She welcomes the courtship in either case: she assigns to these outcomes high value. The chance arises, but Sue stays silent, because Max and Joe are both present, and she prefers not to induce known rivalry between them. The value of having Max and Joe court her is, it turns out, not the sum of having each court her. There is essential emergent structure in this blend of Max-and-Joe-as-rivals, and it includes an emergent value that is not the linear sum of the values of its inputs.

But now suppose that Todd is also present. Sue thinks Todd's reaction to seeing Max and Joe court her will be at first painful brooding but later a determination to court her, which she welcomes highly. Then the high positive value of being courted by both Max and Joe is unrelated to the positive values of being courted by each of them separately.

The game theorist takes the conceptual content of the nodes and the matrix of values for the outcomes as given, and begins the game-theoretic analysis after this point. But from the cognitive perspective, these things are not given; they are instead constructed mentally by conceptual integration and other basic cognitive operations.

The game theorist proceeds in the sequence: (1) chart, or if that is impractical, characterize formally the tree of decisions and actions; (2) assign values to the outcomes; (3) analyze the resulting arithmetic of the game tree. There may be a few cases of decision making, like the Battle of the Bismarck Sea, where this procedure comes close to fitting actual choice. But in actual choice, conceptual integration to assemble the nodes and values is always active. The contents and values of all the nodes are always under construction.

Conceptual integration is additionally indispensable to game theory in a quite different way. It is the basis of deciding, at the specific level, what game one is playing, and, at the general level, whether or not one is playing a game at all. First let us consider the question of what game one is playing. We use conceptual frames (e.g., seduction, debate) in understanding specific situations. The conceptual frame is part of the integration network that constitutes our understanding of the specific situation. Since conceptual frames carry default inferences and principles of inference, it is natural to assume that decision making in any specific situation will depend on what frames are used by the decision maker as conceptual inputs.

Yet Von Neumann and Morgenstern's *Theory of Games and Economic Behavior* (1947/1944), which launched the application of game theory to economic behavior, offered as one of its great insights that the formal structure of decision making displays certain mathematical regularities that are independent of specific conceptual frames. Some cognitive scientists have argued that at least in certain specific cases this assumption is demonstrably wrong (Simon 1978 and 1982; Kahneman and Tversky 1979; Tversky and Kahneman 1986). If it is wrong as a general principle, then it follows that conceptual integration (of frames and specific situations) is indispensable to decision making. "Positive" social science depends on cognitive mechanisms of framing.

Now let us consider the question of whether one is playing a game at all. It turns out that conceptual integration is also involved in deciding this question. The intellectual concept of *interdependent decision making based on the goal of maxi-*

mizing my utility is itself a (very general) conceptual frame—that is, a conventional bundle of shared schematic knowledge. When we use it to help us think about a choice, consciously or unconsciously, it certainly does exert pressure on how we consider ourselves and our choices. This is especially the case when we are also using as an influencing space a specific conceptual frame (such as the frames for "matching pennies" or "poker," two of Von Neumann and Morgenstern's examples) that has *maximizing utility* as part of its fixed, immutable goal structure. But the general schematic frame of *interdependent decision making based on the goal of maximizing my utility* is far from being the only general frame we have for thinking about interdependent choices. It is not easy for the cognitive scientist to swallow the assumption that people have no choice but to blend that abstract frame of game playing with their current specific situation, all of the time, and always to act on the central inference of that blend.

For some theorists, there may be a latent feeling that evolutionary pressure by itself (succeed rather than fail) must ensure that actors will try to enhance their welfare by maximizing their expected utility, but the mechanisms of evolutionary pressure are not so simple. For example, curiosity and routine action to satisfy it are apparently adaptive for various species of mammal, but curiosity killed the cat. Acting on curiosity may be unrelated to any local or recognizable game or utility, and the details of its downstream utility may be for the most part unimaginable to the actor and beyond his ability to evaluate. The benefit of behavior motivated by curiosity may be absolute but not resident within anything that looks like a strip of interdependent decision making. Acting on curiosity does not have to be *reasoned*, it does not have to involve *decision*, and it does not have to be connected to any utility that is recognizable by the actor or imaginable by the actor. It can be *impulsive*. Much of our action—even our action in explicitly political, financial, or legislative contests—could in principle be driven by curiosity.

If this seems implausible, just imagine that one of our ancestors had a genetic disposition to intense curiosity that raised its chances for causing its own death but raised even more dramatically its chances for genetic reproduction (perhaps, for example, because curiosity brings new experience and thereby places us in positions to develop new and useful skills). Then, with any luck, that genetic disposition would have propagated through the species; the fact that a lot of people die as a result of behavior driven by curiosity would be outweighed by the increased differential reproduction enjoyed by genes disposing us to be curious.

Evolution is not playing the same game as the individual. This is uncontroversial. Human beings for the most part would not choose to die, but genes choose to cash us in to make way for newer models. Genes do not care that this choice obliterates mere individual human choosers. Our fervent desire to live is opposed and defeated by the preference of our genes that we be killed off at the convenient moment. We are bent on survival, but so are they, and the harmony this can produce early in life changes to a pitched conflict later in life, one fatal for human choosers. Necessarily, evolution will tend to make human beings with the kinds of backstage cognition that are adaptive for genes, not, where there is conflict, the kinds that suit the perceived self-interests of the individual chooser. In game-theoretic analysis, the welfare-maximizing player who wants to win and live should never choose deep play, and rarely choose the path of curiosity that threatens loss and death, but if that kind of choice increases genetic replication, natural selection will condition human backstage cognition to deliver it. Behavior that is endogenously irrational for the individual can be superbly rational for the genes. Evolution's game and the individual's game may intersect now and then, of course, but in general, the payoff matrix for genes is not a linear sum of the payoff matrices of individual games played by individual agents.

There is another deep conflict between evolutionary theory and rational choice theory. It is not implausible, from the evolutionary point of view, that most of what happens in human life is a "clinic," in the sports sense: most of life may be essentially a training ground in which we prepare for the comparatively few actions in life that are crucial. From the evolutionary point of view, it may be that the most important outcome of a strip of human activity is usually the training of the individuals involved in it. As a consequence, it can be rational for both the individual, in terms of his perceived self-interest, and his genes, in terms of their replication, if the individual is disposed to make trouble for himself. If most of life is a clinic, then it can be soundly rational for the player to make choices that are, if viewed strictly in terms of the payoff matrix of a specific game, quite irrational. If we are skating effortlessly through a game, headed toward optimal payoff, and our method is just to do the same old thing we have always done, then we are not getting the benefit of any new training, and so we may be depriving ourselves of the most important payoff. In such a circumstance, it can be rational to have an impulse to make things harder on ourselves, to get ourselves into trouble, to play with fire, to place quite unnecessary handicaps on ourselves, to challenge ourselves artificially, provided only that the game we are playing is not one of those rare games with truly life-defining consequences. It can be rational, if we are pleasing our employer, to antagonize her, or rational, if we are coasting easily toward a deadline, to rip up what we have done and start over at the last minute, or rational, if we are traveling comfortably in a strange country, to strike a silly bargain that deprives us of most of our money, and so on, provided the cost is not permanently disabling and provided there is a lot to be learned from the pressure that results. Parents often have no doubt that their young children are dedicated to truly risky behavior even when there is no obvious benefit from the behavior and the possibility of injury is manifest. Childhood, from the evolutionary perspective, is, like most of life, a clinic. Making trouble for ourselves can lead us into parts of the game with which we have no experience, and so deliver a great payoff in training, regardless of the values affixed to the outcomes. Resistance is a value. I am not talking here about whether or not people are "rational" in the sense of "wise" about developing their desires or assigning values. If we cavalierly stipulate that those desires and values are absolutely set exogenously, by factors outside the game, then it may still be rational for the individual, whose controlling game is the overall combined game of Life, to have dispositions that lead him to behave in ways that are endogenously irrational in any particular isolated game.

Rational play—as a mode of thought and action that requires the unconscious suppression of our dispositions toward curiosity, training, and resistance—may be a special talent, a controlled mode of thought and action in which we briefly disengage or resist highly adaptive mental and behavioral dispositions. Perhaps one of the reasons we invent and play strange, isolated, stand-alone games like chess and tic-tac-toe is to train ourselves in how to resist dispositions that are better for us than rational play, but not always better. Sometimes, such as when we are in a relatively isolated strip of activity, truly rational play might be useful. Chess and tic-tac-toe, far from showing us the nature of human choice, may train us in a special-purpose mode of choice that now and then has worth.

Within rational choice theory, the clearest recognition of the distance between game theoretic models and cognitive scientific inquiry appears in the work of Arthur Lupia and Mat McCubbins (1997) and Mat McCubbins and Michael Thies (1997). For example, McCubbins and Thies write,

> [Do] we believe that the actors in question quantify the payoffs and pause for a couple weeks to perform the math before deciding how to behave? Do people consciously decide to employ "mixed strategies"? Of course not. . . . They think, "I've dealt with something like this before, and I know I should do this and not that." People simplify, categorize, and use shortcuts to make decisions. In short, they develop or employ previously developed theories about the world. They may have arrived at the "equilibrium response" through trial and error, or indeed through evolutionary mutation, but no matter how they decide, we can check to see whether they act as our complicated models predict they will. *The models are for us as observers, and we use them because we believe them to be good analogies to the expected behavior, given our assumptions* [original emphasis]. Models rely on mathematical formalization to ensure internal consistency—formalization does not determine equilibrium. Indeed, the

models are necessary only because most analysts lack the intuition to predict behavior without them. (p. 19)

This view of the status and utility of the mathematical models is very far from that originally proposed by von Neumann and Morgenstern (1947/1944):

One would misunderstand the intent of our discussions by interpreting them as merely pointing out an analogy between these two spheres. We hope to establish satisfactorily, after developing a few plausible schematizations, that the typical problems of economic behavior become strictly identical with the mathematical notions of suitable games of strategy. (p. 2)

One of the most complex and disturbing uses of conceptual integration in game theory is backward induction. Recall the game of Watch It Grow, in which the dollar on the table grows to increasingly large sums of money as long as the players can resist picking up the pot. The game theorist, using backward induction, proves that "under rationality" the player at turn one picks up the pot, receiving a payoff of ninety-five cents while the other player receives a payoff of a nickel.

There are many points to be made about the game theorist's argument by backward induction. First, all backward induction is performed by repeated blending. To understand "Angela and Tom in the last turn in the last round of Watch It Grow" requires blending of two inputs. The first is a specific situation: Angela is the first player and Tom is the second; it is the last turn in the last round; the pot is on the table. The second input is an abstract frame of knowledge that defines a round and its conditions. This frame includes the complicated knowledge that if it is round x (where x is a variable that can run from 1 to 100), then there is 10^{x-1} in the pot; that the player whose turn it is can pick up the pot or pass, with the stipulated consequences; that there are no rounds after round 100, and so on.

When we blend these two inputs, we produce a blend in which the two players are Tom and Angela, it is the last turn of the last round, there is an incredibly huge sum of money in the pot (10^{100-1}), Tom can either pick up the pot and keep 95 percent of it or pass and receive no money, and so on, and we develop essential emergent structure in the blend that is not given by either input: *Tom picks up the money.*

Once we have constructed this blend, with its all-important emergent structure, we must then construct another blend, in which it is now the penultimate turn of the game and Angela can contemplate the blend for the final turn of the game. In this new blend, we develop essential emergent structure: Angela picks up the money. But now we must construct yet another blend, in which it is the second turn of the ninety-ninth round, and Tom can contemplate the blend for the penultimate turn of the game, . . . and so on backward, in a cascade of blends whose players always contemplate the blend for the next turn in the game, and we keep doing this, at each step developing for the current blend the emergent structure that the pot must be picked up now, and so on back through the turns until we reach the first turn of the first round and develop the expected emergent structure for that blend: Angela picks up the dollar and keeps ninety-five cents. The mental operation that makes it possible for the game theorist (and the player) to perform this rather impressive reasoning is conceptual integration.

But as Binmore and Brandenburger (1990) have reported, there is a problem with this procedure, because it seems to assume the possibility under rationality of blends that are thereafter demonstrated to be impossible under rationality. In short, if the players were rational, they would never reach the hundredth round, or the ninety-ninth, and so on. These hypothetical blends are impossible. Why should players be influenced by a line of argument that assumes the existence of these rounds if it is then going to show that they do not exist? Why should players be influenced by a line of argument that assumes something is possible only to prove that it is impossible?

We might feel that the obvious and compelling answer to this question comes from mathematics: in mathematics, a *reductio ad absurdum* argument works by assuming that something is true in order to show that it is false. For example, to prove that there is no largest prime integer, we assume that there is a largest prime integer, call it k, and, using that assumption, show that there must be a prime integer larger than k. This creates a situation in which k both is and is not the largest prime integer, and this is a contradiction, which is taken as proving that the assumption must be false: there is no largest prime integer. In any such *reductio ad absurdum* argument, we have assumed that something is true (there is a largest prime integer) in order to prove that it is false (there is no largest prime integer). (Of course, there is some underlying logic here: the mathematical system itself has been built so as to be consistent; therefore the blame for the contradiction falls on the assumption, not on the mathematical system.)

In sum, in a *reductio ad absurdum* argument in mathematics, we certainly do assume something to be true in order to prove that it is impossible. This mathematical process is indeed similar to the reasoning in "Assume that *we reach the last turn of the last round of the game*; then Tom will pick up the money; but Angela during the turn before can figure that out, so she will pick up the money; so we see that in fact *we never reach the last turn of the last round of the game*." If mathematical proof can work this way, why not human choice?

In fact, there is plenty of evidence that we do employ *reductio ad absurdum* argument in everyday life: has the Internal Revenue System deposited my tax refund into my bank account? *Assume that it has.* Then my bank balance must be such-and-such. But a quick check of my bank balance shows that it is much lower than such-and-such. This is a contradiction. Therefore, I conclude that the Internal Revenue System *has not* deposited my tax refund. In such an everyday process of reasoning, I have assumed something to be true and, using that assumption, proved it false.

Moreover, a *reductio ad absurdum* argument can employ backward induction. Suppose we have a set of mathematical elements in which we are interested. This could be a set of numbers, or lines, or angles, or vectors, or anything mathematical. Suppose there are exactly $M+1$ such elements, where M is some fixed integer. We can call this set A and denote its $M+1$ elements, $a_0, a_1, \ldots a_M$. Suppose that we want to prove that so-and-so is false for every one of these $M+1$ elements. We might try to do this by brute force, taking each element individually, one at a time, in a long sequence, and proving for each one that so-and-so is false. But M might be a very large integer, which would make the brute force approach impractical, or at least tiresome. A much quicker and more pleasing proof might go like this: first, make the assumption that so-and-so is true for a_M. Now, armed with that assumption, prove theorems until we arrive at a contradiction. We might, for example, prove that a certain number is odd and also that it is even, or that a certain angle is acute and also that it is obtuse. The contradiction proves (by *reductio ad absurdum*) that the assumption must be false, for this reason: given that the mathematical system was coherent before we introduced the new assumption and also that we have not made any mistakes in our proofs, the only thing left that can be the cause of the contradiction is the assumption. Therefore, the assumption must be wrong. In other words, so-and-so must be false for a_M. Now comes the second part of our logical attack: assume that *if* so-and-so is false for a_n where n is *any* integer between 1 and M, then it is not false but instead true for a_{n-1}. Armed with this assumption, prove theorems until we arrive at a contradiction. In just the same way, this contradiction proves (by *reductio ad absurdum*) that the assumption must be wrong. In other words, if so-and-so is false for a_n, where n is any integer between 1 and M, it cannot be true for a_{n-1}. But now, these two conclusions combine logically to prove that so-and-so is false for all of the $M+1$ element in our mathematical system, as follows. By the first conclusion, we know that so-and-so is false for a_M. By the second conclusion, we know that if it is false for a_M, it must be false for a_{M-1}. But then, using the second conclusion again, we know it must be false for a_{M-2}. And so on all the way down through all $M+1$ elements. In this efficient way, without having to investigate all the elements individually, we have proved that so-and-so is false for all the $M+1$ elements. We have used backward induction, and we have assumed some things to be true in order to prove them false.

This mathematical process of backward induction does indeed resemble the process of reasoning in "Assume we have reached the last turn of the last round and Tom leaves the pot untouched. Then he receives no money. Under rationality, he would not prefer this outcome. So in fact, Tom must pick up the money on the last turn of the game. Now suppose that for any turn n except the last in the game, where n is a variable, the player at turn n leaves the pot untouched even though he calculates that the other player will pick it up on turn $n+1$; but then the player at turn n, who has left the pot untouched, receives less money than he would have received if he had picked up the pot at turn n; under rationality, he would not prefer this outcome; therefore he would indeed pick up the pot on turn n. Combining the conclusion that Tom would pick up the money on the last turn with the conclusion that if a player would pick up the money at turn $n+1$, the other player would pick it up at turn n proves that we never get beyond the first turn of the first round. Angela picks up the money and receives ninety-five cents and Tom a nickel." Again, if mathematics can work this way, why not human choice?

For anyone with mathematical training, these processes of *reductio ad absurdum* and induction on n (including backward induction on n), for the purpose of proving either necessity or impossibility, are basic and habitual cognitive tools, familiar and ready to hand. They have a very low threshold of activation. It is easy for the mathematically trained game theorist to activate them as an input to a blend, where the other input is procedures of human choice. In the blend, human choice takes on features of formal induction on n. Because of selective projection, this blend makes backward induction on n in a *reductio ad absurdum* argument look like an appropriate method of choosing.

But there are fundamental differences between the mathematical situation and the human situation, and they make this blend of formal mathematics and human choice dubious as a source of insight into how human beings choose. In the mathematical space, *reductio ad absurdum* and backward induction, as procedures, make no assumptions about actions or values. They deal only with a mathematical system that has *no temporality*: the mathematical system is timeless, eternal, with all of its truths existing simultaneously. In the mathematical operation, we show definitively and logically that a particular specific mathematical structure must exist or must not exist within a mathematical system. Impossibility is very clearly defined as exactly *not existing in the system*.

But this is not at all what the game theorist means by "impossibility": the game theorist, in attempting to prove that the last turn of the last round will never be reached, and indeed that no turn beyond the first will ever be reached, deals with actions and values over time intervals, and he does not try to show that there is something in the human system that makes reaching the later turns impossible. On the contrary, these turns are fully possible in the human system. They are impossible only if we artificially restrict players to a narrow set of operations called by the game theorist "rationality."

But quite evidently, human beings are not restricted in this way. Therefore, what the mathematician means by "impossible" does not line up with what the game theorist means by "impossible." The mathematical system itself resolutely prevents a particular assumption from being mathematically possible; but the human system itself does not prevent the later turns in Watch It Grow from being humanly possible. The mathematician shows us that there is no way whatever in the mathematical system for the assumption to be true. But the game theorist does not show us that there is no way whatever in the human system for these turns to take place. Far from it.

Given this discrepancy, it is no surprise that the actual players disagree with the game theorists. Why should it be impossible to watch money grow for a few turns? Obviously, it is not.

It is easy to identify with the game theorist who thinks that someone who can reject his conclusion is simply missing the clear and overwhelming mathematical reasoning. But it is also easy to identify with the actual player who thinks that the game theorist is missing the clear human reasoning. The theorists and the players disagree, and this offers an opportunity to the cognitive scientist to ask: what mental work is leading to these two different choices?

The game theorists and the actual players disagree, I propose, because they are using different conceptual blends to guide their choices. The game theorist's conceptual blend warrants his choice, while the player's conceptual blend warrants his choice. Each is using "human choosing in this game" as one input to the blend. The game theorist, working from a mathematical conditioning and aesthetic, has a low threshold for activating backward induction on n in a *reductio* argument, and so uses it as the other input to the blend. The result is a blend of "human choosing in this game through backward induction" that looks entirely natural, even inevitable. Just so, readers who judged the British Airways ad to be sexist had a low threshold for activating both the Oedipal frame and the frame of "sexist representation of stewardesses," and so they used it to construct a blend that looked entirely natural to them, even inevitable.

But the copywriters at the ad agency used quite different inputs to the blend and so presumably did not see the Oedipal blend and dismissed it, when it was pointed out, as bizarre. The players of Watch It Grow who dismiss the game theorist's backward-induction argument might, like the copywriters at the ad agency, be deploying a different input to the blend, such as "something-for-nothing" or, since both players benefit enormously if the pot is allowed to grow, "you scratch my back and I'll scratch yours." There are many other possible in-puts: "if it's not broken, don't mess with it" or "What a curious situation! Let's see what happens!"—and so on. If the players are blending "human choosing in this game" with any of these other familiar cultural inputs, and so constructing a persuasive blend, then they are likely to dismiss the backward induction blend of the game theorist as bizarre. I emphasize that I am not assuming here that the players can collaborate, negotiate, enter into agreements, or even communicate with each other, but only that they have rich cultural knowledge to work from, and perhaps some minimal information about each other (appearance, dress, demeanor, accent) that can serve as the basis for categorizing each other.

Their attitude is entirely reasonable, provided we acknowledge that in mak-ing choices, people draw on their own actual experience and on the reported experience of others—often captured in cultural stories. Regrettably, everyone has suffered (and remembers) an experience of self-defeat: the action we hoped would achieve the goal instead kicked it away. Self-defeat is especially likely in a wide range of social interactions in which appearing to go after something disposes others to withhold it from us: "You'll never get a date if you look desperate." "Never chase the bid; let the bid come to you." "It's harder to get a job if you look as if you need one." In such cases, overt action to obtain the goal can be self-defeating. This experience of self-defeat, expressed in many cultural stories and jokes, under-lies the frames of "play it cool," "sit tight," and "don't blow it."

Here is a story of failing to conform to "play it cool," "sit tight," and "don't blow it." The hatch of one of the Mercury space capsules blew off when it was rocking in the ocean, as the recovery team was hauling it and its astronaut safely aboard. Once the hatch was blown, the capsule sank, and the astronaut was sub-sequently stigmatized, perhaps entirely inaccurately, as having lost his cool. He was accused of hitting the escape button to save his life, which turned out not to have needed saving. Allegedly, in one bold action based on maximally high sub-jective expected utility, he lost all his hard-won glory, for nothing. A player of Watch It Grow can easily recruit this story or similar stories. Does the player have the cool, the nerves of steel, the right stuff to sit tight and get the big money? Or will she prove to be anxious, a squirmer, defeated by paltry self-interest? Will she be a hatch-blower?

The player's choice will depend on her expectations of the other player's ac-tion (this is just the fundamental assumption of game theory). To develop those expectations, she can recruit many frames other than the mathematically abstract process of backward induction. Faced with an opponent known to be a graduate student of game theory, she may, if she knows what game theory is, chuckle and settle for ninety-five cents. But faced with an opponent of almost any other cultural or disciplinary background, and certainly one in which nonchalance, cool, self-command, otherworldly spirituality, resistance to sales pressure, or any similar trait is valued, the player will have every reason to sit tight, at least until she can no longer keep her hand off the escape button.

The advertising agent who dismisses the Oedipal blend for the British Airways ad is like the actual players of Watch It Grow who dismiss the backward-induction blend: they both dismiss the blend they do not construct. Similarly, the formally oriented game theorists are like the women who objected to the sexist ad: they both have confidence in the blend that comes naturally to them. If this sounds like a criticism of game theory, I have failed to express my essential point: conceptual integration is an indispensable, powerful, basic cognitive operation, part of backstage cognition, mostly invisible, used constantly and often to good effect, in activities as disparate as reading ads and developing formal techniques in game theory.

Rational choice theorists have fully recognized the problems posed by the observed behavior of people playing games like Watch It Grow and seem to be eager to develop more cognitively realistic models. Certainly rational choice theorists have provided an important part of the answer—people engaged in interdependent decision making try to take some account of what the other agents might do. Can we keep what is useful from the rational choice approach but supplement it with a cognitive scientific approach?

Suppose I ask myself what I would do if I were playing Watch It Grow. The immediate answer from the cognitive science perspective is that the experiment is not ecologically valid; it isn't tied to anything human beings actually do. We can make Watch It Grow more plausible, and run a modified version of it in a controlled experiment (for example, we start with a penny, double the pot each round, and have only sixteen rounds), but even then my only frame of knowledge for understanding this activity is "goofy white-room experiment run by a social scientist with a grant," and while the experiment might tell us something about how people choose when they frame themselves as subjects in social-science white-room experiments, it isn't clear what it could tell us about actual human systems of choice "in the wild." It is natural to think the controlled experiment is better because it is so much cleaner, but human choice is evolved for a very messy, interconnected world, not for a world of white-room experiments. Tic-tac-toe, chess, and Watch It Grow are alien environments, useful, fun, and interesting, but not central or evolutionarily influential.

This first, dismissive response is inappropriate, however, since there is quite a lot to be gained by paying attention to the concerns of the rational choice theorist, so let us retract the dismissive response and turn to deciding what might be involved in running the thought experiment in which I am a player in Watch it Grow.

In *The Literary Mind*, I discussed some ways in which the construction of stories is fundamental to human cognition. For example, when we see a drop of water fall from the kitchen ceiling to the floor, we imagine a standard situation in which the ceiling is dry and we try to build a plausible story that leads from the standard situation to what we have just seen. Is a water pipe leaking? Is there some reason condensation should be forming on the ceiling? Inventing stories of this sort is our main method of explanation. It is also our main method of planning. If we want to achieve some situation, we build a story from our present situation to the achieved situation, and the story is the plan.

This basic human mode of cognition is, I propose, equally at work in choosing. "Backward invention of the story" is a method of choosing that is probably more important than backward induction on n. Backward induction works by eliminating "bad" strategies from final subgames and repeating this operation backward along the game tree, according to the established rules of the game. My alternative candidate, backward invention of the story, works differently: we blend an actual situation—the one we are supposedly in—with an abstract frame of a desired outcome to produce a blend in which we specifically have the desired outcome, and then ask what else we need to recruit to the blend to turn it into a plausible story leading from the actual situation to the specific desired outcome.

Backward invention of stories is a common cognitive instrument in everyday planning. Consider the following illustration: I once saw a film clip (I never learned anything else about the film, and although I distinctly remember seeing Rock Hudson in it, my memory could easily be replacing the unfamiliar actor I did see with the familiar Rock Hudson I didn't) in which two men attack a woman on the street but are repulsed by the hero (Hudson) who has come to her defense. Actually, the thugs were paid by the hero to attack the woman so he could defend her. The would-be hero's process of reasoning is obvious: he is attracted to the woman; he integrates his current situation with a schematic frame of heterosexual intimacy to achieve an imagined and desired blend of specific heterosexual intimacy; he then casts around for other possible recruitments to the blend that could turn it into a plausible story with the right emergent structure, which is to say, a path leading from where he is now to the intimacy he wants; he hits upon the frame of woman-falling-for-the-man-who-has-saved-her; he manipulates reality to become that game.

What this movie hero has done the players of Watch It Grow can do, rationally: they can put together a blend in which they get what they want. They can then try to recruit other structures to the blend that elaborate it into a plausible story leading from the present situation to that goal. "Sit tight" is an effective recruitment, at least for the early rounds.

We all know that people often act in accord with their backward inventions from blends. The woman in the film knew this, too. After a few electrified moments alone with the hero, she asks him, "So, how much did you pay them?"

If I am imagining myself playing Watch It Grow, I take my present situation (the usual state of academic relative poverty) and blend it with an abstract frame of "winning a lot of money" to create an imaginary blend: in this imaginary blend, I have just won a lot of money playing Watch It Grow. Now I must find other structure I can plausibly build into the blend to give it a history, a story, connecting that wonderful outcome back to my actual present situation.

My cognition and my choosing run, I think, as follows: I have framed the game as a once-in-a-lifetime chance to gain a great deal of money effortlessly, at odds that are entirely in my favor. I must not blow this chance. What does "gaining a great deal of money" mean to me? Five million dollars in "year 2000" U.S. currency would certainly, if I could have it all at once, and relying on the magic of capital investment, cover my foreseeable financial responsibilities and let me do most of what I want or need to do. Anything beyond that is gravy. To get my five million dollars for sure, all I need to do is reach the ninth round in a game of 100 rounds.

Here is where the game theorist's insight comes in: I must consider what the other player might do. Can I rely on the other player to pass eight times? Luckily, in a frame of 100 rounds, picking up the money during the ninth round already counts as losing one's cool early. If the other player thinks at all like me, she will want a lot of money and will not want to lose her cool. Getting to that ninth round is plausible.

If my competitor plays first and picks up the money, there is nothing I can do. I will justifiably berate her and despise her as an idiot. Given the opportunity, I will inform her that while a chimpanzee might have done as she did, even my seven-year-old would have acted so much more wisely than she did as to make her look like a member of a mentally inferior species. Alternatively, if she doesn't pick up the money, I will know straightaway that she is smarter than the ideal "rational" player. In any case, from the beginning I will do everything permitted to try to convey my nonchalance and my robotic, automatic commitment to passing.

But the game theorists are right: she might ruin my story, since she has a role in it. This is a risk I run. Is that risk sufficiently daunting to make me settle for less? I am absolutely confident that, whether I am in the role of the first player or the second, I would certainly pass on every round up to the sixth round, when we reach a truly significant moment—at the beginning of the sixth round, there is now a hundred thousand dollars on the table. I would like to have ninety-five thousand dollars, and I would indeed have ninety-five thousand dollars if I picked up the pot, but I know what it is like to have that amount of money, and it is not sufficiently useful to tempt me to throw away my chance at "riches." I'll pass. Suppose I am the first player and I pass on this sixth round. If she then picks up the pot, I receive only five thousand dollars. So in passing as first player in the sixth round, I have taken the risk that I will receive ninety thousand dollars fewer than I would have received if I had picked up the pot. Now suppose, alternatively, that I am the second player and I pass on the sixth round. The pot then immediately increases to a million dollars. If she then picks up the pot on the first turn of the seventh round, I receive only fifty thousand dollars. So in passing as the second player of the sixth round, I have taken the risk that I will receive forty-five thousand dollars fewer than I would have received if I had picked up the pot. Whether I am first or second player, these are risks I have taken, but not very heavy ones: certainly, for me, these risks are not worth my throwing away a shot at "riches."

The identical pattern of reasoning applies during the next round, the seventh, when there is a million dollars on the table. I will have a little more difficulty conforming to that logic, since I do not have any experience of possessing nine hundred fifty thousand dollars, but I can still imagine it, and I am fairly confident that it is still not enough to induce me to throw away my chance at being "rich" for life, especially when I additionally consider that, if I am the first player when there is a million dollars in the pot, my winnings cannot be fewer than fifty thousand dollars, and if I am the second player, my winnings cannot be fewer than five hundred thousand dollars. During this round, I will repeat to myself, "five million, five million. . . ."

The great challenge of nerve for me will come of course in the eighth round, when there is ten million dollars on the table and it is my turn. I could have nine and a half million dollars just by picking up the pot. If I am the first player, and I do not pick it up, I might have to settle for half a million dollars, but that's not so bad, is it? And if I am the second player, and don't pick it up, I will win at least what I am shooting for: my prized five million dollars.

During that crucial eighth round, I will tell myself the following profoundly encouraging and all-important truth, the one that is in fact drives my entire strategy: if I had to guess before the game begins when the other player will pick the money up during 100 possible rounds, it is exceptionally unlikely that I could do so perfectly, and if I underguess by more than a little, I lose a lot of money by trying. This conclusion derives from purely mathematical reasoning, as follows. Suppose I am the first player, and I guess that my opponent will pick up the money in round n, so I pick up the money first in round n. If my guess is off by as little as two turns, meaning that she would actually have picked up the money in round

$n+2$, then I would have been considerably better off to let her do it. Specifically, by keeping my hands off the pot, I would have won $\$.05(10^{n+1})$, which is much more than the $\$.95(10^{n-1})$ I win by picking it up. For example, if I guess that she will pick up the pot in round four, and this leads me to pick it up first, it is true that I win \$950. Yet if my guess was off by just two turns, and she actually would have picked it up in round six, I would have won \$5,000 by letting her pick up the pot. I lose \$4,050 by taking the money off the table. (In fact, if I was off by only one turn, I win \$500 by keeping my hands off the pot, which, true, isn't \$950, but it's still more than half of the amount I win by picking up the pot.) Unless I think I can guess almost perfectly when she will pick up the pot, it is better for me to pass.

Now suppose I am the second player, and I guess my opponent will pick up the money in round n, where n is greater than 1, and I therefore pick up the pot right before her, in round $n-1$. If my guess was wrong by even only *one turn* this time, and she would actually have picked it up in round $n+1$, then I would have been considerably better off to let her do it. Specifically, I would have won $\$.05(10^n)$ by keeping my hands off the pot, but I win only $\$.95(10^{n-2})$ by picking it up. For example, if I guess that she will pick up the pot in round four, and this leads me to pick it up right before her—that is, on the second turn of round three—it is true that I win \$95. Yet if my guess was wrong by just one turn, and she actually would have picked up the pot in round five, I would have won \$500 by letting her pick up the pot. So if I am the second player, unless I can guess absolutely exactly when she will pick up the pot, I am much better off passing every time.

That very strong, overriding, impeccable logic dictates my strategy. I do not think I can in reality guess so exactly when the other player will pick up the pot, so I am better off not touching it. I will pass every time and I will do everything permitted to indicate to the other player that I will pass every time. Even if she and I cannot even see each other and are allowed only to press buttons for "pass" or "take," I will press my "pass" button every time as quickly as humanly possible, to try to give her an indication of my disposition. It's worth the chance.

What would I actually do? After winning a guaranteed minimum of five million dollars, I would probably be thinking of breaking the news to my wife over a dinner of poached salmon and Corton-Charlemagne and wondering where she would like to travel and what books she would like to buy for her vast collection of children's literature. A few turns later, I might be wondering what charities I would establish. Sure, for every subsequent turn, I would still keep passing, but it would all become unreal to me.

Would I ever get that far? I cannot know without being given a chance to play the game for real. For human choosing, thought experiments unconnected to real choices are merely interesting. In a real game, I might switch strategies in the seventh or eighth round. I might not sit tight through the whole game, but I am sure I would not pick up a pot much smaller than five million dollars.

The analysis I have given of Watch It Grow fits the observable data better than the model given by backward induction on *n*, and yet takes full account of the central tenet of rational choice theory that anyone reasoning about interdependent decision-making considers the possible actions of the other choosers. But my analysis has other elements of the sort familiar in cognitive science: framing ("what kind of person am I up against?"), reference points ("five million dollars is real wealth"), linear scales ("nine rounds out of a hundred rounds is already very early") and, most fundamental, backward invention of the story ("I can get to five million dollars if I can just get her to pass eight times, so what can I do to try to make that happen?"). My analysis does not rely on exhaustive and infinite lookahead to all possible outcomes, or imaginary production of all possible paths through the game, or backward induction on *n* from final outcomes, or elimination of dominated strategies. But that does not mean that what I offer must be inaccurate as a picture of actual and quite successful human choosing.

We are now in a fascinating period in which rational choice theorists are on the verge of taking up cognitive issues like these in earnest, with the ambition of producing better models through a synthesis with cognitive science, on the view that research into the principles of human choice is an empirical endeavor. We are leaving behind the age in which models began with the injunction "Assume Rational Play"—an assumption that rules out at a stroke many fundamental cognitive operations, like backward invention of the story, that may be the most important ones.

I speculated earlier that the most important outcome for most strips of activity is the training of the individuals who engage in it. A similar outcome that people seem to desire intensely is the possession, or appearance of the possession, of an identity, or a character, or a style. People want to impose meaning on their lives, and the construction of selfhood is one of their principal avenues for doing so. Frames of identity and character can be all-important constraints in the backward invention of the story. When an actor wants the invented story to confer upon him, or preserve for him, a certain character, identity, or style, he may see the explicit outcome of an individual game as much less important than the character, identity, or style he carries or develops while enacting the story.

To be sure, there are cultural stereotypes of kinds of character who resemble the stereotypical player of game theory: the smooth operator, cool-headed, working the percentages, able to switch paths when the odds change, always calculating, always looking out for number one, nobody's fool. But there are perhaps as many cultural stereotypes of superb players who grow bored and become interesting when they begin to care more about their character, identity, and style in play than they do about payoffs. In *The Thomas Crown Affair*, for example, the most masterful player imaginable, forty-three-year-old Thomas Crown, head of Crown Mergers and Acquisitions, steals a painting by Monet with his own hands from a maximum-security museum. Immediately and secretly, he has a (gorgeous) forger cover the stolen painting with a forged version of another Monet painting he in fact does own, so he can donate the forgery to the museum to hang in the place of the stolen painting. The museum, of course, thinks Crown has donated the real thing. (Actually, he has, in a secret sense, but I mean that the museum thinks Crown has given them the Monet he does own, not that he has returned to them the stolen Monet.) Then, working in full view of the forewarned police and security guards, he restores the original, stolen painting to its original spot on the museum wall by activating the sprinkler system, which washes away the water-based paint used to paint the forgery, leaving the original, stolen Monet visible on the wall! Certainly, during the course of the film, he gets the woman (not, it turns out, the forger but instead the private detective hired by the insurers to recover the painting), but he had not even met her until after he had donated the forgery to the museum.

Perhaps more importantly, there are strong cultural stereotypes of kinds of character based on absolute adherence to principle and a corollary refusal to calculate over outcomes. When Hector kills Patroclos in battle, Achilles insists that the Greeks take the field immediately to avenge his death by killing the Trojans. Odysseus responds by saying, essentially, "Fine, but it's hard to fight all day on an empty stomach. Let's have a good lunch first." Achilles, viewing such calculation over probable outcomes as mean and dishonorable, scorns Odysseus.

There are plenty of modern parallels to Achilles, from Joan of Arc, unarmed on a white horse and carrying her huge, conspicuous banner fifty yards out in front of her army as she charges the English at Orléans, to Rostand's Cyrano de Bergerac, who rejects instantly ("*Non, merci!*") the prospect of making any deal whatever (even the change of a single comma) to obtain Cardinal Richelieu's support for the production of his tragedy, to Winston Churchill after Dunkirk (whom the cool and calculating Lord Halifax, a member of the War Cabinet, judged to have gone off his rocker for refusing even to weigh the costs and benefts of the secret Nazi peace offer), to nearly every superhero in the comic books from Batman to Sally the Little Witch.

In fact, Achilles is mistaken: Odysseus is a complicated case. To be sure, Odysseus is the shrewdest operator in history, endlessly cunning, efficiently milking every situation for the largest benefit he can get, calmly sacrificing many shipmates because it will preserve at least some of them. His epithet is "wily" Odysseus. In modern terms, he would be the operator who calmly and quickly precipitated the Nash equilibrium that gave him the largest market share. But he also values the possession of a certain character: in a moment of slander, someone accuses him of having gotten his wealth from trade, and he retorts hotly that he did not, he got it honorably, with his sword. Most important of all, he is constantly forging reality to conform to a game that might be called "get me home to my wife, my son, and my kingship with my character intact." In ten years of fighting and especially in ten years of unwilling wandering, his greatest cunning lies in exploiting the activities of other people so as to draw them into helping him make that game real, often without their knowing that any such game is being played. For example, the king of the Phaiakians, an island people, believes that he (the king), his daughter, his wife, his people, and Odysseus, all in his banquet hall, are playing a game whose obvious outcome is "Odysseus marries my daughter." But Odysseus is using the actions of the king to place the king in the end stages of Odysseus's game. At the last, the king has no choice, in the cultural setting, but to offer Odysseus a ship and crew to take him back to Ithaca, even though taking him there will outrage the god Poseidon and so bring a heavy cost to the king and his people.

In his local calculations of benefit, in his choosing to act with a certain character, and in his forging a story that returns him home, the indispensable cognitive operation Odysseus exploits is conceptual integration. It is a basic operation of backstage cognition equally at work, and equally influential, in heroic wandering and rational play.

ANALOGY

Reasoning by analogy is a basic topic in social science, commonly recognized as playing a principal role in law, politics, economics, policy making, cultural development, discovery, judgment, choice, and persuasion. It is also a basic topic in cognitive science. Lately, cognitive science has been gathering evidence that our folk theory of how analogy works is wrong, just as our folk theories of how language, vision, categorization, imagination, and memory work are wrong. In this chapter, I will explore what cognitive science might have to say to social scientists about the conception, analysis, and use of analogy in social science. I begin with an example where many billions of dollars were at stake in how an analogy was constructed.

GRAY MONDAY

On Monday, October 27, 1997, when the Dow Jones Industrial Average fell more than five hundred points, precipitously and unnervingly, on huge volume, in a single day, and the last two hours saw broad panic selling, investors wondered whether the next day would be a bloodbath. Later that evening, the Internet was flooded with thousands of postings analyzing whether this crash was like the infamous crash on Black Monday ten years earlier. I read them all evening.

These professional and amateur investors never questioned the fundamental importance of knowing whether the analogy was true. Evidently, punishment awaited anyone who made the wrong call. If the analogy held, then the investor in equities should preserve positions and buy aggressively into the market, which would rise.

Yet there were reasons to doubt the analogy. Even after their five-hundred-point fall, stocks were expensively valued by traditional measures. Most investors had enjoyed unprecedented capital gains on paper in the previous few years, and many could not resist the argument that it would be prudent to realize those gains before the market plunged into the vortex of Asian currency troubles. Thailand's monetary turmoil—in a domino cascade running through Indonesia, Korea, Hong Kong, Japan, and the United States—could be lethal.

The analysts on the Internet took it for granted that establishing analogy or disanalogy depends upon rebuilding, reconstruing, reinterpreting the two analogs—in this case, the two crashes. They began with provisional background structure and connections—for example, the Dow on Black Monday corresponded to the Dow in October 1997 (even though the thirty companies that comprise the Dow had been changed), the drop on Black Monday in 1987 corresponded to the drop on October 27, 1997, and so on. But this structure and these correspondences provided only a launching pad, not the analogy itself. In particular, they provided none of the inferences investors sought as the basis for their consequential decisions and actions.

The effective claims in the Internet analyses were introduced with phrases like, "What this crash is a case of . . . ," "We must not forget that the 1987 crash . . . ," and "It would be a mistake to think of the 1987 crash as. . . ." There were injunctions like "Don't blur categories—the professionals preserve their careers as professionals but the small investors don't have that motivation." In the picture painted by these analyses, analogy and disanalogy are processes centrally concerned with construction and reconstruction of the inputs—that is, the analogs. The analogs are forged as the analogy is forged. This is the topic I will investigate.

YOUR BABY REFUSES TO BE BORN

Creative forging of analogs and connections is essential for at least an important category of analogies. Consider a French political cartoon that appeared on the front page of *Le Figaro* for January 13, 1997.[1] This cartoon, as is typical of its genre, makes its point unmistakably and instantly. It concerns the politically sensitive debate over a policy of setting a retirement age of fifty-five. Its headline and subhead (translated into English) read "Retirement at 55: Chirac bridles" and "Even though 61% of French citizens support the policy. . . ." The cartoon shows an expectant father in the waiting room of a maternity ward. He has been reading the newspaper report of French president Jacques Chirac's resistance to the retirement policy. The obstetrician has just entered the waiting room, followed by a frowning nurse. The obstetrician, at a loss, throws up his hands and says to the father, "Your baby refuses to allow me to deliver him into the world until he can be told at what age he can take his retirement, if he finds work."

The immediate and powerful inference for French readers is that people demanding the retirement policy are being absurd. Extreme assurances are unavailable in life, and it is nonsense to condition everyday life on obtaining them. For workers to go on strike to secure such a retirement policy would be like a fetus's going on strike in the delivery room. The doctor's last clause, "if he finds work," is biting. Unemployment and underemployment are severe in France, especially among the young. "*Chomage*" is a principal topic of daily news. The inference of this last phrase is that it is spectacularly stupid to demand governmental spending on early retirement when the country faces the far more threatening issue of unemployment. What the baby should demand, if it demands anything, is the opportunity for employment, not a promise of early retirement if it happens to be lucky enough to get a job.

Some readers may make yet other inferences of absurdity. The baby can cause difficulties during delivery but may itself suffer, even die, in the consequence, so it would be irrational for the baby to intend these difficulties. The baby's refusal can even be viewed as silly, vain, and arrogant, since, inevitably, natural and medical processes must compel the baby to be born regardless of the difficulties.

The central inference of this analogy is that the French electorate should drop its support for the retirement policy and focus instead on supporting the government in its fight against a sick economy and high unemployment. This message fits the political dispositions of *Le Figaro*.

Suppose we began to analyze this political analogy by adopting the mistaken but common folk assumption that analogy starts with two pre-existing analogs, aligns and matches them, and projects inferences from one to the other. The analogs to be matched for this cartoon would be a scene with a father in the waiting room of a maternity ward and a scene with French workers demanding a policy of early retirement. I can see no significant matches between these two notions in themselves. I can match the labor of the mother to the labor of the French workers, but that connection has nothing to do with this analogy and leads nowhere. I have no pre-existing knowledge of fetuses according to which I can match them with French workers who make demands about their conditions of employment. There is the possible match between the nondelivery of the baby and the nondelivery of passengers and goods—French transportation workers were at the time striking in support of the policy—but that match is optional, provides no inference of absurdity, and could be fatally misleading since it matches the obstetrician responsible for the delivery with the transportation workers responsible for delivery, and this match destroys the analogy. It seems clear that any straightforward matching between these two pre-existing notions, if there is any, misses the analogy.

Matching does not work, but neither does projection of inferences from source to target. The familiar source space would be birth in a maternity ward, supplemented with the frame of the waiting room, and the target space would be French labor politics. But there are no fetuses in the source space who make ridiculous demands of any kind and no doctors who toss up their hands in exasperation at the absurd ideas of the fetus. In the source space, members of the delivery team do not come into the waiting room to protest the unreasonable views of the fetus. None of this and none of the associated inferences in fact exist in the source to be projected onto the target in the first place.

The absurdity of the situation does not belong to the pre-existing source. Interestingly, it does not belong to the pre-existing target, either. The inference of the cartoon is that the demands of the French workers are so absolutely absurd and unheard-of as to be completely astonishing. They are wild from any perspective. But if such an absurdity were already part of the pre-existing target, there would be no need to make the analogy. The motivation for making the analogy is that 61 percent of the French do in fact support these demands, and those citizens need to be persuaded to drop their support.

The cartoon is unmistakably organized by the abstract conceptual frame of the source space—a maternity ward and a waiting room. It also contains a few specified elements, and it is illuminating to consider what they are doing in the cartoon. Consider the newspaper in the expectant father's right hand. Naturally, an expectant father might read a newspaper while he waits, and the analogist exploits this possibility. But the motivation for including the newspaper in the cartoon is not to evoke the frame of a waiting room and not to lead us to match or project the newspaper to some analogical counterpart in the target space. There is a counterpart newspaper in the target space, in fact this identical newspaper, but the connection between them is identity, not analogy. The newspaper has been incorporated deftly into the frame of the waiting room because it is important in the target: it announces president Chirac's resistance to the policy of retirement. The construal of the waiting room, we see, is driven by the analogy. The source analog is being forged so the analogy can work.

The newspaper headline is the least of the elements in the waiting room that appear there under pressure from the target. The difficulty of the delivery and the doctor's frustration are motivated only by the target. In fact, there are elements in this cartoon that are impossible for the source space of real waiting rooms. The perversity of the fetus, the disapproval of the fetus on the part of the obstetrician and the nurse and presumably the father, the speech of the fetus and its logic, the biting irony of putting the problem of retirement ahead of the problem of unemployment—an irony clearly conveyed by the cartoonist but not recognized by the doctor whose words convey it—come only from the target.

The mental operations that account for this analogy and its work are not retrieval of pre-existing source and target notions, alignment and matching of their elements, and projection of inferences from source to target. Instead, the relevant mental operation is, of course, conceptual integration.

In the example of the cartoon, the contributing or influencing spaces to the blend are the French labor situation, with workers, and the maternity ward, with a fetus. The blend has a single element that is both a faction in the French labor debate and a baby. Of particular importance for this cartoon, construction and interpretation can be done on any space at any time as the conceptual integration network develops. In particular, the contributing spaces can be re-represented, rebuilt, reconstrued, and reinterpreted. For example, although notions of the waiting room in a maternity ward do not include conventionally that the obstetrician comes out to report a problem, or centrally that the expectant father is reading a newspaper, nonetheless these structures can be recruited to the source space, and are in this case, since they are needed for blending, under pressure from the target, which has labor problems and politicians whose views are reported by the media. When an organizing frame of the blend has been borrowed from the source, it can be elaborated for the blend with structure not included in, or in fact impossible for, the source. For example, the baby in the cartoon has highly developed intentional, expressive, and political capacities, projected to it from the workers in the target, but we do not project those abilities back to the source: we do not interpret this cartoon as asking us to revise our notions of fetuses to include these advanced abilities.

We keep the source, the target, and the blend quite distinct in this network and do not become confused. Given the genre of the cartoon, we know that the purpose of this analogy is to project inferences from the blend to the target rather than to the source. (Seana Coulson, 1996, has shown that there are other genres with other standard directions of projection.) In the blend, we develop the inference that something has gone wrong with the natural course of things and that agents dealing with it are exasperated, but we do not project back to the source the inference that when delivery is actually failing, it's fine for the obstetrician to take a walk out to the waiting room to whine for sympathy, instead of redoubling his medical efforts in the delivery room. We do not project back to the source from the blend the inference that in a true medical emergency the reaction of the expectant father and the obstetrician should be dumbfounded astonishment at the uncooperative behavior of the fetus rather than anxiety over the health of the mother and child.

We do project the absurdity of the baby's demand in the blend back to the workers' demand in the target—that is the point of the analogy—but this projection is complicated. The baby in the blend is an individual who has not yet obtained employment. Part of the reason we judge the baby to be irrational is that, for the individual, it would be manifestly illogical to care more about retiring early than about having a job, since retiring at all is conditional upon having a job. Yet this inference cannot project identically to each individual working French citizen, who is in fact already employed. Nor does it seem to project identically to each individual unemployed French citizen, who may in fact be more concerned about having a job than about retiring early. The inference projects not identically but to a related inference for the target, an inference not for individuals but for French citizens as a political body. The baby's individual retirement age projects to the retirement age to be set by policy, and the baby's individual prospects for employment project to general employment trends in France. In the target, these numbers are distributed in a way that does not give wild absurdity—61 percent of French citizens are unruffled by their conjunction—but in the blend, these numbers have become the prospects faced by a single individual, whose passion to know his conditional retirement age but nonchalance about his prospects for employment yield a manifest absurdity and irony, judgments that the cartoonist hopes to induce the reader to project back to the target. The intended implication of the analogical integration network is that since unemployment is a general concern for the nation, French citizens should not ask for expensive retirement policies. The two central inferences of the analogy—manifest absurdity and biting irony—are constructed only in the blend; they are not available from the contributing spaces.

The analogy of this cartoon, which appears on the front page of the newspaper as an illustration of the main story, and which presents no difficulty whatever to its readers, gives us a picture of analogy as a simultaneous forging of contributing spaces, a blend, and connections in a dynamic integration network.

We see a somewhat different picture of the nature of analogy, this time an explicit academic picture, if we look at work in artificial intelligence. Forbus, Gentner, Markman, and Ferguson (1998) take the view that there is consensus in AI on the main theoretical assumptions to be made about analogy, and in particular on the usefulness of decomposing analogical processing into constituent subprocesses such as *retrieving* representations of the analogs, *mapping* (*aligning* the representations and *projecting inferences* from one to the other), *abstracting* the common system, and so on.

This work is a very promising start, not least for its emphasis on mappings, counterparts, and projections as basic events in analogy, but for at least an important range of analogies, including many standard analogies in political science and economics, this decompositional view of analogy needs to be supplemented. There are two reasons that it needs to be supplemented. First, the analogies I have in mind cannot be explained as operating over pre-derived construals that are independent of the making of the analogy. Rather, the construal of the analogs depends upon the attempt to make the analogical mappings.

Second, models in this tradition do not seem to allow a place for analogical meaning to arise that is not a composition of the meanings and inferences of the inputs, yet the analogies I have in mind include essential emergent meaning (e.g., absurdity) that cannot be viewed as a conjunction of structures in the contributing spaces.

Forbus, Gentner, Markman, and Ferguson make their claims about the decomposition of processes involved in analogy as part of a rebuttal to Douglas Hofstadter, or rather a counterrebuttal, since Hofstadter had claimed that their work, and similar work in the relevant AI tradition (see e.g., Falkenhainer, Forbus, and Gentner, 1989; Gentner 1983; Gentner and Gentner, 1983; Gentner and Stevens, 1983; Gick and Holyoak 1980, 1983; Holland, Holyoak, Nisbett, and Thagard, 1986; Holyoak and Thagard, 1989, 1995), is hollow, vacuous, a "dead-end" because it takes as given what Hofstadter calls "gist extraction." Gist extraction is "the ability to see to the core of the matter." Hofstadter views this ability as "the key to analogy making—indeed to all intelligence" (Hofstadter, 1995). In collaboration with David Chalmers and Robert French (1992), Hofstadter argues that there is no illumination to be found in this tradition because the programs compute over merely meaningless symbolic structures, because these formal structures are cooked beforehand in ways that make the matching easy, and, most important, because the cooking is done by the programmer, not the program. In Hofstadter's view, the programmer has already done the all-important gist extractions, boiled the meanings out of them, and substituted in their place formal sets of predicate calculus symbols that already contain, implicitly, the highly abstract, nearly vacuous formal match. The programmer then provides these formal nuggets to the program. A program that detects the formal match between them is not making analogies.

So we see a hot debate within cognitive science itself over the nature of analogy and its mechanisms. It seems to me that a good intuitive understanding of the nature of ecologically valid analogy comes from the practical-minded nonacademics who were actually making analogies and disanalogies and posting them on the Internet on the night of October 27, 1997—Gray Monday, as it came to be called, once its aftermath was known. For them, finding analogy or disanalogy is a process of forging, not merely finding, connections; and forging connections requires forging the analogs as you forge the connections, revising the entire system of contributing spaces and connections dynamically and repeatedly, until one arrives at a network of contributing spaces and connections that is persuasive.

My claim that analogy works by forging such a network may seem at first counterintuitive because it runs against the folk theory according to which "finding an analogy" consists of comparing two things in the world and locating the "hidden" matches. We speak of "seeing" the analogy, which presupposes that the analogy is completely there to be seen. According to this folk theory, things in the world are objectively as they are, things match objectively or not, and analogies and disanalogies are scientific discoveries of objective truth. This view is reassuring and attractive. By contrast, when I speak of forging contributing spaces and connections, with continual revision and backtracking, to build a network of spreading coherence that is "persuasive," it may sound as if I am offering a dismal and barbarous postmodern hash in which anything can be anything, any construal of the analogs will do, and any connections will serve, since all meaning is invented, a mere "construct," anyway.

But not so. Human beings have, over time, invented many human-scale concepts to suit their purposes—*chair, sitting, rich, Tuesday, marriage*—but these inventions are highly constrained by both our biological endowment and our experience. First, there are universal mental phenomena. Human beings all have conceptual framing, categorization, blending, grammar, and memory, for example. There is such a thing as human nature, and it includes certain fundamental kinds of mental phenomena, analogy being one of them. That is one kind of constraint. Second, profound constraints come from success and failure. Some concepts and connections lead to success while others lead to failure. Some help you live, some make you ill. With the right analogies, you make a killing in the market, with the wrong ones, you get slaughtered. I have no hesitation in saying that inventive forging of analogies can result in scientific discovery of true analogies. In fact, it has resulted in scientific discovery of true analogies. When a network is constructed that works, we call it true.

There is another reason that the folk theory of analogy appears attractive: after the fact, in the rearview mirror, an established analogy usually looks exactly like a match between existing structures, and it is easy to forget the conceptual work of forging construals and connections that went into building the network.

LOVELY WHILE IT LASTS

Reforging the inputs while constructing the analogy was common procedure on the night of Gray Monday. The analysts on the Internet expressed revisions of the analogs elaborately and unmistakably, using phrases like "What if what really happened on Black Monday was . . ." and "You need to think of today's events not as X but instead as Y."

I take it that this kind of reforging is typical for analogies in business and finance. Consider the cover of *The Economist* for August 9, 1997, which shows a kite high in the air and a man in a business suit flying it. The kite is labeled "Dow," for the Dow Jones Industrials Average, and the caption reads "Lovely while it lasts." The final conceptual product that comes out of understanding this analogy looks as if it matches source and target and as if it projects an inference from source to target. But that description of the product is not a model of the process.

When I think of someone flying a kite, at least a traditional kite like the one on the cover, rather than a trick kite, I imagine that it is easy to do in good wind. If there is a difficult stage in flying a kite, it is the beginning, when the kite is near the ground. Once the kite is very high, it is much easier to keep aloft, given that at higher altitudes the wind is relatively more constant and there is an absence of obstructions. The traditional kite-flier wants to keep the kite at a single high altitude, and when he has had his fun, he winds up his string.

The phrase "Lovely while it lasts" is conventionally used to suggest that "it" won't last, and interpreting "it" as referring to the Dow suggests that the cartoon is predicting a fall in the market. Under pressure from this target, we can reconstrue the source by recruiting to it some possible but peripheral structure: namely, gravity pulls objects down with constant force, while winds are irregular; therefore, at some moment, the winds will die and the kite will fall.

The inevitability of this fall is the inference to be projected to the target. But it is constructed for the source only under pressure from the target.

If we look at this analogy, we see that it depends crucially on a blended space. Although the organizing conceptual frame of the source space is flying the kite, and that conceptual frame is projected to the blended space to help organize it, much of the central structure that develops in the blended space does not come from that frame, and indeed some of it conflicts strongly with that source. In the blend of flying-a-kite and investing-in-the-stock-market, the kite-flier-investor faces extreme difficulty in keeping the kite-stock-index aloft. In fact, he is physically struggling. Yet the kite is very high and the winds are so good that they are blowing the kite-flier's tie and hair forward. This would be highly unconventional structure for the source because, given the wind, he should not be struggling at all. The blended space therefore has a crucial causal and intentional structure that does not come from the source influencing space.

We also know that this kite-flier is not satisfied merely to keep the kite up; he is a special, bizarre, unique kite-flier with a special kite, who will be content only if the kite constantly gains altitude or meets some more refined measure, such as never dropping in any given period of time lower than eight percent above its low in the previous period. This is highly unconventional for the source influencing space.

In this blended space, it is upsetting if the kite loses two percent of its altitude, dangerous if it loses five percent, a major correction if it loses ten percent, and a complete disaster if it loses thirty percent. Of course, in the source influencing space, none of these events presents any problem at all; indeed, the only great disaster would be the kite's hitting the ground. And yet, in the target influencing space with the Dow, there is no real possibility that the market could fall to zero, or even down by half. We see, then, that the projection of inferences from the source influencing space is very complicated. We need from the source influencing space the structure according to which constant gravity will ultimately find a moment to overcome completely the inconstant winds, but we cannot take from that source the inference that gravity will ultimately make the kite fall to zero altitude and be smashed.

Now consider the man flying the kite. He is wearing a business suit and tie. This is not impossible for the source influencing space of flying a kite, but it is odd, and the only motivation for building it into the source is pressure from the target world of business and investment.

What is the counterpart in the target influencing space of the kite-flier in the source influencing space? Presumably, he has a target counterpart, since the analogy is about harm that will come to people and institutions, not about harm that will come to the kite. This is a more complex question than it might seem. Consider that, in the domain of kite-flying, the actual kite-flier could make the kite crash, raise it by letting out string, lower it by taking in string, or reel in his kite and go home. But this structure is not recruited for the source influencing space, projected to the blended space, or given counterparts in the target influencing space. The kite-flier in the blend cannot be any of these kite-fliers. The kite-flier-investor in the blend cannot sell the market short and then make the kite lose altitude; he cannot make the Dow kite crash to the ground; he cannot sell his stocks and get out of the market at its peak; paradoxically, it is not even clear that he can have any effect on the kite at all, even though he is holding the string. He can be affected by what happens to the kite but probably cannot influence the kite significantly. Moreover, consider that we know that in real investing, a real investor can make money even if the Dow Average stays fixed, by trading stocks as they rise and fall individually. Indeed, this is the standard way to make money in the market, since, if we ignore the effect of new investment in the market, there must be a loser for each winner. But this kite-flier in the blend is not such an investor; he must be someone who is somehow invested in the continuing ascent of the kite that is the Dow, perhaps someone whose money is largely in Dow or S&P 500 index funds, or other more-or-less Dow-oriented mutual funds. But notice that in the source domain of kite-flying, there are no such kite-fliers. These kinds of kite-fliers exist only in the blend, not in the source.

And finally, the string to the kite is not a possible kite string. It is a somewhat smoothed graph of the Dow Index over something like the previous fifteen years. Interestingly, Black Monday of 1987 is not visible in this graph because a sharp fall of that sort, followed by the sharp rise, would deform the string unacceptably far from the strictly increasing smooth curve of the source space. In the source influencing space with the kite, the path of the kite string is a snapshot in time of a line in space, while in the target influencing space, the path of the Dow Average is a graph of the value of a variable over time. (This is why the sky in the cartoon is ruled like graph paper.) In the source, the path of the kite string has to do with the physics of kites, strings, wind power, and gravity, which should be crucial for the analogy, since the central inference of the analogy has to do with this physics—namely, with the fact that gravity will at some moment be stronger than the winds. In the source domain, the kite string is indispensable for raising the kite—without it the kite would surely fall, quickly in light wind. But as we have seen, the blend that provides the inferences of the analogy has structure for the kite string that either ignores the central structure of the kite string in the source or powerfully contradicts it. The view of analogy as retrieving pre-existing representations of analogs, matching and aligning them, and projecting inferences from the source to the target fails for this analogy, which, like the *Figaro* cartoon, is meant to be instantly intelligible and persuasive.

ANALOGY AND ALLEGORY

Literary scholars are familiar with these routine complexities of analogy because literary texts, although they are identical to everyday language in their invisible deployment of backstage cognition, sometimes go to the extra work of displaying these mental and linguistic operations openly on stage. When they do, and a basic mental or linguistic operation is made visible to the reader, the reader often judges the operation to be exotic, special, literary. But these operations are just those used in everyday cognition and action. It is their visibility and the mastery with which they are used that distinguish these literary texts. Consider, for example, Milton's famous portrayal of Satan, Sin, and Death in the second book of *Paradise Lost*, analyzed in Turner (1987).

Milton wishes to make an analogy about a theological complex including evil, sin, and death. Part of this analogy, the personification of evil as Satan, is already conventional and available for Milton's use. The source domain he chooses for this analogy is kinship relations, and his chief motivation for choosing it is that he is dealing with the Holy Trinity of Father, Son, and Holy Ghost. Milton presents an infernal version of this trinity.

Milton's theological space includes evil, disobedience, sin, death, and their relations, as well as the psychology of the prototypical sinner confronted with spiritual death. Milton's kinship space includes progeneration and kinship relations, especially the role *father*. He supplements this standard kinship space with yet a third influencing space, which is itself a pre-existing blend, of the birth of Athena from the brow of Zeus.

In Milton's blend, Satan conceives of the concept of sin; a fully grown woman, Sin, leaps from his brow. Satan is attracted to sin/Sin: he has sex with her. Although he does not know it at the time, his involvement with sin/Sin has a consequence, namely death—in the blend, Death is the male offspring of Satan's incestuous union with Sin. The analogy with the Holy Trinity is clear: Satan corresponds to God, and both are Fathers. Sin corresponds to Christ, the re- deemer; both Christ and Sin are offspring who further in some fashion their father's work. Death corresponds to the Holy Ghost, who, we recall, is the Spiritus Sanctus, the breath that put life into Mary's womb and that makes the human spirit immortal, free of death. Milton adds something that has no analogy with the Holy Trinity: Death rapes his mother Sin, causing her to give birth to a small litter of allegorical monsters.

After Satan has been sent to Hell and has determined to escape, he meets two characters at the gates of Hell who have been stationed there to prevent his exit. They are Sin and Death. But he does not recognize them.

The principal mental spaces that contribute to this analogical blended story— the kinship space and the theological space—correspond in some ways but not others. Milton draws from both of them, selectively. For example, he takes exclusively from the kinship space Sin's intercession between Death and Satan— father and son—when they are on the brink of terrible combat. He takes exclu- sively from the theological space many central features, as follows. In the theologi- cal space, the cast of mind that goes with thrilling sin ignores the fact that mortality and spiritual death are sin's consequences and is appalled to acknowledge them. Hence, in the blend, Sin is surprised to have conceived Death, and she finds her son odious. Next, in the theological space, mortality and spiritual death overshadow the appeal of sin and are stronger than sin; acknowledging death devalues sin; willful, sinful desires are powerless to stop this devaluation. Hence, in the blend, Sin is powerless to stop her horrible rape by Death. In the theological space, the fact of spiritual death brings ceaseless remorse and anguish to the sinful mind, and the torments of hell bring eternal punishment. Hence, in the blend, the rape of Sin by Death produces monstrous offspring whose birth, life, actions, and rela- tionship to their mother are impossible for the domain of human kinship:

> These yelling Monsters that with ceaseless cry
> Surround me, as thou saw'st, hourly conceiv'd
> And hourly born, with sorrow infinite
> To me, for when they list, into the womb
> That bred them they return, and howl and gnaw

My Bowels, thir repast; then bursting forth
Afresh with conscious terrors vex me round,
That rest or intermission none I find.

Milton creates unobvious correspondences between the kinship space and
the theological space. For example, he blends the less than stereotypical scenario
of disliking a child with feeling horror at the fact of death. He blends the unusual
scenario of a son raping a mother with the effect of death on sin.

Perhaps most ingeniously, he blends the unusual medical frame of traumatic
vaginal birth that physically deforms the mother, making her less attractive, with
the way sin becomes less attractive once death is acknowledged as its outcome:

At last this odious offspring whom thou seest,
Thine own begotten, breaking violent way
Tore through my entrails, that with fear and pain
Distorted, all my nether shape thus grew
Transform'd.

In his analogy between a family and a theological complex, Milton reforges
the source influencing space as he forges the connections. He aggressively
reconstrues that source to recruit marginal but not impossible structure such as
incest, the incestuous conception of a son upon a daughter, the mother's finding the son odious, the medical frame of a disfiguring vaginal birth, and the
impregnating rape of the mother by the son. He also recruits to the blended space
some structure from other, lesser influencing spaces, and this structure helps the
blend to extend the source in ways that are impossible for the source itself, as
follows. Under pressure to find a source analog for mental conception, he recruits
to the blend from the story of Zeus and Athena the birth of the daughter from
the brow of the father. Under pressure to find a source analog for the many vile
consequences of sin, he recruits the birth of a litter of vile monsters as the product
of the conjunction of Sin and Death. Under pressure to find a source analog for
the effect of sinning on the sinner, he invents the ability of these monsters to crawl
back into the womb and gnaw on their mother's bowels. Under pressure to find
a source analog for the fact that individual acts of sin take place because of the
existence of sin in the world and its place in the sinful soul, he invents a way for
the offspring of Sin to depend on her for nourishment even though they have
been weaned.

Noticing the way in which the source is reforged and the way in which the
blend is constructed under pressure to make the analogy work should not distract
us from the central effect of this analogy: it is meant to project inferences to the

target. But those inferences are projected to the target influencing space not from the source influencing space but from the blended space.

This integration network may look antiquated to us now, and that may be the reason we are able to inspect it dispassionately, but it is important to remember that not only was it intelligible and compelling for Milton and many of his readers, it was also the most serious possible analogy in human life.

ATTACKING THE TUMOR-FORTRESS

The examples of the cartoon from *Le Figaro*, the cover of *The Economist*, and the Infernal Trinity from *Paradise Lost* are all serious analogical arguments, meant to be persuasive on central issues of politics, economics, and religion, but because they are in the form of cartoons and poetry, it might be tempting to dismiss them as exceptional. When we turn to celebrated examples discussed in the literature on analogy in fields like psychology and computer science, however, we find the same operations of blending and forging, although they are more easily overlooked because they are somewhat less visible. Consider the well-known analogy discussed by Keith Holyoak and Paul Thagard in *Mental Leaps: Analogy in Creative Thought* (1995) and earlier in Gick and Holyoak (1983), in which the target analog is a tumor to be destroyed and the source analog is a fortress to be stormed. The problem in the target is that a laser beam of high intensity that can kill the tumor also kills every other cell it encounters on the way and a beam of low intensity harmless to the patient is also harmless to the tumor. The source analog is a fortress whose roads are mined to blow up under the weight of many soldiers; a few can get through without harm, but they will be too few to take the fortress. The solution to taking the fortress is to send many small groups of soldiers along many roads to converge simultaneously on the fortress and take it. Analogically, the solution to killing the tumor is to send many laser beams of low intensity along many paths at the tumor, to arrive simultaneously and there combine to have the effect of a beam of high intensity.

The analogy looks, after the fact, like a straightforward matching of source and target and a projection of useful inferences, but if we look more closely we see, I think, that the details of this source were contrived in the first place only so the analogy could be forged. Of course, after the target and source are assembled in the right ways so that the analogy will work, they can be handed to someone as analogs to be connected in a straightforward fashion, but connecting these prebuilt representations is not understanding analogy.

Consider the actual military situation in the source. When combat resources are plentiful and easily replaced, commanders facing a crucially important military objective have historically not hesitated to sacrifice pack animals or soldiers and simply replace them. The straightforward solution for the source is to run donkeys or dogs or soldiers up the road, sacrificing as many as necessary to clear the mines. With a sufficient supply of them, the mines will present no problem and the fortress will be taken. After all, there cannot be many mined places. The residents of the fortress must be able to move vehicles over the roads, which they could do only by avoiding the few places that are mined. Moreover, only some spots on a road are suitable for mining in any event. Bridges, for example, are rarely mined because the mines are too easily detected. There is no point in mining the road if the soldiers can simply walk through a field alongside it, so someone planting mines must either install entire fields of mines or place them in very narrow passes in the topography.

But these straightforward and conventional military framings of the source do not serve the analogy, so the representations of the source given in the scholarship typically rebuild the source artificially so as to disallow them. For example, the representation given in Gick and Holyoak and again in Holyoak and Thagard is this: the attacking general has just enough men to storm the fortress—he needs his entire army, so cannot sacrifice any of them. (No mention is made of using animals instead.) The purpose of this weird representation of the source is clearly to disallow normal military ideas, because disallowing them helps the analogy work.

That particular forging of the source in the service of the analogy is explicit, but some other crucial forgings are only implicit. For example, I have told the fortress story to military officers of various ranks. One of them responded, "it says the fortress is situated in the middle of the country, surrounded by farms and villages. Why doesn't the general just send his troops through the fields?" This is an excellent objection. However, that construal is implicitly disallowed. The Fortress Story tells us that the attacking general is a "great general," and that he solves this problem by dividing up his army and sending them charging down different roads. We know that a "great general" could not have missed so obvious a solution as marching his troops through the field, and we also suspect that the defender of the fortress is unlikely to be so inept as to mine roads running through open fields, so we conclude that in some unspecified way the source does not allow this possibility, even though nothing explicit forbids it. The officer asking the excellent question was answered by a companion officer, "All of the roads must go through narrow passes or something."

The most profound conceptual reforging in the service of making analogical connections between tumor and fortress is the most subtle. In the source, it is an unchangeable truth and a central point in military doctrine that the armed force one can bring to bear is also a vulnerable asset one does not wish to lose. For example, the British Home Fleet during World War I was exceptionally strong, but its sheer existence as a "force-in-being" was so important that it was almost never risked in actual battle, the single exception being the Battle of Jutland in 1916, the only major naval battle of the war. In the source, the force and the vulnerability cannot be separated, and their inseparability is crucial. But if the tumor-fortress analogy is to go through, they must somehow be separated, because in the target, the force is not vulnerable. As Holyoak and Thagard note, the laser beam and the laser are not at risk. Nor can the vulnerability of the force in the source be ignored, because vulnerability is indispensable structure for the target. The solution is to take what cannot be separated in the source and to conceive of it as having two aspects— a force whose intensity varies with the number of soldiers that constitute it, and the physical soldiers who are vulnerable. These aspects are projected to the blend separately. The military force with variable intensity is blended with the laser beam; the vulnerable soldiers are blended with the patient. Again, we see that the important work of analogy is not to match analogs but, more complexly, to create an integration network, and this creation often requires reinterpretation of the analogs.

URBAN BLIGHT

It may still be tempting to dismiss all these examples as inconsequential. Two are cartoons, one is poetry, and one is a hypothetical problem of the sort dreamed up by psychologists and inflicted upon college students as subjects. However, my last example is a historical analogy that set policy, changed law, altered the urban landscape, and cost an enormous amount of money. It is Justice William O. Douglas's invention of a policy as expressed in his opinion in a case in 1954 on the constitutionality of the Federal Urban Renewal Program in Washington, D.C. Douglas needed to justify a policy according to which the federal government would be authorized to condemn and destroy entire urban areas, even though nearly all of the privately owned properties and buildings to be destroyed met the relevant legal codes, and most of those were in fact individually unobjectionable. Douglas hit upon the analogical inference that, just as an entire crop, nearly all of whose individual plants are healthy, must be destroyed and entirely replanted when some small part of it is blighted, so an urban area, nearly all of whose individual buildings, utilities, and roads are satisfactory, must be completely destroyed and redesigned from scratch when it has become socially unsavory. The following paragraph suggests his reasoning:

> The experts concluded that if the community were to be healthy, if it were not to revert again to a blighted or slum area, as though possessed of a congenital disease, the area must be planned as a whole. It was not enough, they believed, to remove existing buildings that were unsani-

tary or unsightly. It was important to redesign the whole area so as to eliminate the conditions that cause slums—the overcrowding of dwellings, the lack of parks, the lack of adequate streets and alleys, the absence of recreational areas, the lack of light and air, the presence of outmoded street patterns. It was believed that the piecemeal approach, the removal of individual structures that were offensive, would be only a palliative. The entire area needed redesigning so that a balanced, integrated plan could be developed for the region including not only new homes but also schools, churches, parks, streets, and shopping centers. In this way it was hoped that the cycle of decay of the area could be controlled and the birth of future slums prevented. (Quoted in Schön and Rein, 1994, p. 24)

It might seem as if this invention of a justification for policy is the product of straightforward analogy: agricultural blight, a biological scenario, is mapped analogically onto urban distress, a social scenario. But that analysis of this analogy, although appealing, is inadequate. It is based on the assumption that the thinker first locates all the central structure in the familiar source scenario (here, blight) and then attempts to project it onto the other target scenario (here, slums), so as to create the "strongest match," where "strongest" means least difference between the relations in the two notions. According to such an analysis, we look first for causal structure in blighted crops: there are organisms that inhabit the crop and that directly cause the problem. Are there organisms that inhabit the slum and that directly cause the problem? Certainly: the slum-dwellers. For the blighted crops, there is a solution: destroy the crop completely so as to destroy the organisms completely, and then replant the crop identically, so that it becomes exactly what it was before it was inhabited. Projecting this to slums, we have a straightforward solution: raze the slum areas entirely so as to kill all the residents, and then rebuild the area identically so that it becomes what it was before it was inhabited.

Of course, this analysis, when spelled out this way, is absolutely outrageous. Douglas began instead with distinct preferences in thinking about the slums: the residents must not be harmed, and even inconvenience to them must be attenuated; they are not to be stigmatized or viewed as the important cause of the problem, even though the causal chain must inevitably run through their actions; the federal government is to be viewed as responsible for correcting such problems; the extension of power to the federal government in its dealing with social ills is desirable; and so on. In order to invent his justification, Douglas was obliged to use conceptual blending. I do not mean in the least that Douglas was doing something unusual or roundabout in inventing his conceptual blend. On the contrary, he was doing just what anybody does when coming up with an analogy. One might want to argue that his analogy was true or false, in this respect or that, but not because he was using conceptual blending. Nearly all analogies, purely true and purely false and everything in between, appear to depend on conceptual blending.

Justice Douglas's blend leads to emergent structure not contained in the analogs. For example, before this blending, the concept of urban distress does not by itself yield the policy of razing perfectly acceptable buildings and ripping up useful roads that are in good repair. In Douglas's "urban blight" blend, the agents that cause blight are blended *not* with the biological agents in the area of urban distress but rather with the area itself. So in the blend, but in neither of the pre-existing analogs, the problem is handled by saving the resident organisms but razing the crop/area. A summary of Douglas's argument as "areas with slums are like crops with blight, so we should do to them what we do to the crops" misses the conceptual work in the invention of this policy. Douglas and the experts used elaborate conceptual blending to create a warrant for a major legal decision that set expensive and highly aggressive governmental policy. Again, the purpose of the analogy is in fact to create inferences for the target, and after the fact, in hindsight, the analogy can be viewed as consisting of retrieving pre-existing analogs, matching and aligning them, and projecting inferences from the source to the target. But that hindsight analysis misses, I propose, the essential cognitive operations and conceptual work.

In general, analogy involves dynamic forging of mental spaces, connections between them, and blends as we create a conceptual integration network of spreading coherence, whose final version contains a set of what we recognize, after the fact, in the rearview mirror, as systematic, even "obvious" analogical connections. This view accords with neither the folk theory of analogy nor the view of analogy common in social science, but it is the view, I propose, that is truest to the actual evidence of actual analogies that human beings actually do construct and, even more important, the view that best recognizes the creative power of the mental capacities routinely deployed by cognitively modern human beings.

♔ 5 ♛

DESCENT OF MEANING

I N THE *Meno*, Plato disarmingly proposes that meaning is never created, only remembered. One can sympathize with Plato, for although absolute nativism seems to deny the experience of having a new idea and the evidence of cultural evolution, there isn't a good technical explanation for how new meaning could arise. Plato's nativism at least gives an answer on the side of process, to the extent that collapsing imagination and innovation into memory reduces the number of processes. For if we reject Plato's ingenious dodge, we must discover some process through which new local meanings can be constructed. How did the terrestrial making of meaning advance from what lizards do to what human beings do? We are not even allowed to assume cumulative increase—the lizard emerges from its leathery shell able to hunt and fight, while the human newborn cannot walk or see. How did the universe get, by some evidently circuitous path, from the simplicity present at the big bang to the complex construction of meaning that is the subject of social science? Social scientists study particular elaborate constructions of meaning, taking it for granted that there is construction of meaning. Is there? If so, what makes it possible?

Cognitive science gives no clear answer. Evolutionary psychology offers the interesting hypothesis, aimed at answering a different question, that certain frames of meaning are carried genetically. In a sense, these frames are placed in the genotype by natural selection and provided to the developing brain through genetic instruction. For example, so goes the logic, human beings have a genetically instructed brain capacity for recognizing certain kinds of predators and taking appropriate evasive action. Fair enough, but this hypothesis covers only a relatively small number of universal or universally available frames of meaning and offers little explanation for the sort of meaning that varies dramatically from culture to culture or person to person. Indeed, it offers little explanation for the sort of meaning that could have developed during the last two thousand years. Granted that human beings, like lizards, are built to be able to distinguish predators from potential mates, what we want to know is how the vast world of diverse human meaning could arise, and there is relatively little answer to be found in the hypothesis that natural selection has built human beings to develop a relatively few universal frames.

The best attempt in cognitive science at providing an explanation for how human beings can create new meaning comes in the form of the theory of conceptual schemata. This theory proposes that we detect regularities in environments and compress them into much less detailed conceptual templates that then guide our behavior. We adjust these schemata a little under further experience. So, for example, we have a schema for *door* that lets us interpret and otherwise handle new doors. We have a schema for *restaurant* that makes it possible for us to eat in other cities.

This view—that we recognize regularities in our environments and compress them into templates for the sake of future recognition and behavior—inspired the subfield of cognitive science known as parallel distributed processing, also called "connectionism." In connectionism, a (mildly) neurally inspired computer "network" learns to recognize patterns by adjusting local thresholds of activation on a wide array of individual computational units, each of them quite stupid. The idea is that although individual units are stupid, the overall network can be quite smart.

In connectionism, trial-and-error change of activation weights produces a variety of schemas, which are selected for or selected against by mechanisms that calculate success. In "structured connectionism," by contrast, formation of schemas is powerfully assisted by what are hoped to be analogs of genetic guidance, cellular developmental mechanisms, and ontogenetic experience.

Although this theory of conceptual schemata goes part of the way in explaining how meaning can be attributed, how behavior can be guided, why regularities are detected in our experience, and why there is regularity in the way we attribute meaning, it is less useful as an account of the invention of new meaning. I turn now to the way in which the theory of conceptual schemata does not address the essential problem of invention and variation.

What the theory of conceptual schemata intends to explain is how a human being can have a conceptual system. What it proposes is that when the world changes, we detect new regularities and then represent those regularities in compressed templates. For example, if diseases and earthquakes destroy our adversaries, we detect the new regularity and form a schema.

But not so fast. Most change in the world is caused not by earthquakes and viruses but by people. It arises because people—individuals and groups—engage in mental invention of new meaning, and this new meaning *results* in new regularities in the world. The new meaning is often available before it has produced new regularities in the world. Clearly, an account of the invention of meaning cannot assume as its beginning point that the world has already changed, for the invention of meaning is, in good measure, prior to those changes in the world. We need a theory of invention that accounts for the kind of invention of meaning that precedes the changes it induces in the world.

Most social change involves mental operation—changes in ideas or ideologies or policy, innovations in technology or production or dissemination, compromise and arbitration, confrontation and negotiation—and all these changes depend upon prior invention of meaning. While the theory of conceptual schemata may tell us something about the creation of new meaning in response to a regularity that has arisen in the world, it does not tell us anything about the creation of new meaning that enables that new regularity to arise in the first place. To say, "the social world changes, and we detect the new regularities" does not explain how the social world can change in the first instance. For that, we need an account of invention of new meaning that does not consist exclusively of compression of regularities already in environments.

Floating in orbit around the problem of invention, variation, and diversity, we find the theory of complex adaptive systems. The human gene pool is a complex adaptive system. In a complex adaptive system, many small units interact repeatedly with environments and with each other; these interactions are relatively simple; interaction results in variety; the variety is heritable; there is selection pressure on the resulting units; and the result is complexity, self-organizing diversity, principled order, just on the edge of chaos. The system is considerably more than the sum of its parts. It arises nonlinearly.

To begin to answer the question, "How can cognition create new meanings out of old?" we need to find a way in which existing meanings can interact to produce new meanings that inherit some of their meaning from the original meanings but have new, emergent meaning of their own. This is the problem of "the descent of meaning." How can existing meanings interact to produce descendent meanings that are not copies of the originals? We need to discover the cognitive processes by which "meaning descends."

In using phrases like "meaning descends" and "the descent of meaning," I am relying on an analogy with evolutionary biology. "Descent of Humankind" refers to the evolutionary mechanisms involved in our phylogenetic "descent." We "descend" from "apes." In evolutionary descent, some organisms interact with others to produce descendents, and even in a single generation, the children, the "descendents," are not the same as their ancestors, their parents. After very many generations, the group of living "descendents" can be quite dissimilar to the group of "ancestors" who lived during a particular age long ago. *The Descent of Man* is the title of Charles Darwin's book on this and related subjects.

Evolutionary biologists talk about the way in which anatomically and cognitively modern human beings "descended from" ancestors. They propose hypotheses about "our descent"—that is, the history and mechanisms by which our ancestors interacted with each other sexually in environments to produce "descendents." This process of "descent" involves modifications, where modifications introduce variety and are heritable and where selection pressures bear on the offspring.

By the "descent of meaning" I mean the way in which some meanings interact, in environments, to produce new meanings that inherit some of their aspects from the prior meanings but that have emergent meaning of their own that is not contained in the prior meanings. I am focusing not on the *evolutionary biological* processes for producing something new—processes which take place over extremely long time spans—I am focusing instead on the *cognitive* processes that produce something new. These cognitive processes work very much faster than evolutionary biological processes. They work in cultural time rather than evolutionary time. Indeed, they often work in the blink of an eye.

To say that "meaning descends" is to say that some meanings that exist at any given moment interact to produce descendent meanings that inherit something from the earlier meanings but are not copies of them or even cut-and-paste assemblies of some of their parts. The earlier meanings are the "ancestors" and the meanings that arise from their interaction are the "descendents." The descendents have emergent meaning.

Suppose that conceptual schemata themselves are analogous to agents in a complex adaptive system. Suppose they interact. Suppose there is a process of interaction between conceptual schemata that introduces variation and resembles sexual reproduction—call it "conceptual sex." In conceptual sex, two schemata would come together like parents to produce an offspring that is, in crucial ways, unlike them. Suppose conceptual sex happens all the time, as a routine activity in thought, society, and culture. Suppose that it typically takes place backstage, and that pressures of selection bear on the results. Suppose also that there are regular principles and constraints on conceptual sex. Then the products would inherit meanings from the prior meanings but could have new, emergent meaning of their own not available from the prior meanings.

If meaning does arise through some kind of "conceptual sex," then it could be a dynamic, never-resting, self-organizing system. Simple meanings, in this system, could result in complex "descendent" meanings. Meaning could develop intricate patterns. Alternative intricate patterns would exist and descend side by side, sometimes branching, sometimes converging. This conceptual development would be evolutionary, in the theoretical sense, and path-dependent. It would exploit accidents in its environments and in its resources. Meaning would have no fundamental elements, but would show strong regularities and entrenchments. Conceptual sex would produce new elements, but not unintelligible new elements.

Of course, my candidate for "conceptual sex" is the basic mental operation I have called "conceptual integration," or "blending."

As I have mentioned, Steven Mithen, who works with notions drawn from archeology and evolutionary psychology, has made a loosely similar proposal, that "cognitive fluidity" is the mechanism that underlies the rapid innovation of meaning we see in art, science, and religion. He observes that the descent of meaning among human beings brings amazing innovation and variety that cannot be explained by the existence of a few genetically provided conceptual frames. "Cognitive fluidity" is his name for what he views as a mysterious mental operation that allows human beings to combine quite different concepts. Fauconnier and I have offered a technical analysis of the mental operation that allows human beings to combine quite different concepts, under the name "conceptual integration." The rest of this chapter is a consideration of some issues involved in the proposal that conceptual integration is what makes descent of meaning possible, that conceptual integration is the mechanism of conceptual sex.

IS IT POSSIBLE TO MODEL CONCEPTUAL REPRODUCTION AT ALL?

Meaning is nonlinear—brains in bodies in environments, groups of brains, interacting dynamically, in actual, local circumstances, produce new meaning that is not just the sum of some previous meanings. How can groups of brains—three-pound biological organs—in environments do this? The nuances of religious ritual, the connotations of trust funds, the variation in concepts of freedom, the rhetorical justifications for racism—what operations make it possible to get from genetically set behavior patterns to these curiosities?

There are two general features of the way human beings construct meaning that I will take as being beyond argument. The first general feature is extreme *variety and diversity* of meaning, along with continuous change and evolution. Cultural anthropology, sociology, and the rest of the comparative social sciences have shown undeniably that the human construction of meaning is extraordinarily diverse.

The second general feature is strong *regularity* in the construction of meaning and of procedural *stability* across diverse constructions. Specific regularities concern, for example, color vision, color constancy, and our visual capacity for the perception of motion; language and grammar; categorization; prototyping; conceptual projection and integration; schematic cognition (framing and other compressions, the relation of schematic cognition to grammatical constructions); recursion; symmetry in perception and production; interpretation of other minds on the basis of visible bodily expression, gesture, and movement; focal point reasoning (reference points, focus, viewpoints, and the relationship of focal point reasoning to grammatical constructions); memory (and the drawing of inference on the basis of its performance, such as speed, rather than on the basis of its content); assembly and connection of mental spaces (and their relationship to reference and inference); counterfactual reasoning; narrative; figure/ground organization; profiling; pragmatic scales; and so on.

I will take it as established that human meaning has this character—extreme diversity, complexity, and variety, along with strong regularity—and turn my attention to the problem of why human meaning should look like this. Absent some explanation, it is not clear why this co-occurrence should be inevitable.

THE ANALOGY WITH EVOLUTIONARY BIOLOGY

Evolutionary systems have descent of elements with modification. Modification leads to variety. The variety is heritable. There is selection pressure on the resulting elements. In evolutionary biology, "descent with modification and selection" means "self-replication with heritable variation and selection."

Evolutionary biology has yielded the more abstract concept of a "complex adaptive system." Several systems have been nominated for the status of complex adaptive system—the immune system, the central nervous system, economies, language, proteins, marriage. The work on complexity is suggestive for the study of meaning. I attach Appendix A, "Some Features of Complex Adaptive Systems," for those who are interested in seeing some of the details.

For most of us, the only complex adaptive system we will ever think of involves genetic descent. But the principles of "descent with modification" involved in genetic descent are general. For example, Gerald Edelman (1992) helped demonstrate that the vertebrate immune system operates according to evolutionary principles of variation and selection. Variation and selection operate on descent of lymphocytes in the individual organism, not on descent of genetic material through organisms; and they operate over the life span of the organism, not over generations of organisms. Edelman calls the human immune system a "somatic selection system" to distinguish it from a system of selection of genetic material as it descends through generations. Both are complex adaptive systems, evolutionary, path-dependent, self-organizing.

Part of the difficulty in approaching the construction of meaning lies in the possibility that it is the most hyper-complex adaptive system of all, a nonlinear result of the interaction of several complex adaptive systems, each itself highly nonlinear. The list of candidates involved in the construction of meaning includes genetic, neurobiological, and linguistic systems, in individuals, communities, species, and biota.

THE APPEAL OF EVOLUTIONARY THEORY OF MEANING

There are several related reasons for viewing evolutionary biology and the more general notion of a complex adaptive systems as providing guidance in thinking about the nature of meaning.

• *Comprehensiveness.* In a complex adaptive system, the principles of descent, modification, variation, heritability, and selection apply to everything. For example, principles of evolutionary biology apply to every organism, no matter how strange or unusual.

• *No core-versus-periphery.* In a complex adaptive system, elements or phenomena that seem most exotic are as important for the theory as any other elements or phenomena. The fat island bird that cannot fly is as much an evolutionary phenomenon as grass.

• *No dismissal of data.* Anything in the system is potentially a counterexample to the theory.

• *No problem with "scaling up."* Partial models of meaning (such as those based on notions of semantic primitives, innate concepts, language bioprograms, or symbolic artificial intelligence representations) have problems "scaling up" to include the "rest" of the system. By contrast, it is assumed for a complex adaptive system that the system cannot be partitioned into entirely separate modules, or into rudiments plus overlays. A complex adaptive system cannot be approached by modeling the "rudiments" or the "core" and then scaling the model up to include the rest of the system, because a complex adaptive system has very many interactions throughout the system and regularity arises as a nonlinear consequence of all those interactions. The complexity does not reside in a part of the system; it is emergent in the whole system.

• *Historical process.* Events in a complex adaptive system are fully historical— path-dependent, exploiting accidents, contingent, nonteleological, nonnecessary, and existing side-by-side with alternatives. In principle, patterns of historical descent may stretch over time intervals of any length. Seeing the historical patterns that led to an event may require looking at connections across centuries or millennia. In work on meaning, cognition, action, or language, seeing the important historical pattern behind an event may require looking at developments over thousands of years. Drawing a path of strong descent from classical antiquity to the present is not necessarily ahistorical; failing to do so can be ahistorical. In genetic evolution, history operates over many generations, while in the immune system it can operate effectively within hours. Evolutionary theories of brain activity propose intervals of variation and selection that range from as short as milliseconds to as long as individual human lifetimes.

• *No foundations, but profound entrenchments.* In a complex adaptive system, fully historical, contingent processes, acting over accidents, can and do develop profoundly entrenched patterns that, in practice and for small enough intervals of time, look foundational, rigid, fixed, universal. For example, the eukaryotic cell with its nucleus seems for any practical purpose absolutely fundamental to human life, indispensable, never to be displaced from its role in our bodily life, but it was the result of a historical, contingent process, acting over accidents. Entrenched patterns are in theory malleable and even dispensable, but their liquidity, like the liquidity of glass, may be evident only if observed over very long periods of time, and their eradication may in fact be, as a practical and statistical matter, so highly unlikely for the projected life of the system as to make them look fixed for all time.

CONCEPTUAL SCHEMATA

A conceptual schema, like any schema in a complex adaptive system, offers compressions of regularities in experience, guides future interaction, undergoes descent with modification under further experience, and is subject to selection pressures.

The most recent sophisticated summary of the theoretical notion of a conceptual schema in cognitive science is provided in Martin (1993), which repeats David Rumelhart, Donald Norman, and Andrew Ortony's elaboration of the notion of a conceptual schema, previously summarized in Rumelhart (1980).

Rumelhart (1980) analyzes three ways in which new meaning can arise. (He calls this "learning.") All three ways involve conceptual schemata. First, there is accretion: learning happens when we lay down a memory of an experience as an instantiation of existing schemata. For example, if we have a schema for *restaurant* and visit a new one, then we have a memory of the new restaurant; we remember it as an experience that conformed to the schema *restaurant*. Second, there is tuning: we slightly adjust an existing schema to make it match experience better. For example, under inflation over years, we might slightly adjust our notion now and then of how much a dinner in a good restaurant should cost. Accretion and tuning, Rumelhart notes, *do not lead to new schemata.* So they offer very little in the way of explaining the invention of new schemata. Third, there is restructuring, of two kinds: patterned generation and schema induction. Patterned generation happens infrequently and schema induction almost never. Patterned generation is the construction of a new schema by making a slight change in an old one, where the possibilities for change are few: a constant can be replaced with a variable, a variable can be replaced with a constant, and so on, as motivated by new experience. For example, we may have begun with a frame for *restaurant* in which the maître d' is male, but, under experience, have come to change that constant into a variable: male or female. The second kind of restructuring is schema induction, which is the process of making a new schema that is simply the conjunction of old schemata. So if we always follow dinner at the restaurant with a walk through the park to take coffee at a café, we may develop a *dinner-walk-coffee* schema. I attach Appendix B: "What Is a Conceptual Schema?" presenting further details.

The theory of conceptual schemata is useful for explaining how the making of meaning exhibits regularity. In fact, under the theory of conceptual schemata, regularity is inevitable. But, as I say, the notion of a conceptual schema is nearly useless for explaining how a new schema can arise *before* it is manifest in our regular experience.

CONCEPTUAL REPRODUCTION

Sexual reproduction, a spectacularly successful source of innovation and diversity in genetic descent, blends two genotypes into a third that takes substantial portions from each of them but that delivers something quite different from either of them—a new person. Just so, I propose, "conceptual reproduction" blends two (often quite different) schemata into an offspring schema that takes substantial portions from each of its conceptual parents but that delivers meaning not available in either of them—conceptual reproduction can deliver a new schema.

The analogy is inexact: conceptual reproduction has dynamic features that clash with the dynamic features of sexual reproduction. For example, conceptual reproduction permits extensive inheritance during the lifetime of the offspring. The offspring can return to the parents to take new elements from them. It can inherit an element from a parent provisionally and later abandon it to take a different element. In contrast, the human offspring, although subject to cultural inheritance throughout its life, cannot after fertilization go back to inherit different genetic structure from its parents.

TRASH CAN BASKETBALL

Trash can basketball provides an everyday example of the way in which conceptual reproduction can deliver a new schema. Coulson (1997) analyzes a scenario in which two college students are up late studying for an exam and one of them crumples up a piece of paper and tosses it at the trash can. They quickly develop a shared mental blend in which the wastepaper is a basketball, the person disposing of the paper is a basketball player, and the trash can is the basket. One parent schema is *disposing of wastepaper* and the other is *conventional basketball.*

In the blend, a new schema with new structure is conceived. For example, in the blend, the player must make wastepaper into a ball as a precondition of play. This meaning is not available from the parent of *basketball*, where the players do not make the balls, and it is not available from the parent of *disposing of wastepaper*, where there is no play and where crumpling the wastepaper is not a precondition of disposal.

In the blend, the action of crumpling a piece of paper in frustration and hurling it at the trash can acquires a conceptual standing that serves as the basis of a game, with emergent structure and rules that guide action. The exact details of the blend will be a matter of negotiation between the players and will depend upon the room. Are there obstructions? How close is the player allowed to get to the basket? Must the player be sitting? May the opposing player try to block the shot? How much noise is permitted?

The resulting offspring schema will be a double-scope blend—that is, it will develop its own organizing schema by drawing on the organizing schemata of both parents. For example, the propulsive force needed for success and the details of grasping the "ball" will depend partly upon the object's being a piece of paper, which comes from the *disposing of wastepaper* parent, and partly on its being a "ball," which comes from the *basketball* input. The idea that trash can basketball has rules of competitive play comes from the *basketball* input, although the exact rules will certainly be quite different from those of basketball—for example, there might be a rule that the ball must be thrown rather than rolled down a sloping bookshelf that ends just above the trash can. Lay-ups are permitted in basketball but the counterpart action with the crumpled paper may be forbidden in trash can basketball on the ground that it requires no skill. There is running and picking and dribbling and body contact in basketball, but these activities may be disallowed in trash can basketball. In *disposing of wastepaper*, the crumpled paper is supposed to stay in the trash can, but in basketball, the ball is supposed to come back out of the net. The new schema of *trash can basketball* will have to handle this conflict. Will a player lose if she has no more wastepaper to turn into a ball? Must it be true wastepaper, or will a blank sheet count? Will she be allowed to retrieve her ball from the wastebasket? The social frame of trash can basketball is also quite different from social frames for conventional basketball and from social frames for throwing paper into the trash can.

In trash can basketball, we have all the constitutive structural and dynamic features of blending:

1. There is a *partial cross-space mapping* of counterparts between the parents. (For example, the crumpled paper and the basketball are counterparts; the trash can and the hoop are counterparts; the disposer and the player are counterparts.)
2. There is *selective projection* of structure from the parents to the offspring.
3. There is *emergent structure* in the offspring.

Structure emerges in three ways:

- *Composition.* Taken together, the projections from the parents make new relations available in the offspring that did not exist in the separate parents. For example, we do not think of basketball courts and dorm rooms as inhabiting the same space, but that spatial composition is available in the blend.
- *Completion.* Structure in the offspring can be interpreted as part of a background schema, and so that partial structure can be "completed" by bringing in the background schema to give the blend emergent structure. For example, once we have wads of paper bouncing off walls in a dorm room, it is easy to complete that structure with the schema for *disturbing the neighbors*, which might bring, as emergent structure in the blend, fine distinctions about appropriate levels of noise in trash can basketball.
- *Elaboration.* The structure in the offspring can be elaborated. This is "running the blend." It arises through cognitive work performed within the offspring, according to its own emergent logic. For example, once the blend has the possibility of disturbing the neighbors by playing trash can basketball, we may run the blend to develop rules about how hard the ball can be thrown, which walls can be used as backboards, what patterns of laughter are disallowed since they would give away the secret that the students are having fun instead of studying, and so on.

THROUGH

Here is a more basic, less amusing example of the way in which conceptual reproduction can deliver a new schema. Image schemata are skeletal patterns that recur in our sensory and motor activity under experience. *Motion along a path*, *bounded interior*, *balance*, and *symmetry* are typical image schemata. Mark Johnson and Leonard Talmy—followed more recently by Claudia Brugman, Eve Sweetser, George Lakoff, Ronald Langacker, me, and many others—have analyzed linguistic evidence for the existence of image schemata. Neurobiological studies of visual processing have focused on the development of recognition patterns that seem to be kinds of image schemata. (For summaries, see Hubel, 1995, and Zeki, 1993.) For example, the primary visual cortex responds to moving bars of light in an interesting way: a given neuron will have a preferred "orientation tuning"—it will respond best to a bar at a given angle. Other neurons in the column appear to have the same preferred stimulus, so that the column constitutes a unified group of neurons that fire together in time in an organized manner to recognize a line at a preferred angle. Different orientation columns prefer different angles. In this way, orientation tuning columns work like neurobiological image schemata for structuring certain kinds of visual experience and for understanding it. These orientation tuning columns in the primary visual cortex are connected to neuronal groups in another, separate visual map, known as V2, and these two connected visual maps respond coherently to the same preferred stimulus, which suggests that image schemata in the primary visual cortex are coordinated with image schemata in V2.

Consider the image schema for *bounded interior* and the separate image schema for *directed motion along a path*. (Human beings are extremely good at recognizing directed motion of an object against a background.) Blending the image schema for *directed motion along a path* with the image schema for *bounded interior* such that the path begins outside the boundary, crosses the bounded interior, and proceeds past the boundary on the other side gives the complex image schema *through*. Alternatively, blending them so that that the path begins in the interior but proceeds outside the interior gives the complex image schema *out of*. Alternatively, blending them so that the path begins outside the interior but ends inside the interior gives the complex image schema *into*.

CATEGORIZATION

Conceptual reproduction is also at work in the invention of new categories and in the provisional and exploratory extension of categories: "military democracy," "artificial life," "That lifeguard is a real fish."

For example, there are air-launched smart weapons that are directed to their targets by shining a laser beam on the target. Soldiers can be dropped behind enemy lines to illuminate targets briefly so these target-seeking smart weapons can find the targets. The soldier, at a distance from the target, moves a hand-held device up and down to do the illuminating. The standard verb for the soldier's action is "paint": the soldier "paints" the target. This is a blend of our standard frame of "painting" and the soldier's scenario of indicating the target. The cross-space mapping between counterparts in these two contributing spaces is rich: in each contributing space, there is a hand-held device; it is moved up and down by a person; it causes the surface of the object to change in appearance; and so on. In the blend, the soldier's action counts as "painting." In the blend, the possible purposes of painting are not only to decorate the object, to preserve it, to amuse the painter, and so on, but also to destroy the object. This is an amazing extension of the standard category of "painting"!

When a blended space is viewed as extending a category, there can be backtalk to one of the original parents. Eve Sweetser reports that the label on a flour package asserts that the flour, sold as especially suitable for use in bread machines, is also excellent for "manual bread." In this way, the original input conception of *bread* is altered: it becomes emphatically marked as *made by hand*. So we see that the process off conceptual reproduction can produce changes in the original parents. Sexual reproduction, by contrast, produces no genetic changes in the parents.

In another example, the invention of *front-loaded Individual Retirement Account* (IRA) as a new schema conflicts with the original schema for IRA, and so the original schema comes to be called a "classic IRA."

There are standard grammatical forms for expressing these new categories, analyzed in Turner and Fauconnier (1995). "Houseboat," "Chunnel," "computer virus," "military democracy," "dolphin-safe tuna," and "artificial life" are by now conventional compounds for expressing categories. "Bond ghoul" has become one in the financial community.

These provisional categorizations can result in new social categories. "Same-sex marriage" is at present the most obvious example. Consider also an idiosyncratic example: A citizen of Paris has two lovers, whose knowledge of each other's existence is certain but not acknowledged. They all carefully ensure that neither lover is introduced into the other's social world. The Seine forms the symbolic geographical boundary: one Left Bank lover, one Right. Our citizen refers to this as "French fidelity." This new category extension has two conceptual parents—sexual fidelity and a stereotype of Parisian sexual pleasure. One might think that these are incompatible schemata, but the offspring provides a new normative schema that guides the intricate social behavior of three people.

NON-EUCLIDEAN GEOMETRY

The invention of non-Euclidean geometry (Fauconnier 1997, Turner and Fauconnier 1999) is a clear case in which conceptual reproduction began with conventional meanings and, using them as conceptual parents, produced a new conceptual offspring. Euclidean geometry provided the conceptual parents for the creation of a branch of non-Euclidan geometry that differs radically from Euclidean geometry. I do not mean that non-Euclidean geometry can be derived within

Euclidean geometry according to the derivation procedures allowed within Euclidean geometry. It cannot. But non-Euclidean geometry can be conceptually derived from Euclidean geometry, and was so derived, through conceptual blending.

It might be difficult to believe that non-Euclidean geometry, indispensable for modern theoretical physics, arose by taking two simple, entirely Euclidean schemata, blending them in a simple way, and then using entirely routine Euclidean reasoning on the offspring, but that is the history. Gerolamo Saccheri (1667–1733) wanted (mistakenly) to prove something quite profound about Euclidean geometry. Essentially, he wanted to show that we could eliminate one of its axioms as unnecessary. Even without that suspect axiom, he believed, it should be possible to prove all the theorems of Euclidean geometry. The suspect axiom, he imagined, could be proved as a conclusion from the others, rather than assumed as an independent axiom on its own. We need a name for the system of geometry that follows from the set of all the traditional Euclidean axioms except that one suspect axiom, so let us call this system of geometry "Euclid minus one." Saccheri's task, then, was to prove that Euclidean geometry was identical to "Euclid minus one," that the excluded axiom could be proved inside "Euclid minus one" as a theorem.

In trying to do this, he needed at one point to show that a certain plane figure could not exist in "Euclid minus one." The crucial part of this history lies in how he arrived at that plane figure and what he then did with it. Essentially, he took some geometric parts that do exist in Euclidean geometry, and he blended them together to make a kind of blended geometrical chimera. (It happens that this blended figure was a quadrilateral polygon whose top and bottom sides are equal. The two interior angles on the left are right angles, and the two interior angles on the right are acute angles.) Crucially, this blended figure is incompatible with the suspect axiom of Euclidean geometry that is excluded from "Euclid minus one." Saccheri wanted to show that it is also incompatible with "Euclid minus one." But he could not do that. He worked very hard, proving one strange theorem after another inside "Euclid minus one," but he could never find a contradiction that would let him rule the chimerical quadrilateral out of "Euclid minus one." He did not realize it at the time, but his work proved that there could be a fully consistent geometry—now called "hyperbolic" geometry—that was incompatible with Euclidean geometry. In our age, hyperbolic geometry is recognized as indispensable to the analysis of physical reality. The essence of Saccheri's effort was to take normal Euclidean conceptual parents, blend them selectively to form a new geometric figure, and then run the blend. The result was something strikingly new: hyperbolic geometry. I attach Appendix C, "Conceptual Integration and Math," with figures and details.

This invention of hyperbolic geometry—a non-Euclidean geometry—came about through blending. Not surprisingly, it is routine for blending to play a role in mathematical invention. Fauconnier and Turner (1998) show how complex numbers were invented by elaborating an age-old blended offspring of two parents: *numbers* and *physical space*. George Lakoff and Rafael Núñez (2000) have provided other analyses of blending in the history of mathematical invention.

CONCLUSION

In *After the Fact*, Clifford Geertz writes of the faculty of the School of Social Science in the Institute for Advanced Study that, "We are hardly of one mind on everything and we have different interests and different problems before us; but we are all suspicious of casting the social sciences in the image of the natural sciences, and of general schemes which explain too much" (1995, p. 127).

My proposal in this chapter certainly looks like "a general scheme that explains too much." There are many challenges to be posed to the theory of conceptual reproduction, but the criticism that it is a one-size-fits-all reduction of social and cultural complexity would be misconceived. The general schemes out of favor in the School of Social Science are those that try to reduce the diversity and complexity of meaning. My purpose here is not to reduce this diversity and complexity but to embrace it, and, importantly, to begin to take it seriously as a fact whose existence needs explaining. In itself, embracing diversity and complexity does nothing to explain their existence. We need an explanation of the birth and evolution of diversity and complexity. How can the landscape of human meaning look like this? How did we get from what lizards do to what human cultures do?

There are not many attempts to answer this question, perhaps because, although it is important, it is difficult. There is Plato's nativism, which has defenders today, but as Mithen has argued, modern nativism in the form of evolutionary psychology could at best give us a relatively few universal frames of meaning and offers little explanation for the complexity and diversity of human meaning we see. There are models of how we recognize regularities in environments. There are attempts to see how much of the job can be done by linear composition. There are also several interesting suggestions that somehow mental life must be a complex adaptive system.

The theory of conceptual integration is an attempt to provide substance to the intuition that meaning—in individual lives and in cultures—descends through elaborate, perpetual, and distributed processes of modification, inheritance, and selection, to develop all the great richness, diversity, and nuance that characterize cognitively modern human beings and the complex societies they make.

✑ 6 ✑

COGNITIVE SOCIAL SCIENCE

I T IS no surprise that the fundamental topic of study in cognitive science is mental events, viewed as occurring in single brains or distributively across as few as two brains or as many as all the brains of an entire community and its descendent communities, and lasting as briefly as a few milliseconds or as long as tens of thousands of years.

It is also no surprise that political science, economics, sociology, and anthropology share with cognitive science this fundamental topic of study—mental events, however distributed. Nonmental facts (the location of coal, the date of the potato blight in Ireland) can mean something in social science only because they bear on mental events. The distribution of oil in the earth's crust can mean something in economics because the geological facts of the matter are enmeshed in a mental world of belief, desire, need, demand, value, utility, pricing, judgment, decision, competition, cooperation, conflict, and persuasion. The study of oil without mental events is natural science, not social science.

Mental events provide the defining problems of the social sciences. What are our basic cognitive operations? How do we use them in judgment, decision, action, reason, choice, persuasion, expression? Do voters know what they need to know? How do people choose? What are the best incentives? When is judgment reliable? Can negotiation work? How do cognitive conceptual resources depend on social and cultural location? How do certain products of cognitive and conceptual systems come to be entrenched as publicly shared knowledge and method? Economists, political scientists, sociologists, and anthropologists refer as a matter of course to mental events and typically must assume some general outline of what those mental events can be and how they can arise.

Given this convergence of cognitive science and the social sciences at their intellectual cores, under the general umbrella of the nature of thought and meaning, it would be natural to conclude that they must converge as disciplines. They have not done so. Although cognitive science is a natural and inevitable part of research in the social sciences, so far technical research in cognitive science has had little effect on the social sciences. The study of cognition is not part of the professional formation of the graduate student of economics, political science, sociology, or anthropology. Cognitive science has been vibrant, but its motion has been contained.

It may be that history is to blame. Paul DiMaggio (1997) observes that "thirty years ago, behaviorism made psychology essentially irrelevant to the study of culture," and, we can add, to any social scientist who needs a view of mental events. After the grand collapse of behaviorism, there arose a subsequent program of research by cognitivists and developmentalists into perception, long- and short-term memory, recognition tasks, acquisition of motor skills, and similar psychological phenomena. These good traditions of research also offered little to address the questions that interest the social scientist.

There was once, and in pale reduction still is, a discipline of historical influence and prestige whose defining focus is just this convergence of social science around the topic of mental events. Greek rhetoricians took a complex view of cognition, in which individual human beings are equipped with large toolkits of powerful and generative cognitive operations and conceptual structures, which they use for understanding, judgment, decision, and persuasion, including self-persuasion. The rhetorician strives for conscious awareness of these cognitive operations and conceptual structures, in the hope of discovering ways in which to manipulate them. The effectiveness of the manipulations depends on the shared nature of these cognitive operations and conceptual structures—they are part of the backstage cognition of the members of the audience. It is in virtue of this backstage cognition that the rhetorician can prompt the audience in one way or another. The rhetorician in effect invites the members of the audience to recruit from their background cognitive resources and to use those recruitments for some purpose. What can be recruited to mental work depends on social and cultural location. Parts of the repertoire are common and can be assumed for any audience while other parts are special to special communities or special situations. Consequently, it is a basic principle of rhetorical theory that what works in one situation may not work in another. One of Aristotle's definitions of rhetoric is "the mental ability to see the available means of persuasion *in any particular situation.*"

Rhetoricians undertook the study of why and how people judge credibility, plausibility, and truth-value; of how people reach judgments under uncertainty;

of how they erect schemes of payoffs and costs; of the instruments they possess for making sense of situations and for constructing new meaning. Rhetoricians paid special attention to the relationship between language and mental events, since language is itself a surprisingly complex cognitive toolkit of refined instruments for prompting people to do conceptual work. Over two millennia, it was routinely assumed with varying degrees of emphasis that politicians, lawyers, diplomats, leaders in business, military leaders, and other practical agents of the social world must have a formation in rhetoric, and equally assumed that technical training in the theory of rhetoric is indispensable to scholars of what we now call the social sciences.

It seems that there is no modern equivalent for the view once provided by rhetoric. We lack a cohesive disciplinary view of how cognitive science, economics, political science, sociology, and anthropology converge. It is tempting in these circumstances to return to the tradition of rhetoric, but in trying to exhume it we would, for sociological reasons, only dig our own grave. Rhetoric in our time has fallen on abject and humiliating circumstances. It is now associated for the most part not with research but with fraud, poverty, and the humanities. We cannot afford these connotations; we must have others: bold scientific research, emerging syntheses, new paradigms, wealth, rigor, power, truth. The National Science Foundation, the Russell Sage Foundation, the McDonnell-Pew Foundation, the Alfred P. Sloan Foundation, and the National Institutes of Health will not fund rhetoric (although the Luce Foundation might). Apparently, we must toss a handful of earth on the memory of the discipline of rhetoric—*sit terra tibi levis*—and prefer in its place a modern name for our project, perhaps something like "cognitive social science."

In the present moment, the social sciences face what appears to be challenging terrain as they look for a conception of themselves and their professional activity. With social science on one hand and cognitive science on the other hand, we might arrange a powerful blended future, a good intellectual marriage. The courtship has begun, but it will take some help getting to the altar.

This book began with the a set of large questions for the future of social science, posed by the organizers of the twenty-fifth anniversary conference of the School of Social Science in the Institute for Advanced Study on new directions in social science. The motivations behind these questions were partly intellectual and partly institutional. In this book, I have tried to point the way to some of what I think might be intellectual answers. In brief, cognitive science and social science should be brought together under the general umbrella of the study of backstage cognition, or, more specifically, the study of meaning, reason, choice, concept change, and concept formation, as they are subtended by human neurobiology and played out over the world's societies and cultures.

These intellectual suggestions also lead to an institutional recommendation. The combined university and foundation resources for the study of social science are large. Perhaps some of those resources could be devoted to the founding of cognitive social science.

ᴥᓯ Appendix A ᴥᓯ

SOME FEATURES OF
COMPLEX ADAPTIVE SYSTEMS

Tʜᴇʀᴇ are several good summaries of complex adaptive systems. The following is based partly on (Gell-Mann, 1993). A complex adaptive system exhibits the following features:

- Very many highly connected simple parts interact repeatedly and constantly.
- Complexity arises from the interaction.
- The organization of the system arises from the interaction.
- Both the complexity and the organization arise nonlinearly. That is, the complexity and the organization are not compositions of components and structure at lower levels.
- The system is self-organizing.
- The system has experience.
- The system develops compressed templates, schemata, codings that play a large role in the system's interaction under future experience. (There is no implication or requirement here of objective, veridical "copying" of the world into the schemata or of objective "mirroring" between the experience and the schemata. Indeed, in principle, a schema might arise that is unrelated to past experience—by random mutation, for example—but that nonetheless guides future interaction well.)
- These schemata do not carry anything near the level of detail of past or future experience. They are compressed. Much of their power lies

in what they discard. They actively guide the system to ignore or disattend to aspects of experience.

- There is variation in the proliferation of these schemata (descent with modification).
- There is some selection pressure on the various schemata. The selection need not be sharply defined and the direction of the pressure can vary, even reverse itself. All that is required is some pressure that results in some partial tendency in the system's generation of variety, and a loose match, at times, between the time interval of variation and the time interval of selection. Without such a match, the system could not be effectively adaptive: if selection pressures change much more rapidly than the mechanisms of schema generation can operate, then while each new schema has been "selected for" under old selection pressures, its having been selected for gives it no adaptiveness under the new selection pressures.
- Given the way complex adaptive systems develop, they are attracted to good-enough operation rather than exact solutions.
- The schemata get expanded in some sense as the system has actual experience. This expansion depends upon interaction with the environment, and leads to much fuller structures, often highly local and provisional. Genotypes are expanded into phenotypes. Gene pools are expanded into populations and through those populations selection pressure is brought to bear on genetic structures. Compressed scientific theories are expanded into explanations (and predictions) of highly specific events, and the perceived fitness of those explanations brings selection pressure to bear on competing theories. It is useful to remember that the level of abstractness or generality of the schemata and the level of experience or local interaction can be quite different.
- The compressed patterns generated by the complex adaptive system serve as "recognition" devices.
- There are many opportunities for maladaptation: entrenchment, mismatch of time scales of generation and selection, misgeneration of expectations of regularities on the basis of selected random events, and interaction between distinct complex adaptive systems.

☙ Appendix B ❧
WHAT IS A CONCEPTUAL SCHEMA?

THE MOST advanced description of a conceptual schema comes from joint and individual work by David Rumelhart, Donald Norman, and Andrew Ortony. Rumelhart (1980) gives a summary of the history of the notion of a schema and provides a summary of the work of Rumelhart, Norman, and Ortony. As he reports, Rumelhart and Ortony (1977) listed four major characteristics of schemata:

- Schemata have variables. (E.g., a schema for *room* has lots of variables—number and kinds of entrances, dimensions, etc.)
- Schemata can embed, one within another. (E.g., a schema for *room* can embed in a schema for *house*)
- Schemata represent knowledge at many levels of abstraction.
- Schemata represent knowledge rather than definitions.

Rumelhart adds two more features:

- Schemata are active processes.
- Schemata are recognition devices whose processing is aimed at the evaluation of their goodness of fit to the data being processed.

Martin (1993) gives a fuller summary, including features of conceptual schemata discussed by Rumelhart, Norman, Ortony, and others:

- Internalization. There is some correlation between conceptual schemas and environments.
- Compression.

- Assimilation. "Schemata inform what they represent; they assimilate states of the environment in a manner consistent with their organization."
- Accommodation. The schema can be adjusted under experience.
- Diagnosticity. "Schemata are diagnostic; they convey information about history that can be used to predict future states of the environment."
- Recursiveness. Another name for embedding. "Schemata can contain other schemata."
- Generativity. "Schemata can be created from other schemata."

It is, of course, *generativity* that I am concerned with. "Schemata can be created from other schemata." But just how? Where do schemata come from, how are they learned, and how can schemata generate other schemata?

Norman and Rumelhart (1978) had given a taxonomy of kinds of learning. Rumelhart (1980) gives a summary of that taxonomy, as follows. There are three processes: accretion, tuning, and restructuring.

1. *Accretion*. Accretion is the process of forming traces of comprehension, in which schemata are instantiated but not generated. Accretion causes no new schemata to be formed.

> Learning by accretion is probably the most common sort of learning. It is also the sort of learning that has least effect on the operation of the system. Whenever new information is encountered, there is assumed to be some trace of the comprehension process laid down in memory. This memory trace is the basis for recollections. Generally, these traces are assumed to be partial copies of the original instantiated schemata. Thus, memory traces are assumed to be very much like schemata themselves. They differ only inasmuch as they are fragmentary and they have representations for particular aspects of the original situation in the place of the variables of the original schemata. (p. 53)

2. *Tuning*. An existing schema can be tuned to make it better aligned with experience. Again, no radically new schemata are formed, but an existing schema can undergo continual if modest change.

> Tuning involves the actual modification or evolution of existing schemata. First, our knowledge of the variable constraints and default values can be upgraded continuously as we continue to use the schemata. Whenever we find a case in which we determine that a certain schema offers an adequate account of a particular situation, we can modify the vari-

able constraints and default values in the direction of the current experience. This will make the schema sensitive to slow changes in the population of cases to which the schema is applied. As this process continues, it will continue to sharpen the variables and default values to make the schema better represent the population of situations to which it is applied. Note, however, that this sort of tuning will only occur when the schema is deemed to offer an adequate account of the situation at hand. Thus, because cases that deviate widely from the appropriate variable constraints and default values will not be accommodated by the schema in question, change must be slow.

The second sort of tuning involves replacing a constant portion of a schema with a variable one—that is, adding a new variable to a schema. This sort of schema modification amounts to *concept generalization*—making a schema more generally applicable. Presumably, the occasion for such learning is the discovery, at some point in time, that a particular schema would offer a good account for a particular situation if only some presumably constant feature of the schema were allowed to vary. To the degree that a constant is merely a variable with very tight constraints, this can be seen as a special case of the previous kind of tuning, namely, a case in which the change is from a variable with highly constrained constraints that becomes one with somewhat more relaxed constraints.

The third sort of tuning is, in a sense, the opposite of the last one, namely, the process of making a variable into a constant or specializing the use of the concept. One occasion for such learning would be the discovery that certain "outlier" situations are better accounted for by other schemata and that the apparent variable is better thought of as a constant. As before, this can also be thought of as a special case of changing variable constraints—in this case tightening them. (pp. 53–54)

3. *Restructuring.* Restructuring gives new schemata. However, Rumelhart claims that restructuring is quite unusual. There are two kinds of restructuring: *patterned generation* and *schema induction*. Patterned induction occurs when we make a new schema by making a few changes in an old one. We can put constants where an old schema had variables, or variables where it had constants, or substitute a new variable or constant for an old variable or constant of the original schema. Schema induction, very rare, occurs when an organized combination of existing schemata becomes a schema in its own right.

If accretion and tuning were the only learning mechanisms, no new schemata could be created. The third learning mode [restructuring] discussed previously involves the creation of new schemata. There are basically two ways in which new schemata can be formed. Norman and Rumelhart (1978) called these *patterned generation* and *schema induction*.

Patterned generation involves the creation of a new schema by copying an old one with a few modifications. Such learning is, in essence, learning by analogy. We learn that a new concept is like an old one except for a few differences. A new schema can differ from an old one by having variables where the old one had constants (a generalization of the old schema), by having constants where an old schema had variables (a further specification of the old schema), or by substituting a new variable or constant for an old variable or constant of the original schema. Once a new schema is created by such processes, the process of tuning will continue to modify the newly created schema to bring it more into line with experience.

The second way in which new schemata can be formed is through the process of schema induction. The notion here is that if a certain spatiotemporal configuration of schemata is repeated, there is reason to assume that the particular configuration forms a meaningful concept and a schema can be formed that consists of just that configuration. This, of course, is the classical contiguity learning. It is interesting that, in spite of the ubiquity of the notion of contiguity learning in learning theories of the past, there is no real *need* for it in a schema-based system. Provided we begin with a sufficiently general set of schemata, the processes of tuning, accretion, and patterned generation can carry us a long way. Schema induction does cause some difficulty for the notion of schemata as I have outlined them. In order for schema induction to work properly, we must posit some aspect of the system sensitive to the recurrence of configurations of schemata that do not, at the time they occur, match any existing schemata. Such a system is not a natural part of a schema-based system. (p. 54)

ᴈ Appendix C ᴁ
CONCEPTUAL INTEGRATION AND MATH

Iᴛ ɪs easy to think of two rays drawn at right angles in the same direction away from a line segment (see the figure at the top left in Figure A-1). It is equally easy to think of the same two rays now diverging from each other (see the figure at the top right in Figure A.1). It is strange to blend these two figures, with the result that the two rays make right angles with the line segment yet diverge from each other (see the figure at the bottom in Figure A.1).

If we swallow this counterintuitive offspring and proceed to elaborate it with nothing other than familiar Euclidean logic, the result is non-Euclidean geometry, or more accurately, the hyperbolic branch of non-Euclidean geometry.

The painful and laborious birth of non-Euclidean geometry took fifteen hundred years. Kline (1972) and Bonola (1955 [1912]) survey the efforts of many geometers, apparently beginning with Euclid, to come to terms with, or to disprove the possibility of, two coplanar lines that never meet even though they share a transversal perpendicular to one but not the other, or two coplanar lines that do meet yet share a perpendicular, and so on. Popular celebrations of the theory of relativity explain that non-Euclidean geometry revolutionized both mathematics and physics. But the only magic in this invention is the offspring. The conceptual parents are familiar. The reasoning is familiar. Only the offspring is unfamiliar. Here are the details:

Euclid had defined parallel lines as straight lines in a plane that, when extended indefinitely in both directions, never meet. Without using the "parallel axiom," he had proved that two straight lines are parallel when they form with one of their transversals equal interior alternate angles, or equal corresponding

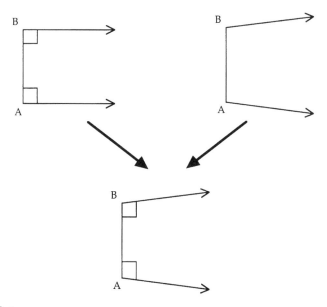

Figure A.1

angles, or interior angles on the same side which are supplementary. To prove the converse of these propositions, he made use of the parallel axiom: "If a straight line falling on two straight lines makes the interior angles on the same side less than two right angles, the two straight lines, if produced indefinitely, meet on that side on which the angles are less than two right angles." This axiom seemed to many geometers to lack the necessary feature of self-evident truth. Rather than assume it as an axiom, they sought to derive it from the other axioms and from Euclid's first twenty-eight theorems, none of which uses or in any way depends on the parallel axiom.

Consider the crucial attempt made by Gerolamo Saccheri (1667–1733), reported by Bonola. Saccheri focused on a quadrilateral ABCD where angle DAB and angle ABC are right angles, and where line segments AD and BC are equal (see Figure A-2).

Without using the parallel axiom, it is easy to prove that angles BCD and CDA must be equal. Saccheri did this. If we assume the parallel axiom, BCD and CDA are right angles. (In fact, the implication works in both directions—the parallel axiom is equivalent to the assumption that BCD and CDA are right angles—but all we need for this analysis is the first direction: the parallel axiom implies that BCD and CDA are right angles.) Therefore, if we deny that BCD

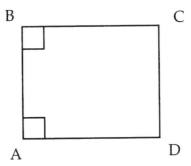

Figure A.2

and CDA are right angles, we thereby deny the parallel axiom. Saccheri did just this, in the hope of deriving a contradiction from the denial, which would prove the parallel axiom by reductio ad absurdum.

But if BCD and CDA are not right, they are still equal, and so they must be either obtuse or acute. Saccheri attempted to show that, in either case, a contradiction follows. He assumed that they are acute; that is, he performed the following conceptual blend:

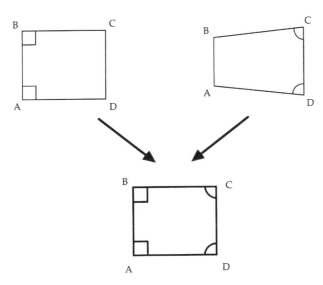

Figure A.3

Both inputs are routine Euclidean figures. Both have a quadrilateral ABCD, equal line segments AD and BC, equal angles DAB and ABC, and equal angles BCD and CDA. The offspring takes this structure from both parents. But the first parent has right internal angles DAB and ABC, and the second parent has acute internal angles BCD and CDA. The offspring takes the right angles from the first parent and the acute angles from the second. The offspring is impossible in Euclidean geometry, but Saccheri never found a contradiction for this offspring. In fact, he produced many astonishing theorems that are now recognized as belonging to hyperbolic geometry. These theorems were so repugnant to commonsense notions that he concluded they must be rejected.

It is important to see that all of Saccheri's elaboration of the offspring followed everyday procedures of Euclidean geometry. The parent spaces are Euclidean and familiar; the elaboration procedures are Euclidean and familiar. The only new thing in the process is the selective, two-sided projection to create the offspring.

One of the theorems Saccheri derived was another blend having to do with parallel lines: given any point A and a line b, there exist in the pencil (family) of lines through A two lines p and q that divide the pencil into two parts. The first of these two parts consists of the lines that intersect b, and the second consists of those lines (lying in angle α) that have a common perpendicular with b somewhere along b. The lines p and q themselves are asymptotic to b.

In Euclidean geometry, α is 0 and p and q are identical. But for Saccheri's new geometry, derived from the acute-angle offspring, α is positive and p and q are distinct, so there is an infinity of lines through A that have a common perpendicular with b and never meet it. This is a blend of two standard notions: the first is a schema of a parallel line through a point outside a line; the second is a schema of a bundle of lines through a point. If we blend these, we have multiple lines through a point outside a line that are all parallel to the line.

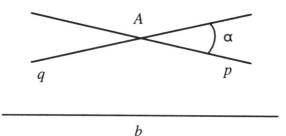

Figure A.4

Saccheri is not credited with the invention of non-Euclidean geometry. As Kline summarizes and simplifies the history, "If non-Euclidean geometry means the technical development of the consequences of a system of axioms containing an alternative to Euclid's parallel axiom then most credit must be accorded to Saccheri and even he benefited by the work of many men who tried to find a more acceptable substitute axiom for Euclid's" (p. 869). Credit is given instead to Gauss, Bolyai, and Lobatchevsky for recognizing (but not proving) that hyperbolic non-Euclidean geometry is mathematically consistent, and to Gauss for recognizing that physical space might be non-Euclidean.

Bolyai, Lobatchevsky, and, it is thought, Gauss all did essentially the same technical work as each other. Lobatchevsky, for example, presents a situation nearly identical to Saccheri's "pencil of parallel lines" (see Figure A.5).

Lobatchevsky showed that, in absolute geometry, there are two classes of lines through A: lines that meet b and lines that do not meet b. The lines that do not meet b include two lines p and q that form the boundary between the two classes; if a perpendicular is dropped from A to b, the perpendicular forms the same angle β with p and q, and all lines through A that make an angle less than β with the perpendicular will intersect b. Euclid's parallel axiom is equivalent to specifying that β is a right angle. Otherwise, β increases and approaches a right angle as the length of the perpendicular approaches 0, and β decreases and approaches zero as the length of the perpendicular becomes infinite. And so on.

These results give a striking demonstration of the counterintuitive notion that the offspring is not the sum of the parents, that the offspring may be quite new. Conceptual reproduction using what you have gives you something you don't have, often something remarkably new. Conceptual reproduction is non-linear.

This history also shows the power of entrenchment. Kline writes, "The efforts to find an acceptable substitute for the Euclidean axiom on parallels or to prove that the Euclidean assertion must be a theorem were so numerous and so futile

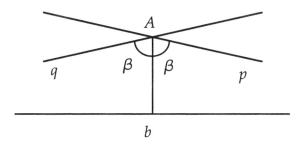

Figure A.5

that in 1759 d'Alembert called the problem of the parallel axiom 'the scandal of the elements of geometry'" (p. 867).

In this history, conceptual reproduction produced offspring so incompatible with schemata used in everyday experience of physical space and with Euclidean geometry that the offspring were resisted for many centuries. This shows something interesting: a new conceptual understanding is not only a matter of hitting upon the basic composition of the offspring. The offspring needs to be worked until it no longer seems random, arbitrary, without coherence.

✎ NOTES ❦

CHAPTER 2

1. I thank Mat McCubbins for this observation.
2. I thank Bruce Bueno de Mesquita for conversation on this point.

CHAPTER 3

1. See Sidney Verba, Kay L. Schlozman, and Henry E. Brady, "Rational Action and Political Activity," paper presented at the 1997 Annual Meeting of the American Political Science Association. In Appendix A, "An Inventory of Rational Choice Theories," under "Procedural Definitions of Practical Rationality Employed by Economists," they write:

> Economists have chosen to take another approach in which they describe a procedure that can be used to test for practical rationality. They assume that individual desires are fixed and that beliefs are fixed (this second assumption can be relaxed) as feasible sets are changed. Then, if we denote the set of all alternatives by M, any subset of these alternatives by J, and the actions taken from this subset as $A(J)$, they make the assumption of the *Independence of Irrelevant Alternatives* (*IIA*):
>
> $$\text{If } M \supseteq J \text{ and } M \supseteq K, \text{ then } A(J) \cap A(K) = A(J \cup K) \cap J \cap K$$

That is, for any two subsets of M, the intersection of the alternatives chosen from J and those chosen from K must equal the set of those alternatives that are chosen from the union of J and K and which are in J and in K. This condition implies that if an individual confronted with a set of alternatives $J = \{j, k, l, \ldots, m\}$ chooses j, then the person will choose j from any subset K of J which includes j. And if j is chosen from L as well as from J, then j will be chosen from the superset composed of J and L. In short this requires some consistency in actions as feasible sets change.

It can be shown that if we define the preference of j over k (written jPk or j preferred to k) as identical to choice from pairs of alternatives (so that A({j,k}) = j if and only if jPk) then the *IIA* condition is equivalent to the following *Choice Function Assumption* (CFA):

For any J such that M⊇J: A(J) = {all $j \in$ J such that for no $k \in$ J is kPj}.

This assumption says that the alternatives chosen from J are all those for which there is no j in J which is preferred to them. The choice function assumption implies that there is a preference relationship underlying choices which does not change from one feasible set to another. It follows directly from the CFA that there always exists some asymmetric relationship P (an asymmetric relationship is one for which if jPk then not kPj—if you prefer j to k then you do not prefer k to j) over all pairs of alternatives in M that will correctly predict the person's choices over any subset J of M. Note that the relationship P only has to be asymmetric—there is no assumption that it is transitive. The choice function assumption is compatible with the possibility that there are intransitivities so that jPk, kPl, and lPj. Therefore, the CFA is a very weak assumption. It appears to be the assumption that Debra Satz and John Ferejohn want to make the basis of their theory of rational choice, and they argue that it is so weak that it really does not need verification. In fact, they seem to be arguing that we could not do social science without an assumption like this that implies that a person remains consistent from one situation to the next.

The CFA provides a definition of practical rationality that is much easier to accept than one which requires us to review an individual's desires and beliefs to see if the person chose the best alternative. The CFA provides an easily acceptable definition of rationality because it substitutes a requirement for consistency for the substantive review of desires, beliefs, and actions. Economists who accept the CFA only need to believe that people will act consistently, according to the IIA, from one choice situation to another. They do not need to know the person's desires or beliefs. These desires and beliefs are then imputed to them through revealed preference because they act as if they had them. A great deal might be made of the possibility that they may not "really" have them, but this seems more like a curious feature of the theory than a likely empirical fact. If someone always acted according to the CFA in every possible situation, then it seems realistic to say that they really do have the desires and beliefs that we would impute to them from this behavior.

2. I thank Bruce Bueno de Mesquita and Bary Weingast for illumination on this point.

CHAPTER 4

1. I thank Francis-Noël Thomas for providing this example.

✎ REFERENCES ✐

Aristotle. 1991. *On Rhetoric: A Theory of Civic Discourse.* Translated by George A. Kennedy. New York: Oxford University Press.

Barkow, Jerome H., Leda Cosmides, and John Tooby, editors. 1992. *The Adapted Mind: Evolutionary Psychology and the Generation of Culture.* New York: Oxford University Press.

Binmore, Ken, and A. Brandenburger. 1990. "Common Knowledge and Game Theory." In *Essays on Foundations of Game Theory*, edited by K. G. Binmore (pp. 105–150). Oxford: Blackwell.

Blakeslee, Sandra. 1995. "How the Brain Might Work." *The New York Times*, 21 March, pp. B5 and B7. [A journalistic sketch of the binding problem and of a proposal by Rodolfo Llinás to solve it.]

Bonola, Roberto. 1955/1912. *Non-Euclidean Geometry: A Critical and Historical Study of Its Development.* Translated by H. S. Carslaw. Chicago: Open Court Publishing Company.

Boynton, Robert S. 1999. "Thinking the Unthinkable: A Young Historian Proposes that the Great War Was England's Fault," *The New Yorker*, 12 April, pp. 43–50.

Brady, Henry, and Stephen Ansolabehere. 1989. "The Nature of Utility Functions in Mass Publics." *American Political Science Review* 83:1 (March 1989), 143–163.

Brown, Margaret Wise. 1942. *The Runaway Bunny.* Pictures by Clement Hurd. New York: Harper and Row.

Bryant, Adam. 1996. "Advertising." *The New York Times*, June 6, p. D7.

Chalmers, D. J., R. M. French, & D. R. Hofstadter. 1992. "High-level Perception, Representation and Analogy: A Critique of Artificial Intelligence

Methodology." *Journal of Experimental and Theoretical Artificial Intelligence* 4, 185–211.

Collier, David, and Stephen Levitsky. 1997. "Democracy with Adjectives: Conceptual Innovation in Comparative Research." *World Politics* 49:3 (April), 430–451.

Colman, Andrew M. 1995. *Game Theory and Its Applications in the Social and Biological Sciences*. Second edition. Oxford: Butterworth-Heinemann.

Coulson, Seana. 1995. "Analogic and Metaphoric Mapping in Blended Spaces." *Center for Research in Language Newsletter* 9:1, 2–12.

———. 1996. "The Menendez Brothers Virus: Analogical Mapping in Blended Spaces." In *Conceptual Structure, Discourse, and Language*, edited by Adele Goldberg (pp. 67–81). Stanford: Center for the Study of Language and Information.

———. 1997. "Semantic Leaps: The Role of Frame-Shifting and Conceptual Blending in Meaning Construction." Ph.D. dissertation, University of California, San Diego.

Cowan, George A., David Pines, and David Meltzer, editors. 1993. *Complexity: Metaphors, Models, and Reality*. Reading, MA: Addison-Wesley. [Santa Fe Institute Studies in the Science of Complexity, Proceedings Volume XIX.]

Damasio, Antonio R. 1994. *Descartes' Error*. New York: G. P. Putnam.

D'Andrade, Roy. 1995. *The Development of Cognitive Anthropology*. Cambridge: Cambridge University Press.

DiMaggio, Paul. 1997. "Culture and Cognition: An Interdisciplinary Review." *Annual Review of Sociology* 23: 263–287.

Durham, William H. 1991. *Coevolution: Genes, Culture, and Human Diversity*. Stanford: Stanford University Press.

Edelman, Gerald. 1989. *The Remembered Present: A Biological Theory of Consciousness*. New York: Basic Books.

———. 1992. "The Sciences of Recognition." In Gerald Edelman, *Bright Air, Brilliant Fire: On the Matter of the Mind*. New York: Basic Books.

Falkenhainer, B., K. D. Forbus, and D. Gentner. 1989. "The Structure-Mapping Engine: Algorithm and Examples." *Artificial Intelligence* 41:1, 1–63.

Fauconnier, Gilles. 1994/1985. *Mental Spaces: Aspects of Meaning Construction in Natural Language*. Second edition. Cambridge: Cambridge University Press.

———. 1997. *Mappings in Thought and Language*. Cambridge: Cambridge University Press.

Fauconnier, Gilles, and Mark Turner. 1994. "Conceptual projection and middle spaces," UCSD Cognitive Science Technical Report 9401. San Diego. [Available from <cogsci.ucsd.edu> and from <www.wam.umd.edu/~mturn>]

———. 1996. "Blending as a Central Process of Grammar." In *Conceptual Structure, Discourse, and Language*, edited by Adele Goldberg (pp. 113–

130). Stanford: Center for the Study of Language and Information. [An expanded web version is available at <www.wam.umd.edu/~mturn/WWW/blending.html>]

———. 1998a. "Conceptual Integration Networks." *Cognitive Science* 22:2 (April-June), 133–187.

———. 1998b. "Principles of Conceptual Integration." In *Discourse and Cognition*, edited by Jean-Pierre Koenig (pp. 269–283). Stanford: Center for the Study of Language and Information.

———. *The Way We Think*. Manuscript in preparation.

Fearon, James D. 1991. "Counterfactuals and Hypothesis Testing in Political Science." *World Politics* 43:2, 169–195.

Feldman, Jerome. 1988. "Connectionist Representation of Concepts." In *Connectionist Models and Their Applications: Readings From Cognitive Science*, edited by David Waltz and Jerome A. Feldman (pp. 341–361). Norwood, NJ: Ablex Publishing.

Forbus, K., D. Gentner, A. B. Markman, and R. W. Ferguson. 1998. "Analogy Just Looks Like High Level Perception: Why a Domain-General Approach to Analogical Mapping Is Right." *Journal of Experimental and Theoretical Artificial Intelligence* 10:2 (April), 231–258.

Freeman, Margaret. 1997. "Grounded Spaces: Deictic -Self Anaphors in the Poetry of Emily Dickinson." *Language and Literature* 6:1, 7–28.

Geertz, Clifford. 1962. "The Growth of Culture and the Evolution of Mind." In *Theories of Mind*, edited by Jordan M. Scher (pp. 713–740). New York: Free Press. Reprinted in Geertz (1973a), 55–83.

———. 1972. "Deep Play: Notes on the Balinese Cockfight." *Daedalus* 101: 1–37. Reprinted in Geertz (1973a), 412–453.

———. 1966. "Religion as a Cultural System." In *Anthropological Approaches to the Study of Religion*, edited by M. Banton (pp. 1–46). London: Tavistock Publications. Reprinted in Geertz (1973a), 87–125.

———. 1973a. *The Interpretation of Cultures*. New York: Basic Books.

———. 1973b. "Thick Description: Toward an Interpretive Theory of Culture." Chapter 1 of Geertz (1973a).

———. 1995. *After the Fact: Two Countries, Four Decades, One Anthropologist*. Cambridge: Harvard University Press.

Gell-Mann, Murray. 1993. "Complex Adaptive Systems." In *Complexity: Metaphors, Models, and Reality*, edited by George A. Cowan, David Pines, and David Meltzer (pp. 17–28). Reading, MA: Addison-Wesley.

Gentner, D. 1982. "Are Scientific Analogies Metaphors?" In *Metaphor: Problems and perspectives*, edited by D. S. Miall (pp. 106–132). Brighton, Sussex: Harvester Press.

———. 1983. "Structure-Mapping: A Theoretical Framework for Analogy." *Cognitive Science* 7, 155–170.

Gentner, D., and Donald Gentner. 1983. "Flowing Waters or Teeming Crowds: Mental Models of Electricity." In *Mental Models*, edited by D. Gentner and A. L. Stevens (pp. 99–130). Hillsdale, NJ: Lawrence Erlbaum.

Gentner, D., and A. L. Stevens, editors. 1983. *Mental Models*. Hillsdale, NJ: Lawrence Erlbaum.

Gick, M. L., and K. J. Holyoak. 1980. "Analogical Problem Solving." *Cognitive Psychology* 12, 306–355.

———. 1983. "Schema Induction and Analogical Transfer." *Cognitive Psychology* 15, 1–38.

Goldberg, Adele. 1995. *Constructions: A Construction Grammar Approach to Argument Structure*. Chicago: University of Chicago Press.

Grush, Rick, and Nili Mandelblit. 1997. "Blending in Language, Conceptual Structure, and the Cerebral Cortex." In *Roman Jakobson Centennial Symposium: International Journal of Linguistics Acta Linguistica Hafniensia*, edited by Per Aage Brandt, Frans Gregersen, Frederik Stjernfelt, and Martin Skov, volume 29, pp. 221–237. C.A. Reitzel: Copenhagen.

Harmon, Gilbert. 1986. *Change in View*. Cambridge: MIT Press.

Hofstadter, Douglas. 1995. "A Review of *Mental Leaps: Analogy in Creative Thought*." *AI Magazine*, Fall, pp. 75–80.

Hogarth, Robin M., and Melvin Reder. 1987. *Rational Choice: The Contrast Between Economics and Psychology*. Chicago: University of Chicago Press.

Holland, J. H., K. J. Holyoak, R. E. Nisbett, and P. R. Thagard. 1986. *Induction: Processes of Inference Learning and Discovery*. Cambridge: MIT Press.

Holland, Paul W. 1986. "Statistics and Causal Inference." *Journal of the American Statistical Association* 81:396 (December), 945–960.

Holyoak, K. J., and P. Thagard. 1989. "Analogical Mapping by Constraint Satisfaction." *Cognitive Science* 13:3, 295–355.

———. 1995. *Mental Leaps: Analogy in Creative Thought*. Cambridge: MIT Press.

Hubel, David H. 1995. *Eye, Brain, and Vision*. New York: Scientific American Library.

Hutchins, Edwin. 1995. "How a Cockpit Remembers Its Speeds." *Cognitive Science* 19, 265–288.

———. 1994. *Cognition in the Wild*. Cambridge: MIT Press.

Kahneman, Daniel. 1995. "Varieties of Counterfactual Thinking." In *What Might Have Been: The Social Psychology of Counterfactual Thinking*, edited by Neal J. Roese and James M. Olson (pp. 375–396). Hillsdale, NJ: Lawrence Erlbaum.

Kahneman, Daniel, and Amos Tversky. 1979. "Prospect Theory: An Analysis of Decision under Risk." *Econometrica* 47:2 (March), 263–291.

Kahneman, Daniel, Paul Slovic, and Amos Tversky, editors. 1982. *Judgment under Uncertainty: Heuristics and Biases.* Cambridge: Cambridge University Press.

King, Gary, Robert O. Keohane, and Sidney Verba. 1994. *Designing Social Inquiry: Scientific Inference in Qualitative Research.* Princeton, NJ: Princeton University Press.

Kline, Morris. 1972. *Mathematical Thought from Ancient to Modern Times.* New York: Oxford University Press.

Lakoff, George, and Rafael Núñez. 2000. *Where Mathematics Comes From.* New York: Basic Books.

Lakoff, George, and Mark Turner. 1989. *More than Cool Reason: A Field Guide to Poetic Metaphor.* Chicago: University of Chicago Press.

Lévi-Strauss, Claude. 1963. *Structural Anthropology.* Translated by Claire Jacobson and Brooke Grundfest Schoepf. New York: Basic Books.

Lewin, Shira. 1996. "Economics and Psychology: Lessons for Our Own Day from the Early Twentieth Century." *Journal of Economic Literature* 34 (September), 1293–1323.

Lobachevski, Nicholas. 1914/1840. *Geometrical Researches on the Theory of Parallels.* Translated by George Bruce Halsted. Chicago: Open Court Publishing Company. [First edition of the translation, 1891.]

Lupia, Arthur, and Mat McCubbins. 1997. *The Democratic Dilemma: Knowledge, Persuasion, and the Foundations of Reasoned Choice.* Cambridge: Cambridge University Press.

Lupia, Arthur, and Matthew D. McCubbins, and Samuel L. Popkin, editors. 2000. *Elements of Reason: Cognition, Choice, and the Bounds of Rationality.* Cambridge: Cambridge University Press.

Mandelblit, Nili. 1996. "Formal and Conceptual Blending in the Hebrew Verbal System: A Cognitive Basis For Morphological Verbal Pattern Alternations." Unpublished manuscript.

———. 1997. "Grammatical Blending: Creative and Schematic Aspects in Sentence Processing and Translation." Ph.D. dissertation, University of California, San Diego.

Mandelblit, Nili, and Oron Zachar. 1998. "The Notion of Dynamic Unit: Conceptual Developments in Cognitive Science." *Cognitive Science* 22:2 (April–June), 229–268.

McCubbins, Mat, and Michael Thies. 1997. "Rationality, Positive Political Theory, and the Study of Law." Unpublished manuscript, University of California, San Diego.

Martin, Ben. 1993. "The Schema" In *Complexity: Metaphors, Models, and Reality*, edited by George A. Cowan, David Pines, and David Welzer (pp. 263–279). Reading, MA: Addison-Wesley.

Norman, Donald, and David E. Rumelhart. 1978. "Accretion, Tuning, and Restructuring: Three Modes of Learning." In *Semantic Factors in Cognition*, edited by John W. Cotton and Roberta L. Klatzky (pp. 37–53). Hillsdale, NJ: Lawrence Erlbaum.

Oakley, Todd. 1995. "Presence: The Conceptual Basis of Rhetorical Effect." Unpublished Ph.D. dissertation, University of Maryland.

Ramey, Martin. 1997. "Eschatology and Ethics." Chapter 4 of "The Problem Of the Body: The Conflict Between Soteriology and Ethics in Paul." Ph.D. dissertation, Chicago Theological Seminary. [Contains a discussion of blending in 1 Thessalonians.]

Reddy, Michael. 1979. "The Conduit Metaphor." In *Metaphor and Thought*, edited by Andrew Ortony (pp. 284–324). Cambridge: Cambridge University Press.

Rilke, Rainer Maria. 1961/1922. *Duino Elegies*. Translated by C. F. MacIntyre. Berkeley: University of California Press.

Robert, Adrian. 1998. "Blending in the Interpretation of Mathematical Proofs." In *Discourse and Cognition*, edited by Jean-Pierre Koenig (pp. 337–350). Stanford: Center for the Study of Language and Information.

Rumelhart, David. 1980. "Schemata: The Building Blocks of Cognition." In *Theoretical Issues in Reading Comprehension: Perspectives from Cognitive Psychology, Linguistics, Artificial Intelligence, and Education*, edited by Rand J. Spiro, Bertram C. Bruce, and William F. Brewer (pp. 33–58). Hillsdale, NJ: Lawrence Erlbaum.

Rumelhart, David E., and Andrew Ortony. 1977. "The Representation of Knowledge in Memory." In *Schooling and the Acquisition of Knowledge*, edited by Richard C. Anderson, Rand J. Spiro, and William E. Montague (pp. 99–135). Hillsdale, NJ: Lawrence Erlbaum.

Schön, Donald, and Martin Rein. 1994. *Frame Reflection: Toward the Resolution of Intractable Policy Controversies*. New York: Basic Books.

Simon, Herbert A. 1978. "Rationality as Process and Product of Thought." *American Economic Review: Proceedings* 68:1–16.

Simon, Herbert A. 1982. *Models of Bounded Rationality*. 2 volumes. Cambridge: MIT Press.

———. 1986. "Rationality in Economics and Psychology." *Journal of Business* 59: 4, 2. Reprinted in Hogarth and Reder (1987), pp. 25–40.

Smith, Vernon L. 1991. "Rational Choice: The Contrast between Economics and Psychology." *Journal of Political Economy* 99:4 (August), 877–897.

Sun, Douglas. 1994. "Thurber's Fables for Our Time: A Case Study in Satirical Use of the Great Chain Metaphor." *Studies in American Humor* 3:1, 51–61.

Suskind, Ron. 1999. "Ordinary People Show Faith, Reaping Rich Rewards." *Wall Street Journal*, 30 March, p. A1.

Tetlock, Philip, and Aaron Belkin, editors. 1996. *Counterfactual Thought Experiments in World Politics.* Princeton, NJ: Princeton University Press.

Thaler, Richard. 1991. *Quasi Rational Economics.* New York: Russell Sage Foundation.

Turner, Mark. 1987. *Death Is the Mother of Beauty: Mind, Metaphor, Criticism.* Chicago: University of Chicago Press.

———. 1989. "Categories and Analogies." In *Analogical Reasoning: Perspectives of Artificial Intelligence, Cognitive Science, and Philosophy*, edited by David Helman (pp. 3–24). Dordrecht: Kluwer.

———. 1991. *Reading Minds: The Study of English in the Age of Cognitive Science.* Princeton, NJ: Princeton University Press.

———. 1996a. "Conceptual Blending and Counterfactual Argument in the Social and Behavioral Sciences." In *Counterfactual Thought Experiments in World Politics*, edited by Philip Tetlock and Aaron Belkin (pp. 291–295). Princeton, NJ: Princeton University Press.

———. 1996b. *The Literary Mind: The Origins of Thought and Language.* New York: Oxford University Press.

Turner, Mark, and Gilles Fauconnier. 1995. "Conceptual Integration and Formal Expression." *Metaphor and Symbolic Activity.* 10:3, 183–203.

———. 1998. "Conceptual Integration in Counterfactuals." In *Discourse and Cognition*, edited by Jean-Pierre Koenig (pp. 285–296). Stanford: Center for the Study of Language and Information.

———. 1999. "A Mechanism of Creativity." *Poetics Today* 20:3 (Fall), 397–418.

Tversky, Amos, and Daniel Kahneman. 1986. "Rational Choice and the Framing of Decisions." *Journal of Business* 59:4, 2. Reprinted in Hogarth and Reder (1987), 67–94.

Veale, Tony. 1996. "Pastiche: A Metaphor-Centered Computational Model of Conceptual Blending, with special reference to Cinematic Borrowing." Unpublished manuscript. [Available from <www.wam.umd.edu/~mturn/WWW/blending.html>.]

von Neumann, John, and Oskar Morgenstern. 1947/1944. *Theory of Games and Economic Behavior.* Princeton: Princeton University Press.

Zbikowski, Lawrence. In press. "Conceptual Blending in Music: The Nineteenth-Century *Lied*." In *Cognitive Linguistics and the Verbal Arts*, edited by Vimala Herman. Cambridge: Cambridge University Press.

Zeki, Semir. 1993. *A Vision of the Brain.* Oxford: Blackwell.

✧ INDEX ✧